BIBLE DIFFICULTIES
—GENESIS—
CPH Apologetic Commentary

EXAMINE THE
SCRIPTURES DAILY

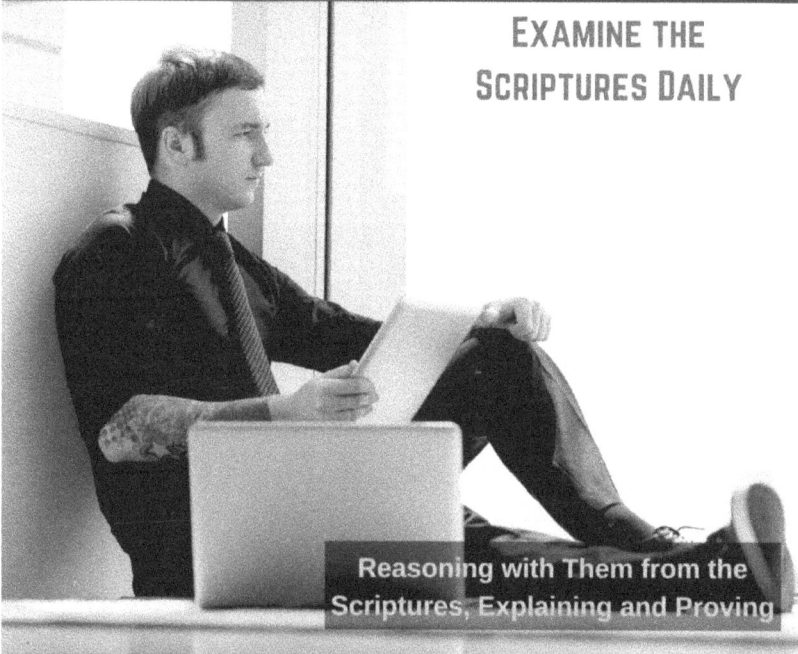

Reasoning with Them from the
Scriptures, Explaining and Proving

Edward D. Andrews

BIBLE DIFFICULTIES
—GENESIS—

CPH Apologetic Commentary

Edward D. Andrews

Christian Publishing House
Cambridge, Ohio

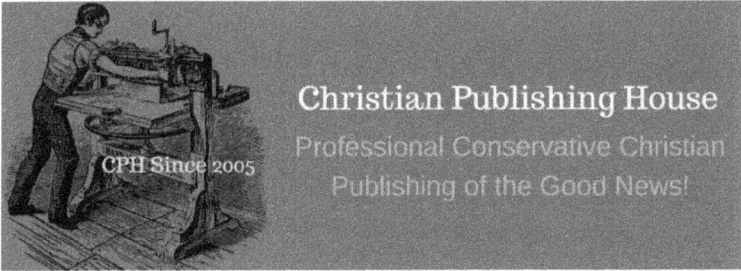

Christian Publishing House

CPH Since 2005

Professional Conservative Christian
Publishing of the Good News!

Unless otherwise indicated, Scripture quotations are from the *Updated American Standard Version of the Holy Scriptures*, 2016 edition (*UASV*).

BIBLE DIFFICULTIES —GENESIS—CPH Apologetic Commentary

Authored by Edward D. Andrews

ISBN-13: **978-1-945757-17-4**

ISBN-10: **1-945757-17-5**

PREFACE Apologetic Evangelism

Apologetic Evangelism "is tilling the soil of people's hearts of people's minds and hearts to help them be more willing to listen to the truth. - Norman L. Geisler

Evangelism is the work of a Christian evangelist, which seeks to persuade other people to become Christian, especially by sharing the basics of the Gospel, but also the deeper message of biblical truths. Today the Gospel is almost an unknown, so what does the Christian evangelist do? **Preevangelism** is laying a foundation for those who have no knowledge of the Gospel, giving them background information, so that they are able to grasp what they are hearing. The Christian evangelist is preparing their mind and heart so that they will be receptive to the biblical truths. In many ways, this is known as apologetics.

Christian apologetics [Greek: *apologia*, "verbal defense, speech in defense"] is a field of **Christian theology** which endeavors to offer a reasonable and sensible basis for the **Christian faith**, defending the faith against objections. It is reasoning from the Scriptures, explaining and proving, as one instructs in sound doctrine, many times having to overturn false reasoning before he can plant the seeds of truth. It can also be earnestly contending for the faith and saving one from losing their faith, as they have begun to doubt. Moreover, it can involve rebuking those who contradict the truth. It is being prepared to make a defense to anyone who asks the Christian evangelist for a reason for the hope that is in him or her.– Jude 1.3, 21-23; 1 Pet 3.15; Acts 17:2-3; Titus 1:9

What do we mean by **obligated** and what we mean by **evangelism** are at the heart of the matter and are indeed related to each other.

EVANGELISM: An evangelist is a proclaimer of the gospel or good news, as well as all biblical truths. There are levels of evangelism, which is pictured in first-century Christianity. All Christians evangelized in the first century, but a select few fit the role of a full-time evangelist (Ephesians 4:8, 11-12), like Philip and Timothy.

Both Philip and Timothy are specifically mentioned as evangelizers. (Ac 21:8; 2 Tim. 4:5) Philip was a full-time evangelist after Pentecost, who was sent to the city of Samaria, having great success. An angel even directed Philip to an Ethiopian Eunuch, to share the good news about Christ with him. Because of the Eunuch's already having a knowledge of God by way of the Old Testament, Philip was able to help him understand that the Hebrew Scriptures pointed to Christ as the long-awaited Messiah. In the end, Philip baptized the Eunuch. After that, the Spirit again sent Philip on a mission, this time to Azotus and all the cities on the way to Caesarea. (Ac 8:5, 12, 14, 26-40) Paul evangelized in many lands, setting up one congregation after another. (2 Cor. 10:13-16) Timothy was an evangelizer or missionary, and Paul placed distinct importance on evangelizing when he gave his parting encouragement to Timothy. – 2 Timothy 4:5; 1Timothy 1:3.

The office of apostle and evangelist seem to overlap in some areas, but could be distinguished in that apostles traveled and set up congregations, which took evangelizing skills, but also developed the congregations after they were established. The evangelists were more of a missionary, being stationed in certain areas to grow and develop congregations. In addition, if we look at all of the apostles and the evangelists, plus Paul's more than one hundred traveling companions, it seems very unlikely that they could have had Christianity at over one million by the 125 C.E. This was accomplished because all Christians were obligated to carry out some level of evangelism.

OBLIGATED: In the broadest sense of the term for evangelizer, all Christians are obligated to play some role as an evangelist.

- *Basic Evangelism* is planting seeds of truth and watering any seeds that have been planted. [In the basic sense of this word (euaggelistes), this would involve all Christians.] In some cases, it may be that one Christian planted the seed, which was initially rejected, so he was left in a good way because the planter did not try to force the truth down his throat. However, some time later he faces something in life that moves him to reconsider those seeds and another Christian water what had already been planted. This evangelism can be carried out in all of the methods that are available: informal, house-to-house, street, phone, internet, and the like. What amount of time is invested in the evangelism work is up to each Christian to decide for themselves.

- *Making Disciples* is having any role in the process of getting an unbeliever from his unbelief state to the point of accepting Christ as his Savior and being baptized. Once the unbeliever has become a believer, he is still developed until he has become strong. Any Christian could potentially carry this one person through all of the developmental stages. On the other hand, it may be that several have some part. It is like a person that specializes in a certain aspect of a job, but all are aware of the other aspects, in case they are called on to carry out that aspect. Again, each Christian must decide for themselves what role they are to have, and how much of a role, but should be prepared to fill any role needed.

- *Part-Time* or Full-Time Evangelist is one who sees this as their calling and chooses to be very involved as an evangelist in their local church and community. They may work part-time to supplement their work as an evangelist. They may be married with children, but they realize their gift is in the field of evangelism. If it is the wife, the husband would work toward supporting her work as an evangelist and vice-versa. If it were a single person, he or she would supplement their work by being employed part-time, but also the church would help as well. This person is well trained in every aspect of bringing one to Christ.

Congregation Evangelists should be very involved in evangelizing their communities and helping the church members play their role at the basic levels of evangelism. There is nothing to say that one church could not have many within, who have the calling of an evangelist, which would and should be cultivated.

Legal Terms as to How We Should Objectively View Evidence

There are approximately 3,000+ of these supposed errors and contradictions in the Bible. It will take us several volumes to consider such an undertaking. Please do not be disheartened by such a large number, because there are compelling reasons why we have so many Bible difficulties, not errors or contradictions. This will be discussed further in chapter one. These volumes are to serve as an essential source in dealing with Bible difficulties. If we offer reasonable responses and satisfactory answers for these challenging passages, it can be inferred that there would be a reasonable answer for the few that may not have a reply as of yet as well.

One reason for having such publications as this is the new atheist. The unbeliever of decades past was satisfied to believe that everything came about by chance, through evolution, and not concern himself with what others believed. This is no longer the case. Sadly, today's atheist is more involved in leading the Christian down the path of doubt, while the Christian denominations are almost entirely inactive in evangelizing the unbeliever. Hundreds of atheistic books and videos are flooding the market in an attempt to discredit the Bible, the foundation of the Christian belief system. Another enemy of God's Word is found in the agnostic. An agnostic teaches that it is hard to know whether God exists and that we are unable to accept the Bible as a revelation of that existence. Before we begin defining Bible difficulties, it is best that we better define how we should view available evidence.

Burden of Proof: The burden of proof falls on the one making the claims. If the Christian is witnessing to another, he has the burden to prove what he says is so if asked for proof. However, if the critic is challenging the Christian, the burden of disproving lies with the critic. The closer the claim is to socially accepted knowledge, less proof is needed, while the further one moves from conventional knowledge, the more evidence is required. I believe that the legal burden of proof offers the best answers to the witnessing of others. It has been refined over the last 200 years to the point of evaluating a life that is held in its balance, just as everlasting life is held in the balance. Below we will list the levels of legal proof and some percentage and wording to indicate the degree of certainty needed. We have used different Bible objects for each one, but any criticism could be plugged into that particular burden of proof.

Warrants Further Investigation

Reasonable (30%): This is a low-level burden of proof in that it is enough to accept something as *reasonably likely*, being so unless proven otherwise by a deeper look, which may bring in more evidence. For example, at this level, it is *reasonably likely* that Jesus Christ lived, died and was resurrected. This may be achieved in the first conversation with the one which we are sharing the good news.

Probable (40%): This is also a low-level burden of proof in that it is enough to accept something as *likely being so* unless proven otherwise by a deeper look, which may bring in more evidence. At this level, it is *probable* that the Bible is the inspired, inerrant Word of God. This may be achieved in the first 2-3 conversations with the one which we are sharing the good news.

Conviction for Claim

Preponderance of Evidence (51%): This is a higher-level burden of proof that makes Noah surviving a worldwide flood *more likely* to be true than not true.

Clear and Convincing Evidence (85%): This is an even higher level of burden of proof that Adam and Eve were historical persons, created by God is substantially *more likely than not*.

Beyond Reasonable Doubt (99%): This is the highest level of burden of proof that over forty major prophecies about Jesus Christ in the Old Testament came true, being beyond reasonable doubt. It must be understood that feeling as though we have no reason doubt is not the same as 100 percent absolute evidence of certainty. If one has doubts that affect their belief of certainty, it is not beyond reasonable doubt. This too must be qualified, because it is reasonable to have doubts about certain aspects of the whole that does not have all the answers as of yet, but it does not affect the level of certainty as a whole.

Evidentialism only becomes self-defeating the moment one tries to raise the level of certainty to the absolute instead of beyond reasonable doubt (sufficient evidence). The argument against the use of evidentialism that the principle simply does not account for the way we come to have most of our beliefs is no real argument at all. A belief that cold weather makes you sick is not the same as believing there is an Almighty God, Creator. Each of us has hundreds of thousands of core beliefs that are accepted as fact until we come across something that tell us otherwise. Ironically, we are told to investigate before buying a car, or especially a house, as it is a big commitment. Yet, are we to equate the acceptance and commitment to Christ the same way we do that a chair will hold our weight, or our car will get us to work?

The Bible critic generally exaggerates the level of his evidence, presenting it in a sly fashion. At the same time, he will arbitrarily dismiss the Christian evidence, by declaring that all who believes in God and the Bible are foolish and naive. The simple principle to be observed here is to ask, 'which is more likely to be true based on what you know.' Of course, as one grows in knowledge, that is subject to change. A Christian that falls away due to atheism or agnosticism (like Dr. Bart D. Ehrman) will after that require absolute evidence rather that evidence beyond a reasonable doubt. From that time on, God must then show him all that his doubting heart desires. The common expression being, "God if you just _____, I will believe."

The Bible critic runs around like a scavenger looking for an error, not reason. As they come upon a pebble of doubt, they throw it out as though it were a boulder of truth against God. Six months later, an archaeologist digging in Bible lands somewhere finds something that utterly and completely removes this critic's evidence. Does the critic even lean a little closer to God? No, because Christian evidence, no matter how weighty, does not exist on the critic's agenda, which is to sow seeds of doubt regarding the Bible's authenticity. Even if the Ark of the Covenant with the Ten Commandments and Aaron's rod that budded were to be located, the critic would still maintain their stand because the unearthing of these objects does not meet their agenda.

For example, the Bible critic will argue from silence, saying 'Belshazzar of the Bible has not been found in secular history, we have no evidence that he ever existed.' Now, say a year later, a piece of a tablet is found that mentions Belshazzar (this has actually happened), and in

5

connection with the historical account in the Bible. Well, that critic does not draw closer to where the evidence is pointing; he throws it out, dismissing it as though he never raised the argument, and runs to look for another. Sadly this circle of madness just keeps going.

INTRODUCTION Always Being Prepared to Make a Defense

1 Peter 3:15 Updated American Standard Version (UASV)

[15] but sanctify Christ as Lord in your hearts, always being prepared to make a defense[1] to anyone who asks you for a reason for the hope that is in you; yet do it with gentleness and respect;

When one, who is sincerely interested in our beliefs as a follower of Christ, asks for a reason as to why we believe this or that, we must defend those beliefs with sound biblical answers. When Peter says that we need always to be prepared to make a defense to anyone who asks us for a reason for the hope that is in us, to whom does this apply? Who is supposed to be able to make a defense? Does this apply just to Bible scholars, pastors, elders, priests, church leaders, or all Christians? If we return to the first verse of Peter's letter, he writes, "To those who reside as aliens, scattered throughout Pontus, Galatia, Cappadocia, Asia, and Bithynia, who are chosen." (1 Pet. 1:1, NASB) The ones, who resided as aliens, were Christians living among the Jews and pagan Gentiles of Asia Minor. Thus, the first letter of Peter, especially 1:3 through 4:1 was directed to those who had just been recently been baptized. Thus, Peter expected all Christians, even newly baptized ones to be able to defend the hope that lies within all Christians, offering reasonable, logical answers to those who are genuinely interested.

This first letter of Peter was penned about 62-64 C.E., meaning that these early Christians in Asia Minor, like others throughout the Roman Empire, were living under very difficult time, being persecuted on two fronts: by the Jews and the pagan population. The early Christians were mostly converts from Judaism, who now followed Jesus as the way, the truth, and the life. After that, pagans were being converted over to Christianity. The Jewish population viewed the Christians as an apostate form of Judaism, who were stumbling their fellow brothers and sisters. The pagan nations were angered because the Christians had given up their former lifestyle and had now become a new person. To the world, these Christians had undergone a life change that was viewed as apostasy from pagan religion and Judaism, and this was a crime! Because Christians refused to be a part of the world, the world hated them, just as it had hated Jesus. (1 Pet. 1.18; 2:1; 4:4) Even worse, Satan himself became enraged at this new Christian faith. Peter warned, "Be sober-minded; be

---

[1] Or *argument*; or *explanation*

watchful. Your adversary the devil prowls around like a roaring lion, seeking someone to devour."

What counsel within this first letter of Peter would keep these new ones safe, so that they would not return to their former ways? Peter exhorts, "Keep your conduct among the Gentiles honorable, so that when they speak against you as evildoers, they may see your good works and glorify God on the day of visitation."[2] (2:12) Peter goes on to inform them that in those difficult times, they needed to be "be sound in mind[3] and be sober-minded[4] in prayers." (4:7) Again, they needed to be "sober-minded; be watchful" because Satan was 'seeking to devour' them as well. (5:8) Satan uses the enticement of old friends of the world, who were "living in sensuality, lusts, drunkenness, orgies, drinking parties, and lawless idolatry." (4:3) Defending one's hope under normal circumstances is difficult enough, let alone such situations as these. It has even become far more difficult these days and as Paul said that "in the last days difficult times will come," as "evil men and impostors will proceed from bad to worse."–2 Timothy 3:1, 13.

There is one more obligation for these new Christians if they are to maintain their right standing before God and strengthen their faith. Yes, they must also declare and defend their hope. Peter's use of the word "hope" is nearly the same with his use of the word "faith" (1 Pet. 1:3, 13, 21). On this, Thomas R. Schreiner writes, "Believers are to be ready constantly to respond to those who ask about their faith. What Peter emphasized is that they were to be prepared to provide a "defense" (NRSV, apologia–rendered "answer" by NIV) to those who ask about the Christian faith." (Schreiner 2003, p. 175) These new Christians were taught the correct course of conduct by the preaching of the Gospel, through which they had accepted the Christian faith, i.e., "the hope." Peter makes this clear when he writes, "It was revealed to them [the prophets] that they were serving not themselves but you, in the things that have now been announced to you through those who preached the good news to you by the Holy Spirit sent from heaven." (1 Pet 1:12) This now placed what obligation on them. Peter went on to command that they "prepare [their] minds for action." (1:13) What action is Peter talking about? He says, "That [they] may proclaim the excellencies of him who called you out of darkness into his marvelous light." (2:9) When should these ones "proclaim the excellencies"? Peter gives the answer in our main

---

[2] I.e. Christ's second coming to judge

[3] to have understanding about practical matters and thus be able to act sensibly–'to have sound judgment, to be sensible, to use good sense, sound judgment.'– GELNTBSD

[4] to be in control of one's thought processes and thus not be in danger of irrational thinking–'to be sober-minded, to be well composed in mind.'–GELNTBSD

text, "always being prepared to make a defense ... for a reason for the hope that is in you."–1 Peter 3:15

We have far worse conditions today than existed in Asia Minor of 2,000 years ago. Satan is still walking around Christianity like a roaring lion, seeking to devour true Christians. However, he knows his time is far shorter, and he has become desperate in his plight to take as many followers of Jesus Christ with him as possible. The world today under the influence of Satan caters to the fleshly desires of the fallen flesh unlike no other time prior to, because technology has the means of reaching billions in the privacy of their own home. The need to evangelize in our own communities has grown as well because so many are abandoning the faith, and many young ones are not taking up the faith of their parents or grandparents. Christians need to be busy in these last days, sharing the good news, helping a new generation come out of the darkness.

1 Peter 1:13-15 English Standard Version (ESV)

[13] Therefore, preparing your minds for action, and being sober-minded, set your hope fully on the grace that will be brought to you at the revelation of Jesus Christ. [14] As obedient children, do not be conformed to the passions of your former ignorance, [15] but as he who called you is holy, you also be holy in all your conduct,

Defending the Hope That Is In You

We must begin with the fact that we must know accurately what the Bible says on different Bible doctrines and be able to offer substantial reasons for the faith. As to the biblical truths, we do not want to remain a spiritual babe. "For everyone who partakes only of milk is not accustomed to the word of righteousness, for he is an infant. But solid food is for the mature, who because of practice have their senses trained to discern good and evil. Therefore leaving the elementary teaching about the Christ, let us press on to maturity." (Hebrews 5:13-6:1) We can consider a Bible example of one, who lack a deeper knowledge, through no fault of his own, correcting it once it was brought to his attention, namely, Apollos. The account is below; notice how he can defend the faith much better after he received the way of God more accurately, he eagerly helps others discover this hope.

Acts 18:24-28 English Standard Version (ESV)

[24] Now a Jew named Apollos, a native of Alexandria, came to Ephesus. He was an eloquent man, competent in the Scriptures. [25] He had been instructed in the way of the Lord. And being fervent in spirit, he spoke and taught accurately the things concerning Jesus, though he knew

only the baptism of John. [26] He began to speak boldly in the synagogue, but when Priscilla and Aquila heard him, they took him aside and explained to him the way of God more accurately. [27] And when he wished to cross to Achaia, the brothers encouraged him and wrote to the disciples to welcome him. When he arrived, he greatly helped those who through grace had believed, [28] for he powerfully refuted the Jews in public, showing by the Scriptures that the Christ was Jesus.

Just as was true of Priscilla and Aquila, Christian evangelists should be able to share the faith accurately to unbelievers, to those who have started to doubt, and to those in Christian denominations that are not on the true path of salvation. If we are to accomplish these things, we must have an accurate, full, true knowledge of God's Word. Paul wrote to the brothers in Colossae, "For this reason also, since the day we heard of it, we have not ceased to pray for you and to ask that you may be filled with the accurate knowledge[5] of his will in all spiritual wisdom and understanding, so as to walk in a manner worthy of the Lord, fully pleasing to him bearing fruit in every good work and increasing in the accurate knowledge[6] of God." – Colossians 1:9-10

This sharing of the Gospel is not just some basic biblical truth of Jesus's life and ministry, death, resurrection and ascension. Moreover, this is not just being able to string many good sounding words together, but rather words that will lead others to the same hope that we hold so dearly. The principle behind Paul's words to the Corinthians makes this point nicely. He wrote, "I would rather speak five words with my mind in order to instruct others, than ten thousand words in a tongue." – 1 Corinthians 14:19

Yes, Christians looking to share biblical truths with others should seek to do so with words of understanding. They should possess an accurate, full and true knowledge about the Father, the Son , The Holy Spirit, the Kingdom of God, and the Father's will and purpose for mankind, as well as the many other laws and principles found in Scripture. Certainly, if we are going to be successful in sharing or defending our beliefs, we must first fully understand them ourselves. Have we bought out the time and applied our mind meditatively in a study of God's Word so that we can effectively share it with others? Paul exhorted his young traveling companion, Timothy, "Do your best to present yourself to God as one

---

[5] *Epignosis* is a strengthened or intensified form of *gnosis* (*epi*, meaning "additional"), meaning, "true," "real," "full," "complete" or "accurate," depending upon the context. Paul and Peter alone use *epignosis*.

[6] *Epignosis* is a strengthened or intensified form of *gnosis* (*epi*, meaning "additional"), meaning, "true," "real," "full," "complete" or "accurate," depending upon the context. Paul and Peter alone use *epignosis*.

10

approved, a worker who has no need to be ashamed, rightly handling the word of truth." (2 Tim. 2:15) On this the following commentaries write,

God bestows his approval on the one who exhibits truth, love, and godliness in daily living, and who correctly handles the word of truth. The false teachers were mishandling God's words, using them for their own benefit. Timothy was commissioned to handle the words of God correctly. All preaching should present the truth clearly, cutting through erroneous ideas or inaccurate opinions.[7]

Third, this same workman (specifically, Timothy but by application today all believers) was to be accurate in delivering the message of truth. The truth is the gospel. Paul showed concern that Timothy would present the gospel without perverting or distorting it. He was not to be turned aside by disputes about words or mere empty prattle.[8]

Paul develops this concept in the striking phrase ... Paul's use of [epaischunomai, aischunomai, and aischune] means "unashamed" in the sense that he does not need to be ashamed of his work. The participle orthotomounta qualifies [ergates] and together with the words that follow specifically describes how Timothy may be unashamed: by being a worker who handles accurately the word of truth.

The material that this worker is to handle correctly is "the word of truth" ... Only when he handles it correctly will he be unashamed ... The rendering given in several of the modern translations, using a combination of the verb "handle" and some adverb such as "accurately" (NASB), "rightly" (RSV), or "correctly" (NIV), for the compound verb [orthotomounta] with the phrase "the word of truth" as the direct object captures this relationship quite well.[9]

If we are going to be "a worker who has no need to be ashamed, rightly handling the word of truth," we must not always rely on others as being more effective, when we are called upon to share or defend our beliefs. Yes, God expects each of us to be capable of supporting our hope

---

[7] Knute Larson, I & II Thessalonians, I & II Timothy, Titus, Philemon, vol. 9, Holman New Testament Commentary (Nashville, TN: Broadman & Holman Publishers, 2000), 286.
[8] Thomas D. Lea and Hayne P. Griffin, 1, 2 Timothy, Titus, vol. 34, The New American Commentary (Nashville: Broadman & Holman Publishers, 1992), 215.
[9] George W. Knight, The Pastoral Epistles: a Commentary on the Greek Text, New International Greek Testament Commentary (Grand Rapids, MI; Carlisle, England: W.B. Eerdmans; Paternoster Press, 1992), 411–412.

with Scripture. We do not want to fall under those who Paul mentioned to Timothy, "always learning and never able to arrive at a knowledge of the truth." (2 Tim. 3:7) We do not want to remain a spiritual babe for our entire Christian life. What do we think of children, who never really grow up and live with their parents off and on for their entire life? When we think of the many different professions in life, such as medicine, law, science, engineer, mechanic and so on, we know that our hands are held throughout our education, but once in the real world, we are expected to be self-reliant. Even Paul said of himself, "When I was a child, I spoke like a child, I thought like a child, I reasoned like a child. When I became a man, I gave up childish ways." – 1 Corinthians 13:11.

If we ever expect to defend our hope effectively, i.e., the faith, we are going to have to study daily. This should not trouble us because it does not take hours every day, but at least 30 minutes or more. The amount that can be accomplished in 30 minutes a day, after 365 days, will be far more than we might have ever expected. A Christian should study the Bible (not just read) a minimum of thirty minutes a day, he should also prepare the lessons assigned for the Bible study at the church and any other service that allows him to prepare ahead of time. A Christian should participate in any comment sessions that are allowed at their particular church, as this gives them practice in effectively sharing biblical truths. Also, A Christian should attend every Christian meeting, as it offers them an opportunity to build others up. A Christian should share every new thing they learn in their personal studies with at least one new friend, which gives them practice at effectively communicating biblical truths. We must have a deep understanding of the biblical truths that we share and defend, which is going to be presented to all kinds of different persons. Our studying daily needs to be a time on the day when we will not be disturbed. We want to turn the phone off, any music, television, and meditatively go through God's Word. The daily study will be our greatest tool for helping us to share and defend the Word of God and out faith effectively. Paul counsels Titus and by extension us as well, "let our people learn to devote themselves to good works, so as to help cases of urgent need, and not be unfruitful." (Titus 3:14) If we are studying daily, preparing for meetings, answering at meetings, attending all meetings, sharing a new biblical truth with friends, we will be able to apply Paul's thoughts to the Colossians as well. He wrote "Let your speech always be gracious, seasoned with salt, so that you may know how you ought to answer each person." – Colossians 4:6

Using the Bible to Defend Our Hope

It should be noted that many today hold back from sharing or defending their Christian faith. Those who do, tend to do so without using the Bible. If we want to defend our hope successfully, we need to have our Bible as the primary evidence of that hope. Our hope lies within God's Word, so we need to use God's Word to defend it. We must persuade with reason from God's Word, not from what we feel, think, or believe. It should be, 'the Word of God says,' Paul wrote,' 'Jesus said,' 'God said,' not 'I feel,' 'I think,' or 'I believe.' It is our effective use of the Bible when we communicated biblical truths to others that are going to convince the right-hearted ones of the truth and the way. One way that we will become more skilled is by our using our Bible at every opportunity: in our personal study of course, in sharing new truths with friends, and especially in looking up every Scripture that is cited in our religious services. Another way is to start paying attention to how commentaries and other study tools, as well as our pastors, elders tie Scriptures together contextually to establish their biblical point. If you were going to share the hope of salvation, could you walk a listener through 5-10 Scriptures that would paint a picture of that hope? Will our listener tell a friend of what they learned, and say, "He straight to his Bible and showed it to me directly!"

If we are sharing or defending biblical truths, we must do so correctly, persuasively, and in such a way that it is easy to grasp. This means that we know it well ourselves, and we have prepared well by communicating in more relaxed moments, which made us better communicators. For example, can we explain the resurrection hope at this very moment to another if they asked? Will our explanation be from the Bible? Will it be what the author meant by the words he used? Will it be persuasive? Will it be easy to follow and understand? If not, then, how can we honestly say we have a resurrection hope? Is there not irony that many young girls can tell you everything about Taylor Swift, but little if anything about their heavenly Father? The same is true of adult males, who can tear a car apart blindfolded, but cannot string along a handful of verses that defend their resurrection hope. And yes, adult females have an immense amount of knowledge about subject matters that interest them, yet likely cannot support their resurrection hope any better. The above are a bit of a stereotype, which is noted, but it makes the point that we prepare for worldly things with far more vigor than we prepare to share and defend the faith.

If we are going to have any success in defending our Christian faith, we must be able to overcome the objections of others. We will find that the same objections are repeatedly used. Therefore, we will eventually, be able to overcome the standard objections easily. However, a couple words of caution. First, we do not want to become complacent in our response to common objections; because the listener needs to feel as though they are getting an emotionally involved response, not some automatize, robotic response, as if we feel like, 'here we go again.' Second, do not be complacent in thinking that every objection is going to be the common ones. If someone has an objection that we have never addressed, just simply say, "you raise a very good point, and the next time we speak, I will give you a logical and reasonable answer." When we research his objection, do so to the point that we know it inside and out. Moreover, be aware that 99 percent of all Bible difficulties have logical, reasonable answers. On this, R. A. Torrey writes, "Humbly. Recognize the limitations of your own mind and knowledge, and do not for a moment imagine that there is no solution just because you have found none. There is, in all probability, a very simple solution, even when you can find no solution at all."[10] In the end, there are answers, so meditate on the objection that has been raised, search through the literature, looking for Scripture and arguments to refute the objection in defense of the faith. Out of many thousands of Bible difficulties that have answers as to why they are, in fact, Bible difficulties and not errors, mistakes or contradictions, there are but a handful that has yet to be answered. This does not mean there is no answer, just that the information needed may be lacking, or it is something we will have to wait on until, a greater mind comes along, or until the second coming of Christ. However, really, if science had answers to many thousands of issues, but only a few remained unanswered, we would never hear the end of it. It is amazing that we have what we have considering we are dealing with a book where parts of it were penned 2,000 years ago while other parts were written 3,500 years ago.

As a proclaimer and defender of the faith, always be on the alert for points that can be used to overcome objections that we have heard, or what logically sounds like an objection one might raise. Whether we are studying a book, working on the our Bible reading with a commentary or sitting in a pew listening to a talk from our elder or pastor, have our mind attuned to such things. Say, we ae sitting at church, the pastor or elder makes an excellent point that overcomes a particular Bible objection (The Bible is not practical for our day, or there are so many different interpretations, who can know the truth), so we write it down in out notebook, because, yes, we have a notebook and pen. This will further implant the point in our mind. Now, we take it a step further. Find three different people after the meeting and say, "I really enjoyed what the pastor or elder had to say about the objection that the Bible is not

---

[10] http://www.christianpublishers.org/handling-bible-difficulties

practical for our day." Then, we should proceed to reiterate what was said in our own words. This will further embed it in our mind. Our notebook can be used for all kinds of notes at the meetings or during our personal study, but if we take notes on some objection or a Bible difficulty of some sort, highlight it a particular color. Why? We do this because we will also have another notebook that is specifically for Bible difficulties and Bible objections, so we have prepared and refutations. In this special notebook, leave the first few pages blank, as it will serve as out table of content. We can number our pages, so in the front we can write down a phrase that will tell us what the issue is and the page on which it can be found.

Therefore Christian defenders of God's Word and principles,

2 Timothy 2:15 English Standard Version (ESV)

[15] Do your best to present yourself to God as one approved, a worker who has no need to be ashamed, rightly handling the word of truth.

Let us have the spirit of Paul,

1 Corinthians 9:16-17 English Standard Version (ESV)

[16] For if I preach the gospel, that gives me no ground for boasting. For necessity is laid upon me. Woe to me if I do not preach the gospel![17] For if I do this of my own will, I have a reward, but if not of my own will, I am still entrusted with a stewardship.

CHAPTER 1 Bible Difficulties Explained

IT SEEMS THAT the charge that the Bible contradicts itself has been made more and more in the last 20 years. Generally, those making such claims are merely repeating what they have heard, because most have not even read the Bible, let alone done an in-depth study of it. I do not wish, however, to set aside all concerns as though they have no merit. There are many who raise legitimate questions that seem, on the surface anyway, to be about well-founded contradiction. Sadly, these issues have caused many to lose their faith in God's Word, the Bible. The purpose of this books is, to help its readers to be able to defend the Bible against Bible critics (1 Pet. 3:15), to contend for the faith (Jude 1:3), and help those, who have begun to doubt. – Jude 1:22-23.

Before we begin explaining things, let us jump right in, getting our feet wet, and deal with two major Bible difficulties, so we can see that there are reasonable, logical answers. After that, we will delve deeper into explaining Bible difficulties.

Is God permitting Human Sacrifice?

Judges 11:29-34, 37-40? Updated American Standard Version (UASV)

29 Then the Spirit of the Lord was upon Jephthah, and he passed through Gilead and Manasseh; and passed on to Mizpah of Gilead, and from Mizpah of Gilead he passed on to the sons of Ammon. **30** And Jephthah **made a vow** to Jehovah and said, "If You will indeed give the sons of Ammon into my hand, **31** then it shall be that **whatever** comes out of the doors of my house to meet me when I return in peace from the sons of Ammon, it shall be Jehovah's, and I will offer it up as a burnt offering." **32** So Jephthah crossed over to the sons of Ammon to fight against them; and Jehovah gave them into his hand. **33** He struck them with a very great slaughter from Aroer as far as Minnith, twenty cities, and as far as Abel-keramim. So the sons of Ammon were subdued before the sons of Israel.

34 When Jephthah came to his house at Mizpah, behold, **his daughter was coming out to meet him** with tambourines and with dancing. Now she was his one and only child; besides her he had no son or daughter.

37 And she said to her father, "Let this thing be done for me: leave me alone two months, that I may go up and down on the mountains and weep because of my virginity, I and my companions." **38** And he said, "Go." So he sent her away for two months; and **she left with her**

companions, and wept on the mountains because of her virginity. [39] At the end of two months she returned to her father, who did to her according to the vow that he had made; and she never known a man.[11] Thus it became a custom in Israel, [40] that the daughters of Israel went year by year to commemorate[12] the daughter of Jephthah the Gileadite four days in the year.

It is true; to infer that having the idea of an animal sacrifice would really have not been an impressive vow, which the context requires. Human sacrifice will be repugnant if we are talking about taking a life. Jephthah had no sons, so he likely knew it was the daughter, who would come to greet him.

First, the text does not say he killed his daughter. The idea of some that he did kill her is concluded only by inference. While it is not good policy to interpret backward, using Paul on Judges, he does say humans are to be "as a living sacrifice." Therefore, Jephthah could have offered his daughter at the temple, "as a living sacrifice" in service, like Samuel.

This is not to be taken dismissively, because, under Jewish backgrounds, it is no small thing to offer a perpetual virginity as a sacrifice. This would mean Jephthah's lineage would not be carried on, the family name, was no more.

Second, the context says she went out to weep for two months, not mourn her death. It says, "she left with her companions, and wept on the mountains because of her virginity."

If she was facing imminent death, she could have married, and spent that last two months as a married woman. There would be absolutely no reason for her to mourn her virginity if she were not facing perpetual virginity. – Exodus 38:8; 1 Samuel 2:22

Third, it was completely forbidden to offer a human sacrifice. – Leviticus 18:21; 20:2-5; Deuteronomy 12:31; 18:10

Imagine an Israelite believing that he could please God with a human sacrifice that was intended to offer up a human life. To do so would have been a rejection of Jehovah's Sovereignty (the very person you are asking for help), and a rejection of the Law that made them a special people. Worse still, this interpretation would have us believe that Jehovah knew this was coming, allowed the vow, and then aided this type of man to succeed over his enemies.

---

[11] I.e., *never had relations with a man*
[12] Or *lament*

The last point is simple enough. If such a man as one who would make such a vow, in gross violation of the law, and then carry it out; there is no way he would be mentioned by Paul in Hebrews chapter 11 among the most faithful men and women in Israelite history.

In review, there is no way God would have granted and helped in Jephthah's initial success knowing the vow that was coming because both Jehovah and Jephthah would be as bad as the Canaanites. There is no way that God would accept such a vow and then go on to help Jephthah with his enemies yet again. Then, to allow such a vow to be carried out, to then put Jephthah on the wall of star witnesses for God in Hebrews chapter 11.

Does Isaiah 45:7 mean that God Is the Author of Evil?

Isaiah 45:7 King James Version (KJV)	**Isaiah 45:7** English Standard Version (ESV)
7 I form the light, and create darkness: I make peace, and **create evil**: I the Lord do all these things.	7 I form light and create darkness, I make well-being and **create calamity**, I am the Lord, who does all these things.[13]

Encarta Dictionary: (Evil) (1) morally bad: profoundly immoral or wrong (2) deliberately causing great harm, pain, or upset

QUESTION: Is this view of evil always the case? No, as you will see below.

Some apologetic authors try to say, 'we do not understand Isaiah 45:7 correctly, because there are other verses that say God is not evil (1 John 1:5), cannot look approvingly on evil (Hab. 1:13), and cannot be tempted by evil. (James 1:13)' Well, while all of these things are Scripturally true, the question at hand is not: Is God evil, can God approvingly look on evil, or can God be tempted with evil? Those questions are not relevant to the one at hand, as God cannot be those things, and at the same time, he can be the yes to our question. The question is, is God the author, the creator of evil?

We would hardly argue that God was **not just** in his bringing "calamity" or "evil" down on Adam and Eve. Thus, we have Isaiah 45:7 saying that God is the creator of "calamity" or "evil."

Let us begin simple, without trying to be philosophical. When God removed Adam and Eve from the Garden of Eden, he sentenced them and humanity to sickness, old age, and death. (Rom. 5:8; i.e., enforce

---

[13] See Jeremiah 18:11, Lamentations 3:18, and Amos 3:6

penalty for sin), which was to bring "calamity" or "evil" upon humankind. Therefore, as we can see "evil" does not always mean wrongdoing. Other examples of God bringing "calamity" or "evil" are Noah and the flood, the Ten Plagues of Egypt, and the destruction of the Canaanites. These acts of evil were not acts of wrongdoing. Rather, they were righteous and just, because God, the Creator of all things, was administering justice to wrongdoers, to sinners. He warned the perfect first couple what the penalty was for sin. He warned the people for a hundred years by Noah's preaching. He warned the Canaanites centuries before.

Nevertheless, there are times, when God extends mercy, refraining from the execution of his righteous judgment to one worthy of calamity. For example, he warned Nineveh, the city of blood, and they repented, so he pardoned them. (Jonah 3:10) God has made it a practice to warn persons of the results of sin, giving them undeservedly many opportunities to change their ways. – Ezekiel 33:11.

God cannot sin; it is impossible for him to do so. So, when did he create evil? Without getting into the eternity of his knowing what he was going to do, and when, let us just say, evil did not exist when he was the only person in existence. We might say the idea of evil existed because he knew what he was going to do. However, the moment he created creatures (spirit and human), the potential for evil came into existence because both have free will to sin (fall short of perfection). Evil became a reality the moment Satan entertained the idea of causing Adam to sin, to get humanity for himself, and then acted on it.

God has the right and is just to bring the *calamity of* or *evil* down on anyone that is an unrepentant sinner. God did not even have to give us the underserved kindness of offering us his Son. God is the author or agent of evil regardless of the source books that claim otherwise. If he had never created free will beings, evil would have never gone from the idea of evil to the potential of evil, to the existence of evil. However, God felt that it was better to get the sinful state out of angel and human existence, recover, and then any who would sin thereafter; he would be justified in handing out evil or calamity to only that person or angel alone.

Who among us would argue that he should have created humans and angels like robots, automatons with no free will? The moment he chose the free will, he moved evil from an idea to a potential, and Satan moved it to reality. God has a moral nature that does not bring about evil and sin when he is the only person in existence. However, the moment he created beings in his image, which had the potential to sin, he brought about evil. The moment we have a moral code of good and evil that is placed upon one's with free will; then, we have evil as a potential.

19

In English, the very comprehensive Hebrew word ra' is variously translated as "bad," "downcast (sad, NASB)," "ugly," "evil," "grievous (distressing, NASB)," "sore," "selfish (stingy, HCSB)," and "envious," depending upon the context. (Gen 2:9; 40:7; 41:3; Ex 33:4; Deut. 6:22; 28:35; Pro 23:6; 28:22)

Evil as an adjective **describes** the **quality of** a class of people, places, or things, or of a specific person, place, or thing

Evil as a noun, **defines** the **nature** of a class of people, places, or things, or of a specific person, place, or thing (e.g., the evil one, evil eye).

We can agree that "evil" is a thing. Create means to bring something into existence, be it people, places, or things, as well something abstract, for lack of a better word at the moment. We would agree that when God was alone evil was not a reality; it did not exist? We would agree that the moment that God created free will creatures (angels and humans), creating humans in his image, with his moral nature, he also brought the potential for evil into existence, and it was realized by Satan?

Inerrancy: Can the Bible Be trusted?

If the Bible is the Word of God, it should be in complete agreement throughout; there should be no contradictions. Yet, the rational mind must ask, why is it that some passages appear to be contradictions when compared with others? For example, Numbers 25:9 tells us that 24,000 died from the scourge, whereas at 1 Corinthians 10:8, the apostle Paul says it was 23,000. This would seem to be a clear error. Before addressing such matters, let us first look at some background information.

Full inerrancy in this book means that the original writings are fully without error in all that they state, as are the words. The words were not dictated (automaton), but the intended meaning is inspired, as are the words that convey that meaning. The Author allowed the writer to use his style of writing, yet controlled the meaning to the extent of not allowing the writer to choose a wrong word, which would not convey the intended meaning. Other more liberal-minded persons hold with *partial inerrancy*, which claims that as far as faith is concerned, this portion of God's Word is without error, but that there are historical, geographical, and scientific errors.

There are several different levels of inerrancy. *Absolute Inerrancy* is the belief that the Bible is fully true and exact in every way; including not only relationships and doctrine, but also science and history. In other words, all information is completely exact. *Full Inerrancy* is the belief that the Bible was not written as a science or historical textbook, but is phenomenological, in that it is written from the human perspective. In other words, speaking of such things as the sun rising, the four corners of the earth or the rounding off of number approximations are all from a human perspective. *Limited Inerrancy* is the belief that the Bible is meant only as a reflection of God's purposes and will, so the science and history is the understanding of the author's day, and is limited. Thus, the Bible is susceptible to errors in these areas. *Inerrancy of Purpose* is the belief that it is only inerrant in the purpose of bringing its readers to a saving faith. The Bible is not about facts, but about persons and relationships, thus, it is subject to error. *Inspired: Not Inerrant* is the belief that its authors are human and thus subject to human error. It should be noted that this author holds the position of full inerrancy.

For many today, the Bible is nothing more than a book written by men. The Bible critic believes the Bible to be full of myths and legends, contradictions, and geographical, historical, and scientific errors. University professor Gerald A. Larue had this to say, "The views of the writers as expressed in the Bible reflect the ideas, beliefs, and concepts current in their own times and are limited by the extent of knowledge in those times."[14] On the other hand, the Bible's authors claim that their writings were inspired of God, as Holy Spirit moved them along. We will discover shortly that the Bible critics have much to say, but it is inflated or empty.

2 Timothy 3:16-17 Updated American Standard Version (UASV)

[16] All Scripture is inspired by God and profitable for teaching, for reproof, for correction, for training in righteousness; [17] so that the man of God may be fully competent, equipped for every good work.

2 Peter 1:21 Updated American Standard Version (UASV)

[21] for no prophecy was ever produced by the will of man, but men carried along by the Holy Spirit spoke from God.

The question remains as to whether the Bible is a book written by imperfect men and full of errors, or is written by imperfect men, but inspired by God. If the Bible is just another book by imperfect man, there is no hope for humankind. If it is inspired by God and without error, although penned by imperfect men, we have the hope of everything that it offers: a rich, happy life now by applying counsel that lies within and the real life that is to come, everlasting life. This author contends that the Bible is inspired of God and free of human error, although written by imperfect humans.

---

[14] Gerald Larue, "The Bible as a Political Weapon," *Free Inquiry* (Summer 1983): 39.

Before we take on the critics who seem to sift the Scriptures looking for problematic verses, let us take a moment to reflect on how we should approach these alleged problem texts. The critic's argument goes something like this: 'If God does not err and the Bible is the Word of God, then the Bible should not have one single error or contradiction, yet it is full of errors and contradictions.' If the Bible is riddled with nothing but contradictions and errors as the critics would have us believe, why, out of 31,173 verses in the Bible, should there be only 2-3 thousand Bible difficulties that are called into question, this being less than ten percent of the whole?

First, let it be said that it is every Christian's obligation to get a deeper understanding of God's Word, just as the apostle Paul told Timothy:

1 Timothy 4:15-16 Updated American Standard Version (UASV)

[15] Practice these things, be absorbed in them, so that your progress will be evident to all. [16] Pay close attention to yourself and to your teaching; persevere in these things, for as you do this you will ensure salvation both for yourself and for those who hear you.

Paul also told the Corinthians:

2 Corinthians 10:4-5 Updated American Standard Version (UASV)

[4] For the weapons of our warfare are not of the flesh[15] but powerful to God for destroying strongholds.[16] [5] We are destroying speculations and every lofty thing raised up against the knowledge of God, and we are taking every thought captive to the obedience of Christ,

Paul also told the Philippians:

Philippians 1:7 Updated American Standard Version (UASV)

[7] It is right for me to feel thus about you all, because I hold you in my heart, for you are all partakers with me of grace, both in my imprisonment and in the defense and confirmation of the gospel.

In being able to defend against the modern-day critic, one has to be able to reason from the Scriptures and overturn the critic's argument(s) with mildness. If someone were to approach us about an alleged error or contradiction, what should we do? We should be frank and honest. If we do not have an answer, we should admit such. If the text in question gives the appearance of difficulty, we should admit this as well. If we are

---

[15] That is *merely human*

[16] That is *tearing down false arguments*

unsure as to how we should answer, we can simply say that we will look into it and get back to them, returning with a reasonable answer.

However, we do not want to express disbelief and doubt to our critics, because they will be emboldened in their disbelief. It will put them on the offense and us on the defense. With great confidence, we can express that there is an answer. The Bible has withstood the test of 2,000 years of persecution and interrogation and yet it is the most printed book of all time, currently being translated into 2,287 languages. If these critical questions were so threatening, the Bible would not be the book that it is.

When we are pursuing the text in question, be unwavering in purpose, or resolved to find an answer. In some cases, it may take hours of digging to find the solution. Consider this: as we resolve these difficulties, we are also building our faith that God's Word is inerrant. Moreover, we will want to do preventative maintenance in our personal study. As we are doing our Bible reading, take note of these surface discrepancies and resolve them as we work our way through the Bible. We need to make this part of our prayers as well. I recommend the following program. Below are several books that deal with difficult passages. As we daily read and study our Bible from Genesis to Revelation, do not attempt it in one year; make it a four-year program. Use a good exegetical commentary like *The Holman Old/New Testament Commentary* (HOTC/HNTC) or *The New American Commentary* set, and *The Big Book of Bible Difficulties* by Norman L. Geisler, as well as *The Encyclopedia of Bible Difficulties* by Gleason Archer.

We should be aware that men under inspiration penned the originally written books. In fact, we do not have those originals, what textual scholars call autographs, but we do have thousands of copies. The copyists, however, were not inspired; therefore, as one might expect, throughout the first 1,400 years of copying, thousands of errors were transmitted into the texts that were being copied by imperfect hands that were not under inspiration when copying. Yet, the next 450 years saw a restoration of the text by textual scholars from around the world. Therefore, while many of our best literal translations today may not be inspired, they are a mirror-like reflection of the autographs by way of textual criticism.[17] Therefore, the fallacy could be with the copyist error that has simply not been weeded out. In addition, we must keep in mind that God's Word is without error, but our interpretation and understanding of that Word is not.

---

[17] Textual criticism is the study of copies of any written work of which the autograph (original) is unknown, with the purpose of ascertaining the original text. Harold J. Green, Introduction to New Testament Textual Criticism (Peabody, MA: Hendrickson, 1995), 1.

It should be noted that the Bible is made up of 66 smaller books that were hand-written over a period of 1,600 years, having some 40 writers of various trades such as shepherd, king, priest, tax collector, governor, physician, copyist, fisherman, and a tentmaker. Therefore, it should not surprise us that some difficulties are encountered as we casually read the Bible. Yet, if one were to take a deeper look, one would find that these difficulties are easily explained. Let us take a few pages to examine some passages that have been under attack.

This chapter's objective is not to be exhaustive, not even close. What we are looking to do is cover a few alleged contradictions and a couple of alleged mistakes. This is to give us a small sampling of the reasonable answers that we will find in the above recommended books. Remember, our Bible is a sword that we must use both offensively and defensively. One must wonder how long a warrior of ancient times would last who was not expertly trained in the use of his weapon. Let us look at a few scriptures that support our need to learn our Bible well so will be able to defend what we believe to be true.

When "false apostles, deceitful workmen, disguising themselves as apostles of Christ" were causing trouble in the congregation in Corinth, the apostle Paul wrote that under such circumstances, we are to *tear down their arguments* and *take every thought captive*. (2 Corinthians 10:4, 5; 11:13–15) All who present critical arguments against God's Word, or contrary to it, can have their arguments overturned by the Christian, who is able and ready to defend that Word in mildness. – 2 Timothy 2:24–26.

1 Peter 3:15 Updated American Standard Version (UASV)

[15] but sanctify Christ as Lord in your hearts, always being prepared to make a defense[18] to anyone who asks you for a reason for the hope that is in you; yet do it with gentleness and respect;

Peter says that we need to be prepared to make a *defense*. The Greek word behind the English 'defense' is *apologia*, which is actually a legal term that refers to the defense of a defendant in court. Our English apologetics is just what Peter spoke of, having the ability to give a reason to any who may challenge us, or to answer those who are not challenging us but who have honest questions that deserve to be answered.

2 Timothy 2:24-25 Updated American Standard Version (UASV)

[24] For a slave of the Lord does not need to fight, but needs to be kind to all, qualified to teach, showing restraint when wronged [25] with

---

[18] Or *argument*; or *explanation*

gentleness correcting those who are in opposition, if perhaps God may grant them repentance leading to accurate knowledge[19] of the truth,

Look at the Greek word (*epignosis*) behind the English "knowledge" in the above. "It is more intensive than *gnosis* (1108), knowledge because it expresses a more thorough participation in the acquiring of knowledge on the part of the learner."[20] The requirement of all of the Lord's servants is that they be able to teach, but not in a quarrelsome way, and in a way to correct his opponents with mildness. Why? Because the purpose of it all is that by God, and through the Christian teacher, one may come to repentance and begin taking in an accurate knowledge of the truth.

Inerrancy: Practical Principles to Overcoming Bible Difficulties

Below are several ways of looking at the Bible that enable the reader to see he is not dealing with an error or contradiction, but rather a Bible difficulty.

Different Points of View

At times, you may have two different writers who are writing from two different points of view.

Numbers 35:14 Updated American Standard Version (UASV)

[14] You shall give three cities across the Jordan and three cities you shall give in the land of Canaan; they will be cities of refuge.

Joshua 22:4 Updated American Standard Version (UASV)

[4] And now Jehovah your God has given rest to your brothers, as he spoke to them; therefore turn now and go to your tents, to the land of your possession, which Moses the servant of Jehovah gave you beyond the Jordan. [on the other side of the Jordan, ESV]

Here we see that Moses is speaking about the east side of the Jordan when he says "on this side of the Jordan." Joshua, on the other hand, is also speaking about the east side of the Jordan when he says "on the other side of the Jordan." So, who is correct? Both are. When Moses was penning Numbers the Israelites had not yet crossed the Jordan River, so the east side was "this side," the side he was on. On the other hand, when

---

[19] *Epignosis* is a strengthened or intensified form of *gnosis* (*epi*, meaning "additional"), meaning, "true," "real," "full," "complete" or "accurate," depending upon the context. Paul and Peter alone use *epignosis*.

[20] Spiros Zodhiates, *The Complete Word Study Dictionary: New Testament*, Electronic ed. (Chattanooga, TN: AMG Publishers, 2000, c1992, c1993), S. G1922.

Joshua penned his book, the Israelites had crossed the Jordan, so the east side was just as he had said, "on the other side of the Jordan." Thus, we should not assume that two different writers are writing from the same perspective.

A Careful Reading

At times, it may simply be a case of needing to slow down and carefully read the account, considering exactly what is being said.

Joshua 18:28 Updated American Standard Version (UASV)

[28] and Zelah, Haeleph and the Jebusite (that is, Jerusalem), Gibeah, Kiriath; fourteen cities with their villages. This is the inheritance of the sons of Benjamin according to their families.

Judges 1:21 Updated American Standard Version (UASV)

[21] But the sons of Benjamin did not drive out the Jebusites who lived in Jerusalem; so the Jebusites have lived with the sons of Benjamin in Jerusalem to this day.

Joshua 15:63 Updated American Standard Version (UASV)

[63] But as for the Jebusites, the inhabitants of Jerusalem, the sons of Judah could not drive them out; so the Jebusites live with the sons of Judah at Jerusalem until this day.

Judges 1:8-9 Updated American Standard Version (UASV)

[8] And then the sons of Judah fought against Jerusalem and captured it and struck it with the edge of the sword and set the city on fire. [9] And afterward the sons of Judah went down to fight against the Canaanites living in the hill country and in the Negev[21] and in the Shephelah.[22]

2 Samuel 5:5-9 Updated American Standard Version (UASV)

[5] At Hebron he reigned over Judah seven years and six months, and in Jerusalem he reigned thirty-three years over all Israel and Judah.

[6] And the king and his men went to Jerusalem against the Jebusites, the inhabitants of the land, and they said to David, "You shall not come in here, but the blind and lame will turn you away"; thinking, "David cannot come in here." [7] Nevertheless, David captured the stronghold of Zion, that is the city of David. [8] And David said on that day, "Whoever would strike the Jebusites, let him get up the water shaft to attack 'the

---

[21] I.e. *South*
[22] I.e., lowland

lame and the blind,' who are hated by David's soul." Therefore it is said, "The blind and the lame shall not come into the house." [9] And David lived in the stronghold and called it the city of David. And David built all around from the Millo and inward.

There is no doubt that even the advanced Bible reader of many years can come away confused because the above accounts seem to be contradictory. In Joshua 18:28 and Judges 1:21, we see that Jerusalem was an inheritance of the tribe of Benjamin, yet the Benjamites were unable to conquer Jerusalem. However, in Joshua 15:63 we see that the tribe of Judah could not conquer them either, with the reading giving the impression that it was a part of their inheritance. In Judges 1:8, however, Judah was eventually able to conquer Jerusalem and burn it with fire. Yet, to add even more to the confusion, we find at 2 Samuel 5:5–8 that David is said to have conquered Jerusalem hundreds of years later.

Now that we have the particulars let us look at it more clearly. The boundary between Benjamin's inheritances ran right through the middle of Jerusalem. Joshua 8:28 is correct, in that what would later be called the "city of David" was in the territory of Benjamin, but it also in part crossed over the line into the territory of Judah, causing both tribes to go to war against this Jebusite city. It is also true that the tribe of Benjamin was unable to conquer the city and that the tribe of Judah eventually did. However, if you look at Judges 1:9 again, you will see that Judah did not finish the job entirely and moved on to conquer other areas. This allowed the remaining ones to regroup and form a resistance that neither Benjamin nor Judah could overcome, so these Jebusites remained until the time of David, hundreds of years later.

Intended Meaning of Writer

First, the Bible student needs to understand the level that the Bible intends to be exact in what is written. If Jim told a friend that 650 graduated with him from high school in 1984, it is not challenged, because it is all too clear that he is using rounded numbers and is not meaning to be exactly precise. This is how God's Word operates as well. Sometimes it means to be exact, at other times, it is simply rounding numbers, in other cases, the intention of the writer is a general reference, to give readers of that time and succeeding generations some perspective. Did Samuel, the author of judges, intend to pen a book on the chronology of Judges, or was his focus on the falling away, oppression, and the rescue by a judge, repeatedly. Now, it would seem that Jeremiah, the author of 1 Kings was more interested in giving his readers an exact number of years.

Acts 2:41 Updated American Standard Version (UASV)

[41] So those who received his word were baptized, and there were added that day about three thousand souls.

As you can see here, numbers within the Bible are often used with approximations. This is a frequent practice even today, in both written works and verbal conversation.

Acts 7:2-3 Updated American Standard Version (UASV)

[2] And Stephen said:

"Brothers and fathers, hear me. The God of glory appeared to our father Abraham when he was in Mesopotamia, before he lived in Haran, [3] and said to him, 'Go out from your land and from your kindred and go into the land that I will show you.'

If you were to check the Hebrew Scriptures at Genesis 12:1, you would find that what is claimed to have been said by God to Abraham is not quoted word-for-word; it is simply a paraphrase. This is a normal practice within Scripture and in writing in general.

Numbers 34:15 Updated American Standard Version (UASV)

[15] The two and a half tribes have received their inheritance beyond the Jordan opposite Jericho, eastward toward the sunrising."

Just as you would read in today's local newspaper, the Bible writer has written from the human standpoint, how it appeared to him. The Bible also speaks of "to the end of the earth" (Psalm 46:9), "from the four corners of the earth" (Isa 11:12), and "the four winds of the earth" (Revelation 7:1). These phrases are still used today.

Unexplained Does Not mean Unexplainable

Considering that there are 31,173 verses in the Bible, encompassing 66 books written by about 40 writers, ranging from shepherds to kings, an army general, fishermen, tax collector, a physician and on and on, and being penned over a 1,600 year period, one does find a few hundred Bible difficulties (about one percent). However, 99 percent of those are explainable. Yet no one wants to be so arrogant to say that he can explain them all. It has nothing to do with the inadequacy of God's Word but is based on human understanding. In many cases, science or archaeology and the field of custom and culture of ancient peoples has helped explain difficulties in hundreds of passages. Therefore, there may be less than one percent left to be answered, yet our knowledge of God's Word continues to grow.

Guilty Until Proven Innocent

This is exactly the perception that the critic has of God's Word. The legal principle of being "innocent until proven guilty" afforded mankind in courts of justice is withheld from the very Word of God. What is ironic here is that this policy has contributed to these Bible critics looking foolish over and over again when something comes to light that vindicates the portion of Scripture they are challenging.

Daniel 5:1 Updated American Standard Version (UASV)

[1] Belshazzar the king made[23] a great feast for a thousand of his nobles, and he was drinking wine in the presence of the thousand.

Bible critics had long claimed that Belshazzar was not known outside of the book Daniel; therefore, they argue that Daniel was mistaken. Yet it hardly seems prudent to argue error from absence of outside evidence. Just because archaeology had not discovered such a person did not mean that Daniel was wrong, or that such a person did not exist. In 1854, some small clay cylinders were discovered in modern-day southern Iraq, which would have been the city of Ur in ancient Babylonia. The cuneiform documents were a prayer of King Nabonidus for "Bel-sar-ussur, my eldest son." These tablets also showed that this "Bel-sar-ussur" had secretaries as well as a household staff. Other tablets were discovered a short time later that showed that the kingship was entrusted to this eldest son as a coregent while his father was away.

He entrusted the 'Camp' to his oldest (son), the firstborn [Belshazzar], the troops everywhere in the country he ordered under his (command). He let (everything) go, entrusted the kingship to him and, himself, he [Nabonidus] started out for a long journey, the (military) forces of Akkad marching with him; he turned towards Tema (deep) in the west."[24]

Ignoring Literary Styles

The Bible is a diverse book when it comes to literary styles: narrative, poetic, prophetic, and apocalyptic; also containing parables, metaphors, similes, hyperbole, and other figures of speech. Too often, these alleged errors are the result of a reader taking a figure of speech as literal, or reading a parable as though it is a narrative.

---

[23] I.e., held

[24] J. Pritchard, ed., *Ancient Near Eastern Texts* (1974), 313.

Matthew 24:35 Updated American Standard Version (UASV)

[35] Heaven and earth will pass away, but my words will not pass away.

If some do not recognize that they are dealing with a figure of speech, they are bound to come away with the wrong meaning. Some have concluded from Matthew 24:35 that Jesus was speaking of an eventual destruction of the earth. This is hardly the case, as his listeners would not have understood it that way based on their understanding of the Old Testament. They would have understood that he was simply being emphatic about the words he spoke, using hyperbole. What he was conveying is that his words are more enduring than heaven and earth, and with heaven and earth being understood as eternal, this merely conveyed even more so that Jesus' words could be trusted.

Two Accounts of the Same Incident

If you were to speak to officers that take accident reports for their police department, you would find that there is cohesion in the accounts, but each person has merely witnessed aspects that have stood out to them. We will see that this is the case as well with the examples below, which is the same account in two different gospels:

Matthew 8:5 Updated American Standard Version (UASV)

[5] When he[25] had entered Capernaum, a centurion came forward to him, imploring him,

Luke 7:2-3 Updated American Standard Version (UASV)

[2] And a centurion's[26] slave, who was highly regarded[27] by him, was sick and about to die. [3] When he heard about Jesus, he sent some older men of the Jews[28] asking him to come and bring his slave safely through.[29]

Immediately we see the problem of whether the centurion or the elders of the Jews spoke with Jesus. The solution is not really hidden from us. Which of the two accounts is the most detailed account? You are correct if you said, Luke. The centurion sent the elders of the Jews to represent him to Jesus, so; that whatever response Jesus might give, it

---

[25] That is *Jesus*

[26] I.e., army officer over a hundred solderiers

[27] Lit *to whom he was honorable*

[28] Or *Jewish elders*

[29] I.e., *save the life of his slave*

would be as though he were addressing the centurion; therefore, Matthew gave his readers the basic thought, not seeing the need of mentioning the elders of the Jews aspect. This is how a representative was viewed in the first century, just as some countries see ambassadors today as being the very person they represent. Therefore, both Matthew and Luke are correct.

Man's Fallible Interpretations

Inspiration by God is infallible, without error. Imperfect man and his interpretations over the centuries, as bad as many of them have been, should not cast a shadow over God's inspired Word. The entire Word of God has one meaning and one meaning only for every penned word, which is what God willed to be conveyed by the human writer he chose to use.

The Autograph Alone Is Inspired and Inerrant

It has been argued by conservative scholars that only the autograph manuscripts were inspired and inerrant, not the copying of those manuscripts over the next 3,000 years for the Old Testament and 1,500 years for the New Testament. While I would agree with this position as well, it should be noted that we do not possess the autographs, so to argue that they are inerrant is to speak of nonexistent documents. However, it should be further understood that through the science of textual criticism, we can establish a mirror reflection of the autograph manuscripts. B. F. Westcott, F. J. A. Hort, F. F. Bruce, and many other textual scholars would agree with Norman L Geisler's assessment: "The New Testament, then, has not only survived in more manuscripts than any other book from antiquity, but it has survived in a purer form than any other great book—*a form that is 99.5 percent pure.*"[30]

An example of a copyist error can be found in Luke's genealogy of Jesus at Luke 3:35–37. In verse 37 you will find a Cainan, and in verse 36 you will find a second Cainan between Arphaxad (Arpachshad) and Shelah. As one can see from most footnotes in different study Bibles, the Cainan in verse 36 is seen as a scribal error, and is not found in the Hebrew Old Testament, the Samaritan Pentateuch, or the Aramaic Targums, but is found in the Greek Septuagint. (Genesis 10:24; 11:12, 13; 1 Chronicles 1:18, but not 1 Chronicles 1:24) It seems quite unlikely that it was in the earlier copies of the Septuagint, because the first-century Jewish historian Josephus lists Shelah next as the son of Arphaxad, and Josephus

---

[30] Norman L. Geisler and William E. Nix: *A General Introduction to the Bible* (Chicago, Moody Press, 1980), 367. (Emphasis is mine.)

normally followed the Septuagint.[31] So one might ask why this second Cainan is found in the translations at all if this is the case? The manuscripts that do contain this second Cainan are some of the best manuscripts that are used in establishing the original text: 01 B L A¹ 33 (Kainam); A 038 044 0102 A¹³ (Kainan).

Look at the Context

Many alleged inconsistencies disappear by simply looking at the context. Taking words out of context can distort their meaning. *Merriam-Webster's Collegiate Dictionary* defines context as "the parts of a discourse that surround a word or passage and can throw light on its meaning."[32] Context can also be "the circumstances or events that form the environment within which something exists or takes place." If we were to look in a thesaurus for a synonym, we would find "background" for this second meaning. At 2 Timothy 2:15, the apostle Paul brings home the point of why context is so important: "Do your best to present yourself to God as one approved, a worker who has no need to be ashamed, rightly handling the word of truth."

Ephesians 2:8-9 Updated American Standard Version (UASV)

⁸ For by grace you have been saved through faith; and that not of yourselves, it is the gift of God; ⁹ not from works, so that no man may boast.

James 2:26 Updated American Standard Version (UASV)

²⁶ For as the body apart from the spirit[33] is dead, so also faith apart from works is dead.

So, which is it? Is salvation possible by faith alone as Paul wrote to the Ephesians, or is faith dead without works as James wrote to his readers? As our subtitle brings out, let us look at the context. In the letter to the Ephesians, the apostle Paul is speaking to the Jewish Christians who were looking to the works of the Mosaic Law as a means to salvation, a righteous standing before God. Paul was telling these legalistic Jewish Christians that this is not so. In fact, this would invalidate Christ's ransom because there would have been no need for it if one could achieve salvation by meticulously keeping the Mosaic Law. (Rom. 5:18) But James was writing to those in a congregation who were concerned with their status before other men, who were looking for prominent positions within the congregation, and not taking care of those that were in need.

---

[31] *Jewish Antiquities*, I, 146 [vi, 4].

[32] Merriam-Webster, Inc: *Merriam-Webster's Collegiate Dictionary*. Eleventh ed. (Springfield, Mass.: Merriam-Webster, Inc. 2003).

[33] Or breath

(Jam. 2:14–17) So, James is merely addressing those who call themselves Christian, but in name only. No person could truly be a Christian and not possess some good works, such as feeding the poor, helping the elderly. This type of work was an evident demonstration of one's Christian personality. Paul was in perfect harmony with James on this. – Romans 10:10; 1 Corinthians 15:58; Ephesians 5:15, 21–33; 6:15; 1 Timothy 4:16; 2 Timothy 4:5; Hebrews 10:23-25.

Inerrancy: Are There Contradictions?

Below I will follow this pattern. I will list the critic's argument first, followed by the text of difficulty, and conclude with an answer to the critic. What should be kept at the forefront of our mind is this: one is simply looking for the best answer, not absoluteness. If there is a reasonable answer to a Bible difficulty, why are the critics able to set them aside with ease? Because they start with the premise that this is not the Word of God, but only a book by imperfect men and full of contradictions; thus, the bias toward errors has blinded their judgment.

Critic: The critic would argue that there was an Adam and Eve, and an Abel who was now dead, so, where did Cain get his wife? This is one of the most common questions by Bible critics.

Genesis 4:17 Updated American Standard Version (UASV)

¹⁷ Cain had sexual relations³⁴ with his wife and she conceived, and gave birth to Enoch; and he built a city, and called the name of the city Enoch, after the name of his son, Enoch.

Answer: If one were to read a little further along, they would come to the realization that Adam had a son named Seth; it further adds that Adam "became father to sons *and daughters.*" (Genesis 5:4) Adam lived for a total of 800 years after fathering Seth, giving him ample opportunity to father many more sons and daughters. So it could be that Cain married one of his sisters. If he waited until one of his brothers and sisters had a daughter, he could have married one of his nieces once she was old enough. In the beginning, humans were closer to perfection; this explains why they lived longer and why at that time there was little health risk of genetic defects in the case of children born to closely related parents, in contrast to how it is today. As time passed, genetic defects increased and life spans decreased. Adam lived to see 930 years. Yet Shem, who lived after the Flood, died at 600 years, while Shem's son Arpachshad only lived 438 years, dying before his father died. Abraham saw an even

---

³⁴ Lit *knew*

greater decrease in that he only lived 175 years while his grandson Jacob was 147 years when he died. Thus, due to increasing imperfection, God prohibited the marriage of closely related people under the Mosaic Law because of the likelihood of genetic defects.—Leviticus 18:9.

Critic: If God is here hardening Pharaoh's heart, what exactly makes Pharaoh responsible for the decisions he makes?

Exodus 4:21 Updated American Standard Version (UASV)

[21] Jehovah said to Moses, "When you go and return to Egypt see that you perform before Pharaoh all the wonders which I have put in your hand; but I will harden his heart so that he will not let the people go.

Answer: This is actually a prophecy. God knew that what he was about to do would contribute to a stubborn and obstinate Pharaoh, who was going to be unwilling to change or give up the Israelites so they could go off to worship their God. Therefore, this is not stating what God is going to do; it is prophesying that Pharaoh's heart will harden because of the actions of God. The fact is, Pharaoh allowed his own heart to harden because he was determined not to agree with Moses' wishes or accept Jehovah's request to let the people go. Moses tells us at Exodus 7:13 (ESV) that "Pharaoh's heart was hardened, and he would not listen to them, as the Lord had said." Again, at 8:15 we read, "When Pharaoh saw that there was a respite, he hardened his heart and would not listen to them, as the Lord had said."

Critic: The Israelites had just received the Ten Commandments, with one commandment being: "You shall not make for yourself a carved image or any likeness of anything that is in heaven above, or that is in the earth beneath, or that is in the water under the earth." Therefore, how is the bronze serpent not a violation of this commandment?

Numbers 21:9 Updated American Standard Version (UASV)

[9] And Moses made a bronze serpent and set it on the standard;[35] and it came about, that if a serpent bit any man, when he looked to the bronze serpent, he lived.

Answer: First, an idol is "a representation or symbol of an object of worship; *broadly*: a false god."[36] Second, it should be noted that not all images are idols. The bronze serpent was not made for the purpose of worship, or for some passionate devotion or veneration. There were times, however, when images were created with absolutely no intention

---

[35] I.e., *pole*

[36] Merriam-Webster, Inc: *Merriam-Webster's Collegiate Dictionary*. Eleventh ed. (Springfield, Mass.: Merriam-Webster, Inc., 2003).

of it receiving devotion, veneration, or worship, yet were later made into objects of veneration. That is exactly what happened with the copper serpent that Moses had formed in the wilderness. Many centuries later, "in the third year of Hoshea son of Elah, king of Israel, Hezekiah the son of Ahaz, king of Judah, began to reign. He removed the high places and broke the pillars and cut down the Asherah. And he broke in pieces the bronze serpent that Moses had made; for until those days the people of Israel had made offerings to it (it was called Nehushtan)."—2 Kings 18:1, 4.

Critic: Deuteronomy 15:11 (NET) says: "*There will never cease to be some poor people in the land;* therefore, I am commanding you to make sure you open your hand to your fellow Israelites who are needy and poor in your land." Is this not a contradiction of Deuteronomy 15:4? Will there be no poor among the Israelites, or will there be poor among them? Which is it?

Deuteronomy 15:4 Updated American Standard Version (UASV)

⁴ However, there will be no poor among you, since Jehovah will surely bless you in the land which Jehovah your God is giving you as an inheritance to possess,

Answer: If you look at the context, Deuteronomy 15:4 is stating that if the Israelites obey Jehovah's command to take care of the poor, "there should not be any poor among" them. Thus, for every poor person, there will be one to take care of that need. If an Israelite fell on hard times, there was to be a fellow Israelite ready to step in to help him through those hard times. Verse 11 stresses the truth of the imperfect world since the rebellion of Adam and inherited sin: there will always be poor among mankind, the Israelites being no different. However, the difference with God's people is that those who were well off financially were to offset conditions for those who fell on difficult times. This is not to be confused with the socialistic welfare systems in the world today. Those Jews were hard-working men, who labored from sunup to sundown to take care of their families. But if disease overtook their herd or unseasonal weather brought about failed crops, an Israelite could sell himself into the service of a fellow Israelite for a period of time; thereafter, he would be back on his feet. And many years down the road, he may very well do the same for another Israelite, who fell on difficult times.

Critic: Joshua 11:23 says that Joshua took the land according to what God had spoken to Moses and handed it on to the nation of Israel as planned. However, in Joshua 13:1, God is telling Joshua that he has grown old and much of the Promised Land has yet to be taken possession of. How can both be true? Is this not a contradiction?

Joshua 11:23 Updated American Standard Version (UASV)

23 So Joshua took the whole land, according to all that Jehovah had spoken to Moses, and Joshua gave it for an inheritance to Israel according to their divisions by their tribes, and the land had rest from war.

Joshua 13:1 Updated American Standard Version (UASV)

13 Now Joshua was old and advanced in years, and Jehovah said to him, "You are old and advanced in years, and there remains yet very much land to possess.

Answer: No, it is not a contradiction. When the Israelites were to take the land, it was to take place in two different stages: the nation as a whole was to go to war and defeat the 31 kings of this land; thereafter, each Israelite tribe was to take their part of the land based on their individual actions. (Joshua 17:14–18; 18:3) Joshua fulfilled his role, which is expressed in 11:23 while the individual tribes did not complete their campaigns, which is expressed in 13:1. Even though the individual tribes failed to live up to taking their portion, the remaining Canaanites posed no real threat. Joshua 21:44, *ASV*, reads: "Jehovah gave them rest round about."

Critic: The critic would point out that John 1:18 clearly says that "*no one has ever seen God*," while Exodus 24:10 explicitly states that Moses and Aaron, Nadab and Abihu, and seventy of the elders of Israel "*saw the God of Israel*." Worse still, God informs them in Exodus 33:20: "You cannot see my face, for man shall not see me and live." The critic with his knowing smile says, 'This is a blatant contradiction.'

John 1:18 Updated American Standard Version (UASV)

18 No one has seen God at any time; the only begotten god³⁷ who is in the bosom of the Father,³⁸ that one has made him fully known.

Exodus 24:10 Updated American Standard Version (UASV)

10 and they saw the God of Israel; and under his feet was what seemed like a sapphire pavement, as clear as the sky itself.

Exodus 33:20 Updated American Standard Version (UASV)

20 But he [God] said, "You cannot see my face, for no man can see me and live!"

---

³⁷ Jn 1:18: "only-begotten god", P⁶⁶א*BC*Lsyrʰᵐᵍ·ᵖ; **[V1]** "the only-begotten god," P⁷⁵א¹33copᵇᵒ; **[V2]** "the only-begotten Son." AC³(Wˢ)ΘΨfl.¹³ MajVgSyrᶜ

³⁸ Or *at the Father's side*

Answer: Exodus 33:20 is one-hundred percent correct: No human could see Jehovah God and live. The apostle Paul at Colossians 1:15 tell us that Christ is the image of the invisible God, and the writer informs us at Hebrews 1:3 that Jesus is the "exact representation of His nature." Yet if you were to read the account of Saul of Tarsus (the apostle Paul), you would see that a mere partial manifestation of Christ's glory blinded Saul – Acts 9:1–18.

When the Bible says that Moses and others have seen God, it is not speaking of *literally* seeing him, because first of all He is an invisible spirit person. It is a *manifestation* of his glory, which is an act of showing or demonstrating his presence, making himself perceptible to the human mind. In fact, it is generally an angelic representative that stands in his place and not him personally. Exodus 24:16 informs us that "the glory of the Lord dwelt on Mount Sinai," not the Lord himself personally. When texts such as Exodus 24:10 explicitly state that Moses and Aaron, Nadab and Abihu, and seventy of the elders of Israel "*saw the God of Israel*," it is this "glory of the Lord," an angelic representative. This is shown to be the case at Luke 2:9, which reads: "And *an angel of the Lord* appeared to them, and *the glory of the Lord shone around them* [the shepherds], and they were filled with fear."

Many Bible difficulties are cleared up elsewhere in Scripture; for example, in the New Testament, you will find a text clarifying a difficulty from the Old Testament, such as Acts 7:53, which refers to those "who received the law *as delivered by angels* and did not keep it." Support comes from Paul at Galatians 3:19: "Why then the law? It was added because of transgressions until the offspring should come to whom the promise had been made, and it was put in place through angels by an intermediary." The writer of Hebrews chimes in at 2:2 with "For since the message *declared by angels* proved to be reliable, and every transgression or disobedience received a just retribution. . . ." As we travel back to Exodus again, to 19:19 specifically, we find support that it was not God's own voice, which Moses heard; no, it was an angelic representative, for it reads: "Moses was speaking, and God was answering him with a voice." Exodus 33:22–23 also helps us to appreciate that it was the back of these angelic representatives of Jehovah that Moses saw: "While my glory passes by . . . Then I will take away my hand, and you shall see my back, but my face shall not be seen."

Exodus 3:4 states: "God called to him out of the bush, 'Moses, Moses!' And he said, 'Here I am.'" Verse 6 informs us: "I am the God of your father, the God of Abraham, the God of Isaac, and the God of Jacob." Yet, in verse 2 we read: "And the angel of the Lord appeared to him in a flame of fire out of the midst of a bush." Here is another example of using God's Word to clear up what seems to be unclear or difficult to understand at first glance. Thus, while it speaks of the Lord making a direct appearance, it is really an angelic representative. Even today, we hear such comments, as 'the president of the United States is to visit the Middle East later this week.' However, later in the article it is made clear that he is not going personally, but it is one of his high-ranking representatives. Let us close with two examples, starting with,

Genesis 32:24-30 Updated American Standard Version (UASV)

²⁴ And Jacob was left alone, and a man wrestled with him until daybreak. ²⁵ When he saw that he had not prevailed against him, he touched the socket of his thigh; so the socket of Jacob's thigh was dislocated as he wrestled with him. ²⁶ Then he said, "Let me go, for the dawn is breaking." But he said, "I will not let you go unless you bless me." ²⁷ And he said to him, "What is your name?" And he said, "Jacob." ²⁸ And he said, "Your name shall no longer be called Jacob, but Israel,³⁹ for you have struggled with God and with men and have prevailed." ²⁹ Then Jacob asked him and said, "Please tell me your name." But he said, "Why is it that you ask my name?" And he blessed him there. ³⁰ So Jacob named the place Peniel,⁴⁰ for he said, "I have seen God face to face, yet my soul has been preserved."

It is all too obvious here that this man is simply a materialized angel in the form of a man, another angelic representative of Jehovah God. Moreover, the reader of this book should have taken in that the Israelites as a whole saw these angelic representatives, and spoke of them as though they were dealing directly with Jehovah God himself.

This proved to be the case in the second example found in the book of Judges where an angelic representative visited Manoah and his wife. Like the above mentioned account, Manoah and his wife treated this angelic representative as if he were Jehovah God himself: "And Manoah said to the angel of the Lord, 'What is your name, so that, when your words come true, we may honor you?' And the angel of the Lord said to him, 'Why do you ask my name, seeing it is wonderful?' Then Manoah knew that he was the angel of the Lord. And Manoah said to his wife, "We shall surely die, *for we have seen God.*" – Judges 13:3–22.

---

³⁹ Meaning *he contends with God*
⁴⁰ Meaning *face of God*

Inerrancy: Are There Mistakes?

I have addressed the alleged contradictions, so it would seem that our job is done here, right? Not hardly. Yes, there are just as many who claim that the Bible is full of mistakes.

Critic: Matthew 27:5 states that Judas hanged himself, whereas Acts 1:18 says, "Falling headlong, he burst open in the middle and all his intestines gushed out."

Matthew 27:5 Updated American Standard Version (UASV)

⁵ And he threw the pieces of silver into the temple and departed; and he went away and hanged himself.

Acts 1:18

¹⁸ (Now this man acquired a field with the price of his wickedness, and falling headlong, he burst open in the middle and all his intestines gushed out.

Answer: Neither Matthew nor Luke made a mistake. What you have is Matthew giving the reader the manner in which Judas committed suicide. On the other hand, Luke is giving the reader of Acts, the result of that suicide. Therefore, instead of a mistake, we have two texts that complement each other, really giving the reader the full picture. Judas came to a tree alongside a cliff that had rocks below. He tied the rope to a branch and the other end around his neck and jumped over the edge of the cliff in an attempt at hanging himself. One of two things could have happened: (1) the limb broke plunging him to the rocks below, or (2) the rope broke with the same result, and he burst open onto the rocks below.

Critic: The apostle Paul made a mistake when he quotes how many people died.

Numbers 25:9 Updated American Standard Version (UASV)

⁹ The ones who died in the plague were twenty-four thousand.

1 Corinthians 10:8 Updated American Standard Version (UASV)

⁸ Neither let us commit sexual immorality, as some of them committed sexual immorality, only to fall, twenty-three thousand of them in one day.

Answer: We must keep in mind the above principle that we spoke of, the *Intended Meaning of the Writer*. We live in a far more precise age today, where specificity is highly important. However, we round large numbers off (even estimate) all the time: "there were 237,000 people in Time Square last night." The simplest answer is that the number of people slain was in between 23,000 and 24,000, and both writers rounded the number off. However, there is even another possibility, because the book of Numbers specifically speaks of "all the chiefs of the people" (25:4-5), which could account for the extra 1,000, which is mentioned in Numbers 24,000. Thus, you have the people killing the chiefs of the people and the plague killing the people. Therefore, both books are correct.

Critic: After 215 years in Egypt, the descendants of Jacob arrived at the Promised Land. As you recall they sinned against God and were sentenced to forty years in the wilderness. But once they entered the Promised Land, they buried Joseph's bones "at Shechem, in the piece of land that *Jacob bought* from the sons of Hamor the father of Shechem," as stated at Joshua 24:32. Yet, when Stephen had to defend himself before the Jewish religious leaders, he said that Joseph was buried "in the tomb that *Abraham had bought* for a sum of silver from the sons of Hamor." Therefore, at once it appears that we have a mistake on the part of Stephen.

Acts 7:15-16 Updated American Standard Version (UASV)

[15] And Jacob went down to Egypt and died, he and our fathers. [16] And they were brought back to Shechem and buried in the tomb that Abraham had bought for a sum of silver from the sons of Hamor in Shechem.

Genesis 23:17-18 Updated American Standard Version (UASV)

[17] So Ephron's field, which was in Machpelah, which faced Mamre, the field and cave which was in it, and all the trees which were in the field, that were in all its border around, were made over [18] to Abraham for a possession in the presence of the sons of Heth, before all who went in at the gate of his city.

Genesis 33:19 Updated American Standard Version (UASV)

[19] And he bought the piece of land where he had pitched his tent from the hand of the sons of Hamor, Shechem's father, for one hundred qesitahs.[41]

Joshua 24:32 Updated American Standard Version (UASV)

[32] As for the bones of Joseph, which the sons of Israel brought up from Egypt, they buried them at Shechem, in the piece of land that Jacob bought from the sons of Hamor the father of Shechem for one hundred qesitahs.[42] It became an inheritance of the sons of Joseph.

---

[41] Or *pieces of money*; money of unknown value

[42] Or *pieces of money*; money of unknown value

Answer: If we look back to Genesis 12:6-7, we will find that Abraham's first stop after entering Canaan from Haran was Shechem. It is here that Jehovah told Abraham: "To your offspring I will give this land." At this point Abraham built an altar to Jehovah. It seems reasonable that Abraham would need to purchase this land that had not yet been given to his offspring. While it is true that the Old Testament does not mention this purchase, it is likely that Stephen would be aware of such by way of oral tradition. As Acts chapter seven demonstrates, Stephen had a wide-ranging knowledge of Old Testament history.

Later, Jacob would have had difficulty laying claim to the tract of land that his grandfather Abraham had purchased, because there would have been a new generation of inhabitants of Shechem. This would have been many years after Abraham moved further south and Isaac moved to Beersheba, and including Jacob's twenty years in Paddan-aram (Gen 28:6, 7). The simplest answer is that this land was not in use for about 120 years because of Abraham's extensive travels and Isaac's having moved away, leaving it unused; likely it was put to use by others. So, Jacob simply repurchased what Abraham had bought over a hundred years earlier. This is very similar to the time Isaac had to repurchase the well at Beersheba that Abraham had already purchased earlier. – Genesis 21:27–30; 26:26–32.

Genesis 33:18–20 tells us that 'Jacob bought this land for a hundred pieces of money, from the sons of Hamor.' This same transaction is also mentioned at Joshua 24:32, in reference to transporting Joseph's bones from Egypt, to be buried in Shechem.

We should also address the cave of Machpelah that Abraham had purchased in Hebron from Ephron the Hittite. The word "tomb" is not mentioned until Joshua 24:32, and is in reference to the tract of land in Shechem. Nowhere in the Old Testament does it say that Abraham bought a "tomb." The cave of Machpelah obtained by Abraham would eventually become a family tomb, receiving Sarah's body and, eventually, his own, and those of Isaac, Rebekah, Jacob, and Leah. (Genesis 23:14–19; 25:9; 49:30, 31; 50:13) Gleason L. Archer, Jr., concludes this Bible difficulty, saying:

> The reference to a *mnema* ("tomb") in connection with Shechem must either have been proleptic [to anticipate] for the later use of that shechemite tract for Joseph's tomb (i.e., 'the tomb that Abraham bought' was intended to imply 'the tomb location that Abraham bought"); or else conceivably the dative relative pronoun *ho* was intended elliptically [omission] for *en to topo ho onesato Abraam* ("in the place that Abraham bought") as describing the location of the *mnema* near the Oak

of Moreh right outside Shechem. Normally Greek would have used the relative-locative adverb *hou* to express 'in which' or 'where'; but this would have left *onesato* ("bought") without an object in its own clause, and so *ho* was much more suitable in this context. (Archer 1982, 379–81)

Another solution could be that Jacob is being viewed as a representative of Abraham, for he is the grandson of Abraham. This was quite appropriate in Biblical times, to attribute the purchase to Abraham as the Patriarchal family head.

Critic: 2 Samuel 24:1 says that God moved David to count the Israelites, while 1 Chronicles 21:1 Satan, or a resister did. This would seem to be a clear mistake on the part of one of these authors.

2 Samuel 24:1 Updated American Standard Version (UASV)

[1] Now again the anger of Jehovah burned against Israel, and it incited David against them to say, "Go, number Israel and Judah."

1 Chronicles 21:1 Updated American Standard Version (UASV)

[1] Then Satan stood up against Israel and moved David to number Israel.

Answer: In this period of David's reign, Jehovah was very displeased with Israel, and therefore he did not prevent Satan from bringing this sin on them. Often in Scripture, it is spoken of as though God did something when he allowed an event to take place. For example, it is said that God 'hardened Pharaoh's heart' (Exodus 4:21), when he actually allowed the Pharaoh's heart to harden.

Inerrancy: Are There Scientific Errors?

Many truths about God are beyond the scope of science. Science and the Bible are not at odds. In fact, we can thank modern day science as it has helped us to better under the creation of God, from our solar system to the universes, to the human body and mind. What we find is a level of order, precision, design, and sophistication, which points to a Designer, the eyes of many Christians, to an Almighty God, with infinite intelligence and power. The apostle Paul makes this all too clear, when he writes, "For his invisible attributes, namely, his eternal power and divine nature, have been clearly perceived, ever since the creation of the world, in the things that have been made. So they are without excuse." – Romans 1:20.

Back in the seventeenth century, the world-renowned scientist Galileo proved beyond any doubt that the earth was not the center of the universe, nor did the sun orbit the earth. In fact, he proved it to be the

42

other way around (no pun intended), with the earth revolving around the sun. However, he was brought up on charges of heresy by the Catholic Church and ordered to recant his position. Why? From the viewpoint of the Catholic Church, Galileo was contradicting God's Word, the Bible. As it turned out, Galileo and science were correct, and the Church was wrong, for which it issued a formal apology in 1992. However, the point we wish to make here is that in all the controversy, the Bible was never in the wrong. It was a misinterpretation on the part of the Catholic Church and not a fault with the Bible. One will find no place in the Bible that claims the sun orbits the earth. So where would the Church get such an idea? The Church got such an idea from Ptolemy (b. about 85 C.E.), an ancient astronomer, who argued for such an idea.

As it usually turns out, the so-called contradiction between science and God's Word lies at the feet of those who are interpreting Scripture incorrectly. To repeat the sentiments of Galileo when writing to a pupil–Galileo expressed the same sentiments: "Even though Scripture cannot err, its interpreters and expositors can, in various ways. One of these, very serious and very frequent, would be when they always want to stop at the purely literal sense."[43] I believe that today's scholars, in hindsight, would have no problem agreeing.

While the Bible is not a science textbook, it is scientifically accurate when it touches on matters of science.

The Circle of the Earth Hangs on Nothing

Isaiah 40:22 Updated American Standard Version (UASV)

[22] It is he who sits above **the circle of the earth**,
and its inhabitants are like grasshoppers;
who stretches out the heavens like a curtain,
and spreads them like a tent to dwell in.

More than 2,500 years ago, the prophet Isaiah wrote that the earth is a circle or sphere. First, how would it be possible for Isaiah to know the earth is a circle or sphere, if not from inspiration? Scientific America writes, "As countless photos from space can attest, Earth is round–the "Blue Marble," as astronauts have affectionately dubbed it. Appearances, however, can be deceiving. Planet Earth is not, in fact, perfectly round."[44] Scientifically speaking, the sun is not perfectly, absolutely 100 percent round but in everyday speech, this verse is both acceptable and accurate,

---

[43] Letter from Galileo to Benedetto Castelli, December 21, 1613.

[44] Charles Q. Choi (April 12, 2007). Scientific America. Strange but True: Earth Is Not Round. Retrieved Monday, August 03, 2015.
http://www.scientificamerican.com/article/earth-is-not-round/

when we keep in mind it is written from a human perspective, not from a scientific perspective. Moreover, Isaiah was not discussing astronomy; he was simply making an inspired observation that man came to realize once he was in space, looking back at the earth, it is round. See the section about title, "Intended Meaning of Writer."

Job 26:7 Updated American Standard Version (UASV)

⁷ "He stretches out the north over empty space
and hangs the earth on nothing.

Here the author describes the earth as hanging upon nothing. Many have never heard of the Greek mathematician and astronomer Eratosthenes. He was born in about 276 B.C.E. and received some of his education in Athens, Greece. In 240 B.C., the "Greek astronomer, geographer, mathematician and librarian Eratosthenes calculates the Earth's circumference. His data was rough, but he wasn't far off."⁴⁵ While man very early on used their God given intelligence to arrive at some outstanding conclusion that were actually very accurate, we learn two points here. Eratosthenes was a very astute scientist, while Isaiah, who wrote some 500 years earlier, was no scientist at all. Moreover, Moses, who wrote the book of Job over 1,230 years before Eratosthenes, knew that the earth hung upon nothing.

How Is the Sun Standing Still Possible?

Joshua 10:13 Updated American Standard Version (UASV)

¹³ And the sun stood still, and the moon stopped,
until the nation avenged themselves of their enemies.
Is this not written in the Book of Jashar? The sun stopped in the midst of heaven and did not hurry to set for about a whole day.

The Canaanites had besieged the Gibeonites, a group of people that gained Jehovah God's backing because they had faith in Him. In this battle, Jehovah helped the Israelites continue their attack by causing "the sun [to stand] still, and the moon stopped, until the nation took vengeance on their enemies." (Jos 10:1-14) Those who accept God as the creator of the universe and life can accept that he would know a way of stopping the earth from rotating. However, there are other ways of understanding this account. We must keep in mind that the Bible speaks from an earthly observer point of view, so it need not be that he stopped the rotation. It could have been a refraction of solar and lunar light rays, which would have produced the same effect.

---

⁴⁵ Alfred, Randy (June 19, 2008). "June 19, 240 B.C.E: The Earth Is Round, and It's This Big". Wired. Retrieved Monday, August 03, 2015.

Psalm 136:6 Updated American Standard Version (UASV)

⁶ to him who spread out the earth above the waters,
   for his lovingkindness is everlasting;

Hebrews 3:4 Updated American Standard Version (UASV)

⁴ For every house is built by someone, but the builder of all things is God.

2 Kings 20:8-11 Updated American Standard Version (UASV)

⁸ And Hezekiah said to Isaiah, "What shall be the sign that Jehovah will heal me, and that I shall go up to the house of Jehovah on the third day?" ⁹ And Isaiah said, "This shall be the sign to you from Jehovah, that Jehovah will do the thing that he has spoken: shall the shadow go forward ten steps or go back ten steps?" ¹⁰ And Hezekiah answered, "It is an easy thing for the shadow to decline ten steps; no, but let the shadow turn backward ten steps." ¹¹ And Isaiah the prophet cried to Jehovah, and he brought the shadow on the steps back ten steps, by which it had gone down on the steps of Ahaz.

How is it that the stars fought on behalf of Barak?

Judges 5:20 Updated American Standard Version (UASV)

²⁰ From heaven the stars fought, from their courses they fought against Sisera.

Judges 4:15 Updated American Standard Version (UASV)

¹⁵ And Jehovah routed Sisera and all his chariots and all his army with the edge of the sword before Barak; and Sisera alighted from his chariot and fled away on foot.

In the Bible, you have Biblical prose, and Biblical poetry.

Prose: language that is not poetry: (1) writing or speech in its normal continuous form, without the rhythmic or visual line structure of poetry **(2)** ordinary style of expression: writing or speech that is ordinary or matter-of-fact, without embellishment.

Poetry: literature in verse: (1) literary works written in verse, in particular verse writing of high quality, great beauty, emotional sincerity or intensity, or profound insight **(2) beauty or grace:** something that resembles poetry in its beauty, rhythmic grace, or imaginative, elevated, or decorative style.

We have a beautiful example of both of these forms of writing communication in chapters four and five of the book of Judges. Judges,

Chapter 4 is a prose account of Deborah and Barak, while Judges Chapter 5 is a poetic account. As we have learned from the above, poetry is less concerned with accuracy than evoking emotions. Poetry has a license to say things like what we find in of 5:20, which is in the poetry chapter: "from heaven the stars fought." This can be said, and the reader is expected not to take the language literally. What we can surmise from it though, is that God was acting against Sisera in some way, there was divine intervention.

Procedures for Handling Biblical Difficulties

1. You need to be completely convinced a reason or understanding exists.

2. You need to have total trust and conviction in the inerrancy of the Scripture as originally written down.

3. You need to study the context and framework of the verse carefully, to establish what the author meant by the words he used. In other words, find the beginning and the end of the context that your passage falls within.

4. You need to understand exegesis: find the historical setting, determine author intent, study key words, and note parallel passages. You need to slow down and carefully read the account, considering exactly what is being said

5. You need to find a reasonable harmonization of parallel passages.

6. You need to consider a variety of trusted Bible commentaries, dictionaries, lexical sources, encyclopedias, as well as books on Bible difficulties.

7. You should investigate as to whether the difficulty is a transmission error in the original text.

8. You must always keep in mind that the historical accuracy of the biblical text is unmatched; that thousands of extant manuscripts some of which date back to the second century B.C. support the transmitted text of Scripture.

9. We must keep in mind that the Bible is a diverse book when it comes to literary styles: narrative, poetic, prophetic, and apocalyptic; also containing parables, metaphors, similes, hyperbole, and other figures of speech. Too often, these alleged errors are the result of a reader taking a figure of speech as literal, or reading a parable as though it is a narrative.

10. The Bible student needs to understand what level that the Bible intends to be exact in what is written. If Jim told a friend that 650 graduated with him from high school in 1984, it is not challenged, because it is all too clear that he is using rounded numbers and is not meaning to be precise.

CHAPTER 2 View of Bible Difficulties

By R. A. Torrey

Updated By Edward D. Andrews

Every careful student and every thoughtful reader of the Bible finds that the words of the Apostle Peter concerning the Scriptures, that there are some things in them hard to be understood is true. The apostle Peter says of Paul's letters, "as he does also in all his [Paul's] letters, speaking in them about these *things*, in which there are some *things* **hard to understand**, which the ignorant and unstable distort to their own destruction, as *they* also *do* the rest of the scriptures." (2 Peter 3:16, LEB) If this were true of Peter, how much more so of us 2,000 years removed, of a different language and culture? This is abundantly true for us! Who of us has not found things in the Bible that have puzzled us, yes, that in our early Christian experience have led us to question whether the Bible was, after all, the Word of God? We find some things in the Bible, which it seems impossible to reconcile with other things in the Bible. We find some things, which seem incompatible with the thought that the whole Bible is of divine origin and absolutely inerrant.

It is not wise to attempt to conceal the fact that these difficulties exist. It is the part of wisdom, as well as of honesty, to frankly face them and consider them.

What shall we say concerning these difficulties that every thoughtful student will eventually encounter?

The first thing we have to say about these difficulties in the Bible is that from the very nature of the case *difficulties are to be expected.*

Some people are surprised and staggered because there are difficulties in the Bible. For my part, I would be more surprised and staggered if there were not. What is the Bible? It is a revelation of the mind and will and character and being of an infinitely great, perfectly wise and absolutely holy God. God Himself is the Author of this revelation. However, one would ask, to who specifically is the revelation made? To men, to finite beings who are imperfect in intellectual development and consequently in knowledge, and who are imperfect in character and consequently in spiritual discernment. The wisest man measured on the scale of eternity is only a babe, and the holiest man compared with God is only an infant in moral development.

Therefore, there must from the very necessities of the case, be difficulties in such a revelation from such a source made to such persons. In addition, when the finite is attempting to understand the infinite, there

48

is bound to be difficulty. When the ignorant contemplate the utterances of one perfect in knowledge, there must be many things hard to be understood, and some things, which to their immature and inaccurate minds appear absurd. When beings whose moral judgments as to the hatefulness of sin and as to the awfulness of the penalty that it demands, listen to the demands of an absolutely holy Being, they are bound to be staggered at some of His demands, and when they consider His dealings, they are bound to be staggered at some of His dealings. These dealings will appear too severe, too stern, and too harsh.

It is plain that there must be difficulties for us in such a revelation as the Bible has proved to be. If someone should hand me a book that was as simple to me as the multiplication table, and say, "This is the Word of God; in it He has revealed His whole will and wisdom," I should shake my head and say, "I cannot believe it; that is too easy to be a perfect revelation of infinite wisdom." There must be in any complete revelation of God's mind and will and character and being, things hard for the beginner to understand; and the wisest and best of us are but beginners.

The second thing to be said about these difficulties is that a difficulty in a doctrine, or a grave objection to a doctrine, does not in any way prove the doctrine untrue.

Many people think that it does. If they come across some difficulty in the way of believing in the divine origin and absolute inerrancy and infallibility of the Bible, they at once conclude that the doctrine is exploded. That is very illogical. They should stop a moment and think, and learn to be reasonable and fair.

There is scarcely a doctrine in science generally believed today, that has not had some great difficulty in the way of its acceptance.

When the Copernican theory (the earth revolves around the sun and not vice versa), now so universally accepted, was first proclaimed, it encountered a very grave difficulty. If this theory were true, the planet Venus should have phases as the moon has, but the best glass could discover no phases then in existence. However, the positive argument for the theory was so strong that it was accepted in spite of this apparently unanswerable objection. When a more powerful glass was made, it was found that Venus had phases after all. The whole difficulty arose, as most; all of those in the Bible arise, from man's ignorance of some of the facts in the case.

The nebular hypothesis (the formation of the solar system) is commonly accepted in the scientific world today. Nevertheless, when this theory was first announced, and for a long time afterward, the movements of the planet Uranus could not be reconciled with the theory.

49

Uranus seemed to move in just the opposite direction from that in which it was thought it ought to move in accordance with the demands of the theory. However, the positive arguments for the theory were so strong that it was accepted in spite of the inexplicable movements of Uranus.

If we apply to Bible study the commonsense logic recognized in every department of science (with the exception of Biblical criticism, if that be a science), then we must demand that if the positive proof of a theory is conclusive, it must be believed by rational men in spite of any number of difficulties in minor details. He is a shallow thinker who gives up a well-attested truth because there are some apparent facts, which he cannot reconcile with that truth. In addition, he is a very shallow Bible scholar who gives up his belief in the divine origin and inerrancy of the Bible because there are some supposed facts that he cannot reconcile with that doctrine. There are in the theological world today many shallow thinkers of that kind.

The third thing to be said about the difficulties in the Bible is: there are many more, and much greater, difficulties in the way of the doctrine that holds the Bible to be of human origin, and hence fallible, than there are in the way of the doctrine that holds the Bible to be of divine origin, and hence infallible.

Turning the Tables

Oftentimes a man will put forth some difficulty and say, "How do you explain that, if the Bible is the Word of God?" You may not be able to answer him satisfactorily. Then he thinks he has you cornered. Not at all, turn on him, and ask him, "How do you account for the fulfilled prophecies of the Bible if it is of human origin? How do you account for the marvelous unity of the Book? How do you account for its inexhaustible depth? How do you account for its unique power in lifting men up to God?" For every insignificant objection he can bring to your view of the Bible, you can bring very many more deeply significant objections to his view of the Bible. Moreover, any candid man who desires to know and obey the truth will have no difficulty in deciding between the two views.

Some time ago a young man, who was of a bright mind and unusually well read in skeptical, critical, and agnostic literature, told me he had given the matter a great deal of candid and careful thought, and as a result he could not believe the Bible was of divine origin.

I asked him, "Why not?"

He pointed to a certain teaching of the Bible that he could not and would not believe to be true.

I replied, "Suppose for a moment that I could not answer that specific difficulty; that would not prove that the Bible is not of divine origin. I can bring you many things far more difficult to account for on the hypothesis that the Bible is not of divine origin than on the hypothesis that the Bible is of divine origin. You cannot deny the fact of fulfilled prophecy. How do you account for it if the Bible is not God's Word? You cannot shut eyes to the marvelous unity of the sixty-six books of the Bible, written under such divergent circumstances and at periods of time so remote from one another. How do you account for it if God is not the real Author of the Book back of the forty or more human authors? You cannot deny that the Bible has a power—to save men from sin, to bring men peace and hope and joy, to lift men up to God—that all other books taken together do not possess. How do you account for it if the Bible is not the Word of God in a sense that no other book is the Word of God?"

The objector did not answer. The difficulties that confront one who denies that the Bible is of divine origin and authority are far more numerous and vastly more weighty than those which confront the one who believes it to be of divine origin and authority.

The fourth thing to be said about the difficulties in the Bible is: *the fact that you cannot solve a difficulty does not prove it cannot be solved, and the fact that you cannot answer an objection does not prove at all that it cannot be answered.*

It is remarkable how often we overlook this very evident fact. There are many, who meet a difficulty in the Bible and give it a little thought and can see no possible solution, at once jump at the conclusion that a solution is impossible, and so they give up their faith in the inerrancy of the Bible and in its divine origin. Any man should have a sufficient amount of modesty, being so limited in knowledge, to say, "Though I see no possible solution to this difficulty, someone a little wiser than I might easily find one."

If we would only bear in mind that we do not know everything, and there are a great many things that we cannot solve now which we could very easily solve if we only knew a little more, it would save us from all this foolishness. We ought never to forget that there may be a very easy solution to infinite wisdom even for that which to our finite wisdom—or ignorance—appears unsolvable. What would we think of a beginner in algebra who, having tried in vain for half an hour to solve a difficult problem, declared that there was no possible solution to the problem because he could find none!

A man of unusual experience and ability one day left his work and drove a long distance to see me, as he was in great uneasiness of mind because he had discovered what he believed to be a flat contradiction in the Bible. He had lain awake all night thinking about it. It had defied all his attempts at reconciliation, but when he had fully stated the case to me, in a very few moments I showed him a very simple and satisfactory solution of the difficulty. He went away with a happy heart. Nevertheless, why had it not occurred to him at the outset that, though it appeared impossible to him to find a solution, after all, someone else might easily discover a solution? He supposed that the difficulty was an entirely new one, but it was one that had been faced and answered long before either he or I were born.

The fifth thing to be said about the difficulties in the Bible is that *the seeming defects of the Book are exceedingly insignificant when put in comparison with its many and marvelous areas of excellence.*

It certainly reveals great perversity of both mind and heart that men spend so much time focusing on and exaggerating such insignificant points, which they consider defects in the Bible, and pass absolutely unnoticed the incomparable beauties and wonders that adorn and glorify almost every page. This is even taking place in some prominent institutions of learning, where men are supposed to be taught to appreciate and understand the Bible and where they are sent to be trained to preach its truth to others. These institutions are spending much more time on minute and insignificant points that seem to point toward an entirely human origin of the Bible than is spent upon studying and understanding and admiring the unparalleled glories that make this Book stand apart from all other books in the world. What would we think of any man who in studying some great masterpiece of art concentrated his whole attention upon what looked like a flyspeck in the corner? A large proportion of the much boasted about "critical study of the Bible" is a laborious and scholarly investigation of supposed flyspecks. The man who is **not** willing to squander the major portion of his time in this intellectualized investigation of flyspecks but prefers to devote it to the study of the unrivaled beauties and majestic splendors of the Book is counted in some quarters as not being "scholarly and up to date."

The sixth thing to be said about the difficulties in the Bible is that *they have far more weight with superficial readers than with profound students.*

Take a man like Colonel Ingersoll, who was very ignorant of the real contents and meaning of the Bible, or that class of modern preachers who read the Bible for the most part for the sole purpose of finding texts to serve as pegs to hang their own ideas. To such superficial readers of the

Bible these difficulties seem of immense importance, but to one who has learned to meditate upon the Word of God day and night they have scarcely any weight at all. That rare man of God, George Müller, who had carefully studied the Bible from beginning to end more than one hundred times, was not disturbed by any difficulties he encountered; but to the man who is reading it through for the first or second time there are many things that perplex and stagger.

The seventh thing to be said about the difficulties in the Bible is that *they rapidly disappear upon careful and prayerful study.*

How many things there are in the Bible that once puzzled and staggered us, but which have since been perfectly cleared up and no longer present any difficulty whatever! Every year of study finds these difficulties disappear more and more rapidly. At first they go by ones, and then by twos, and then by dozens, and then by scores. Is it not reasonable then to suppose that the difficulties that remain will all disappear upon further study?

CHAPTER 3 Some Types of Bible Difficulties

By R. A. Torrey

Updated by Edward D. Andrews

All the difficulties found in the Bible can be included under ten general headings:

The Text from which our English Bible was Translated

No one, as far as I know, holds that the English translation of the Bible is absolutely infallible and inerrant. The doctrine held by many is that the Scriptures as originally given were absolutely infallible and inerrant, and that our English translation is a *substantially accurate* rendering of the Scriptures as originally given.

We do not possess the original manuscripts of the Bible. These original manuscripts were copied many times with great care and exactness, but naturally, some errors crept into the copies that were made. We now possess so many good copies that by comparing one with another, we can tell with great precision just what the original text was. Indeed, for all practical purposes the original text is now settled.

Update: After Torrey's death in 1928, we have made the extremely important discovery over 100 papyrus manuscripts that date before 300 C.E. Quite a few date to the second century, with one small fragment being dated to about 125 C.E. The modern textual scholar can now say with certainty that we have establish the Greek New Testament to a ninety-nine percent reflect of the originally publish book(s). Moreover, we have more than 100 English translations today, with many of them being a very good representation of the Hebrew and Greek in English: NASB, ESB, HCSB, LEB, and others. **Edward D. Andrews**

There is not one important doctrine, which hangs upon any doubtful reading of the text. However, when our Authorized Version (KJV) was published in 1611, some of the best manuscripts were not within reach of the translators, and the science of textual criticism was not so well understood as it is today, and so the translation was made from an imperfect text. Not a few of the apparent difficulties in the Bible arise from this source.

For example, we are told in John 5:4 that "an angel went down at a certain season into the pool, and troubled the water: whosoever then first after the troubling of the water stepped in was made whole of whatsoever disease he had." This statement for many reasons seems improbable and difficult to believe, but upon investigation, we find that it is all a mistake of the copyist. Some early copyist, reading John's account, added in the margin his explanation of the healing properties of this intermittent medicinal spring. A late copyist embodied this marginal note in the body of the text, and so it came to be handed down and got into the Authorized Version (KJV). Very properly, it has been omitted from the Revised Version.

Note: It is omitted from almost all of our modern-day translations as well, with the exception of the NASB and the HCSB, which retained it out of esteem to the KJV. **Edward D. Andrews**

The discrepancies in figures in different accounts of the same events as, for example, the differences in the ages of some of the kings as given in the text of Kings and Chronicles, doubtless arise from the same cause, errors of copyists. Such an error in the matter of figures would be very easy to make, as in the Hebrew; letters, and letters that appear very much alike have a very different value as figures denote numbers. For example, the first letter in the Hebrew alphabet denotes one, and with two little points above it, no larger than flyspecks, it denotes a thousand. The twenty-third or last letter of the Hebrew alphabet denotes four hundred, but the eighth letter of the Hebrew alphabet that looks very much like it and could be easily mistaken for it, denotes eight. A very slight error of the copyist would therefore make an utter change in figures. The remarkable thing when one contemplates the facts in the case is that so few errors of this kind have been made.

Inaccurate Translations

For example, in Matthew 12:40 Jonah is spoken of as being in "the whale's belly." Many a skeptic has made a mockery over the thought of a whale with the peculiar construction of its mouth and throat swallowing a man. However, if the skeptic had only taken the trouble to look the matter up, he would have found the word translated "whale" really means "sea monster" [or great fish] without any definition as to the character of the sea monster. We will take this up more in detail in considering the story of Jonah. Therefore, the whole difficulty arose from the translator's mistake and the skeptic's ignorance. Many skeptics today are so densely ignorant of matters clearly understood by many Sunday school children that they are still harping in the name of scholarship on this supposed error in the Bible.

False Interpretations of the Bible

What the Bible teaches is one thing, and what men interpret it to mean is oftentimes something widely different. Many difficulties that we have with the Bible arise not from what the Bible actually says, but from what men interpret it to mean.

A striking illustration of this is found in Genesis 1. If we were to take the interpretation put upon this chapter by many, it would indeed be difficult to reconcile it with much that modern science regards as established. However, the difficulty is not with what Genesis 1 says, but with the interpretation put upon it. There is no contradiction whatever between what is really proven by science and what is really said in Genesis 1.

Another difficulty of the same character is with Jesus' statement that He would be three days and three nights in the heart of the earth. Many interpreters would have us believe that He died Friday and rose early Sunday morning, and the time between these two is far from being three days and three nights. However, it is a matter of biblical interpretation, and the trouble is not with what the Bible actually says, but with the interpretation that men put upon the Bible. We will take this matter up at length below by Edward D. Andrews.

Matthew 12:40 How many days was Jesus in the tomb?

Some argue for three days, based on Jesus' words,

Matthew 12:40 English Standard Version (ESV)

[40] For just as Jonah was three days and three nights in the belly of the great fish, so will the Son of Man be three days and three nights in the heart of the earth.

This would seem to suggest a full 72 hours. However, we should not set aside similar expressions that may allow us to get at the intent of the words. Many times in Scripture, three days does not always mean a full 72 hours of three days. For example, look at the words of Rehoboam,

1 Kings 12:5, 12 English Standard Version (ESV)

[5] He said to them, "Go away for three days, then come again to me." So the people went away. [12] So Jeroboam and all the people came to Rehoboam the third day, as the king said, "Come to me again the third day."

You see that the king told the people to go away for three days, and then return to him. But you also will notice that they returned on the

56

third day, which was not a full 72 hours of three days. Now, consider what Jesus said of himself, something that Scripture repeatedly says,

Luke 24:46 English Standard Version (ESV)

⁴⁶ and said to them, "Thus it is written, that the Christ should suffer and **on the third day** rise from the dead

Now, if he had remained in the grave for a full 72 hours of three days, it mean that he would have been raised on the fourth day. Jewish days ran from sundown to sundown. Jesus died on Friday afternoon about 3:00 p.m., Nisan 14, 33 C.E.

- Jesus' death Friday Nisan 14, about 3:00 p.m. (Matt 27:31-56; Mk 15:20-41; Lu 23:26-49; Jn 19:16-30)

- Jesus was in Tomb before sundown Friday evening (Matt 27:57-61; Mk 15:42-47; Lu 23:50-56; Jn 19:31-42)

- Jesus in tomb all of Nisan 15ᵗʰ from sundown Friday to sundown Saturday, which began Nisan 16 (Matt 27:62-66)

- Jesus resurrected early Sunday morning of Nisan 16ᵗʰ (Matt 28:1; Mk 16:1; Lu 24:1; Jn 20:1)

Therefore, Jesus was dead and in the tomb for at least a period of time on Friday Nisan 14, was still in the tomb during the course of the whole day of Nisan 15, and spent the nighttime hours of Nisan 16 in the tomb.

- Now after the Sabbath, toward the dawn of the first day of the week, Mary Magdalene and the other Mary went to see the tomb. (Matt 28:1)

- When the Sabbath was past, Mary Magdalene, Mary the mother of James, and Salome bought spices, so that they might go and anoint him. (Mk 16:1)

- But on the first day of the week, at early dawn, they went to the tomb, taking the spices they had prepared. (Lu 24:1)

- Now on the first day of the week Mary Magdalene came to the tomb early, while it was still dark, and saw that the stone had been taken away from the tomb. (Jn 20:1)

Certain women came to the tomb on Sunday morning, it was still dark, he had already been resurrected. Thus, Jesus had been in the tomb for parts of three days.

A Wrong Conception of the Bible

Many think that when we say the Bible is the Word of God, of divine origin and authority, we mean that God is the speaker in every utterance it contains; but this is not what is meant at all. Oftentimes, it simply records what others say, i.e., what good men say, what bad men say, what inspired men say, what uninspired men say, what angels and demons say, and even what the devil says. The record of what they said is from God and absolutely true, but what those other persons are recorded as saying may be true or may not be true. It is true that they said it, but what they said may not be true.

For example, the devil is recorded in Genesis 3:4 as saying, "You will not surely die." It is true that the devil said it, but what the devil said is not true, but an infamous lie that shipwrecked our race. That the devil said it is God's Word, but what the devil said is not God's word but the devil's word. It is God's Word that this was the devil's word.

Very many careless readers of the Bible do not notice who is talking, God, good men, bad men, inspired men, uninspired men, angels or devil. They will tear a verse right out of its context regardless of the speaker and say, "There, God said that." However, God said nothing of the kind. God's Word says that the devil said it or a bad man said it or a good man said it or an inspired man said it, or an uninspired man said it, or an angel said it. What God says is true, namely, that the devil said it, or a bad man, or a good man, or an inspired man, or an uninspired man, or an angel. However, what they said may or may not be true.

It is very common to hear men quote what Eliphaz, Bildad or Zophar said to Job as if it were necessarily God's own words because it is recorded in the Bible, in spite of the fact that God disavowed their teaching and said to them, "you have not spoken of me what is right" (Job 42:7). It is true that these men said the thing that God records them as saying, but often they gave the truth a twist and said what is not right. A very large share of our difficulties thus arises from not noticing who is speaking. The Bible always tells us, and we should always note it. Below, under the subheadings of "the Case of Job" and "The Comforters" Andrews demonstrates how the erroneous interpretations come about.

The Case of Job

What we have covered thus far will help us understand one of the more complex books of the Bible, the book of Job.

Job was a "blameless and upright man, who fears God and turns away from evil." Job was living the happy life; he had seven sons and the

58

daughters. He was a wealthy landowner. "He possessed 7,000 sheep, 3,000 camels, 500 yoke of oxen, and 500 female donkeys, and very many servants, so that this man was the greatest of all the people of the east." (1:3) Even so, he is not a materialistic person; he was simply following a proverb like the above, 'if you work hard, your efforts will be blessed.'

Job 1:13-19; 2:7-8 English Standard Version (ESV)

[13]Now there was a day when his sons and daughters were eating and drinking wine in their oldest brother's house, [14]and there came a messenger to Job and said, "The oxen were plowing and the donkeys feeding beside them, [15]and the Sabeans fell upon them and took them and struck down the servants with the edge of the sword, and I alone have escaped to tell you." [16]While he was yet speaking, there came another and said, "The fire of God fell from heaven and burned up the sheep and the servants and consumed them, and I alone have escaped to tell you." [17]While he was yet speaking, there came another and said, "The Chaldeans formed three groups and made a raid on the camels and took them and struck down the servants with the edge of the sword, and I alone have escaped to tell you." [18]While he was yet speaking, there came another and said, "Your sons and daughters were eating and drinking wine in their oldest brother's house, [19]and behold, a great wind came across the wilderness and struck the four corners of the house, and it fell upon the young people, and they are dead, and I alone have escaped to tell you." [2:7]So Satan went out from the presence of the LORD and struck Job with loathsome sores from the sole of his foot to the crown of his head. [8]And he took a piece of broken pottery with which to scrape himself while he sat in the ashes.

The Comforters

Job 4:7-8 English Standard Version (ESV)

[7]"Remember: who that was innocent ever perished? Or where were the upright cut off? [8]As I have seen, those who plow iniquity and sow trouble reap the same.

Eliphaz in an attempt at dealing with Job's atrocities assumes Job's tragedies are a result of his own actions. Eliphaz has reasoned wrong by taking a proverb and making it an absolute. In essence, he asks Job, 'do those that are innocent die? When have those that live a righteous life been destroyed?' Eliphaz goes on by saying, 'my experience suggests that it is those who are doing wrong and entertain bad that will get back what they gave out.' In other words, Eliphaz is assuming that only the wicked reap bad times.

Job 5:15 English Standard Version (ESV)

[15]But he saves the needy from the sword of their mouth and from the hand of the mighty.

Eliphaz again assumes that Job is at fault. Eliphaz is assuming that it was Job's great riches, which were ill gotten, and this is why he is suffering. Is Eliphaz's statement wrong in and of itself? No, God does rescue the poor from the oppressive, by their following his counsel on the right way to live. However, this is no absolute; saying all who live by God's will and purposes will never be mistreated. Moreover, the whole idea is misplaced, in that maybe Job is the rich oppressor and this is his punishment from God.

Job 8:3-6 English Standard Version (ESV)

[3]Does God pervert justice? Or does the Almighty pervert the right? [4]If your children have sinned against him, he has delivered them into the hand of their transgression.[5]If you will seek God and plead with the Almighty for mercy, [6]if you are pure and upright, surely then he will rouse himself for you and restore your rightful habitation.

Bildad too is stating true statements, but in absolute terms that are misplaced when it comes to Job, or anyone. Certainly, God does not pervert justice. Therefore, Bildad is right on that, but his application and understanding is what is twisted, as he assumes that children died because they had sinned, and justice was being meted out to them. Again, in verse 5-6, we have a true thought, in that if one is in an impure state, and turns to God with pleadings, he will restore them. However, in verses 5-6, Bildad is assuming that Job is unrighteous, because he sees that proverb as an absolute.

As can be seen from the above, one must be aware that proverbs are not absolutes, but are general truths. True enough, there are likely a couple of exceptions to this rule, but that would not negate this rule, and approach of correct interpretation of proverbs.

In the Psalms, we have sometimes, what God said to man and that is always true; but on the other hand, we often have what man said to God, and that may or may not be true. Sometimes, and far oftener than most of us see, it is the voice of the speaker's personal vengeance or despair. This vengeance may be and often is prophetic, but it may be the wronged man committing his cause to Him to whom vengeance belongs (Romans 12:19), and we are not obliged to defend all that he said. In the Psalms, we have even a record of what the fool said, "There is no God" (Psalm 14:1). Now it is true that the fool said it, but the fool lied when he said it. It is God's Word that the fool said it, but what God reports the fool as saying is not God's own word at all but the fool's own word.

Therefore, in studying our Bible, if God is the speaker we must believe what He says. If an inspired man is the speaker, we must believe what he says. If an uninspired man is the speaker, we must judge for ourselves, it is perhaps true, perhaps false. If it is the devil who is speaking, we do well to remember that he was a liar from the beginning; but even the devil may tell the truth sometimes.

The Language in Which the Bible was Written

The Bible is a book of all ages and for all kinds of people, and therefore it was written in the language that continues the same and is understood by all, the language of the common people and of appearances. It was not written in the terminology of science.

Thus, for example, what occurred at the Battle of Gibeon (Joshua 10:12–14) was described in the way it appeared to those who saw it, and the way in which it would be understood by those who read about it. There is no talk about the refraction of the sun's rays, and so forth, but the sun is said to have *"stood still"* (or tarried) in the midst of heaven. It is one of the perfections of the Bible that it was not written in the terminology of modern science. If it had been, it would never have been understood until the present day, and even now it would be understood only by a few. Furthermore, as science and its terminology are constantly changing, the Bible if written in the terminology of the science of today would be out of date in a few years; but being written in just the language chosen, it has proved the Book for all ages, all lands and all conditions of men.

Other difficulties from the language in which the Bible was written arise from the fact that large portions of the Bible are poetical and are written in the language of poetry, the language of feeling, passion, imagination and figure. Now if a man is hopelessly matter-of-fact, he will inevitably find difficulties with these poetical portions of the inspired Word.

For example, in Psalm 18 we have a marvelous description of a thunderstorm, but let the dull, matter-of-fact fellow get hold of that, for example, verse 8: "Smoke went up from his nostrils, and devouring fire from his mouth; glowing coals flamed forth from him," and he will be head over heels in difficulty at once. However, the trouble is not with the Bible, but with his own stupid, thickheaded plainness.

61

Our Defective Knowledge of the History, Geography and Usages of Bible Times

For example, in Acts 13:7 Luke speaks of "the deputy" (more accurately "the proconsul," see English Standard Version) of Cyprus. Roman provinces were of two classes, imperial and senatorial. The ruler of the imperial provinces was called a propraetor, of a senatorial province a proconsul. Up to a comparatively recent date, according to the best information we had, Cyprus was an imperial province and therefore its ruler would be a propraetor, but Luke calls him a proconsul. This certainly seemed like a clear case of error on Luke's part, and even the conservative commentators felt forced to admit that Luke was in slight error, and the destructive critics were delighted to find this "mistake." Further and more thorough investigation has brought to light the fact that just at the time of which Luke wrote the senate had made an exchange with the emperor whereby Cyprus had become a senatorial province, and therefore its ruler was a proconsul. Luke was right after all, and the literary critics were themselves in error.

Repeatedly further researches and discoveries, geographical, historical and archaeological, have vindicated the Bible and put to shame its critics. For example, the book of Daniel has naturally been one of the books that unbelievers and destructive critics have most hated. One of their strongest arguments against its authenticity and truthfulness was that such a person as Belshazzar was unknown to history, that all historians agreed that Nabonidus was the last king of Babylon, and that he was absent from the city when it was captured. Therefore, Belshazzar must be a purely mythical character, and the whole story legendary and not historical. Their argument seemed very strong. In fact, it seemed unanswerable. However, Sir H. Rawlinson discovered at Mugheir and other Chaldean sites clay cylinders on which Belshazzar (Belsaruzar) is named by Nabonidus as his eldest son. Doubtless he reigned as regent in the city during his father's absence, an indication of which we have in his proposal to make Daniel third ruler in the kingdom (Daniel 5:16). He himself being second ruler in the kingdom, Daniel would be next to him. So the Bible was vindicated again.

The critics asserted most positively that Moses could not have written the Pentateuch because writing was unknown in his day. However, recent discoveries have proved beyond a question that writing far antedates the time of Moses. So the critics have been compelled to give up their argument, though they have had the bad grace to hold on stubbornly to their conclusion.

The Ignorance of Conditions under Which Books Were Written and Commands Given

For example, to one ignorant of the conditions, God's commands to Israel as to the extermination of the Canaanites seem cruel and horrible. However, when one understands the moral condition to which these nations had sunk, the utter hopelessness of reclaiming them and the weakness of the Israelites themselves, their extermination seems to have been an act of mercy to all succeeding generations and to themselves.

The Many-Sidedness of the Bible

The broadest-minded man is one-sided, but the truth is many-sided, and the Bible is all-sided. Therefore, to our narrow thought one part of the Bible seems to contradict another.

For example, religious men as a rule are either Calvinistic or Arminian in their mental makeup. In addition, some portions of the Bible are decidedly Calvinistic and present great difficulties to the Arminian type of mind, while other portions are decidedly Arminian and present difficulties to the Calvinistic type of mind. However, both sides are true. Many men in our day are broad-minded enough to be able to grasp at the same time the Calvinistic side of the truth and the Arminian side of the truth; but some are not, so the Bible perplexes, puzzles and bewilders them. The trouble is not with the Bible, but with their own lack of capacity for comprehensive thought.

Expansion: These schools of doctrinal positions are initially established religious leaders and their followers, such as John Calvin and Jacob Arminius. There are even more, such as the Lutheran, from Martin Luther, The Wesleyan, from John Wesley, and the Mennonites, from Menno Simons, and Society of Friends (Quakers) under George Fox. Actually, I would disagree with Torrey here, I believe that he should have used his earlier point of argument, it boils down to the truth of the Bible as being absolute, but man may misinterpret that truth. Therefore, it will lay concealed until discovered. This misinterpretation does not refute the infallibility or inerrancy of Scripture. Actually, doctrine plays no part in inerrancy of Scripture. Whether one believes the earth was created in six literal 24-hour days, or six creative periods called days, has no impact on the doctrine of inerrancy. The Bible is inerrant and one of those interpretations is wrong and the other is correct. This has to do with the person interpreting the Bible, not the inerrancy of the Bible. **Edward D. Andrews**

Therefore, Paul seems to contradict James, and James seems sometimes to contradict Paul; and what Paul says in one place seems to contradict what he says in another place. However, the whole trouble is that our narrow minds cannot take in God's large truth.

The Bible has to do with the Infinite, and our Minds are Finite

It is necessarily difficult to put the facts of infinite being into the limited capacity of our finite intelligence, just as it is difficult to put the ocean into a pint cup. To this class of difficulties belong those connected with the Bible doctrines of the Trinity and of the divine-human nature of Christ. To those who forget that God is infinite, the doctrine of the Trinity seems like the mathematical monstrosity of making one equal three. However, when one bears in mind that the doctrine of the Trinity is an attempt to put into forms of finite thought the facts of infinite being, and into material forms of expression the facts of the spirit, the difficulties vanish. The simplicity of the Unitarian conception of God arises from its shallowness.

The Dullness of our Spiritual Perception

The man who is farthest advanced spiritually is still so immature that he cannot expect to see everything yet as an absolutely holy God sees it, unless he takes it upon simple faith in Him. To this class of difficulties belong those connected with the Bible doctrine of eternal punishment. It often seems to us as if this doctrine cannot be true, must not be true, but the whole difficulty arises from the fact that we are still so blind spiritually that we have no adequate conception of the awfulness of sin, and especially of the awfulness of the sin of rejecting the infinitely glorious Son of God. However, when we become so holy, so like God, that we see the enormity of sin as He sees it, we shall have no difficulty with the doctrine of eternal punishment.

Expansion: Torrey is like many other Calvinist or Lutheran minded individuals, he wishes to follow the evidence, but instead, desires to call those, who do not find this doctrine Biblical, spiritually blind. I hope that even the most conservative reader can see that as dismissive. Without arguing the evidence, I will say that once again, the truth is biblical, and we must follow it objectively, and not allow theological bias to cloud our judgment. I am recommending that you read, *WHAT IS HELL? Basic Bible Doctrines of the Christian Faith* by Edward D. Andrews[46]

As we look back over the ten classes of difficulties, we see they all arise from our imperfection, and not from the imperfection of the Bible. The Bible is perfect, but we, being imperfect, have difficulty with it. As we grow more and more into the perfection of God, our difficulties grow ever less and less, and so we are forced to conclude that when we become as perfect as God is, we shall have no more difficulties whatever with the Bible.

---

[46] http://www.christianpublishers.org/apps/webstore/products/show/5346167

CHAPTER 4 Dealing With Bible Difficulties

By R. A. Torrey

Updated By Edward D. Andrews

Honestly

Whenever you find a difficulty in the Bible frankly, acknowledge it. Do not try to obscure it. Do not try to dodge it. Look it square in the face. Admit it frankly to whoever mentions it. If you cannot give a good, square, honest explanation, do not attempt any at all. Those, who in their zeal for the infallibility of the Bible have attempted explanations of difficulties that do not commend themselves to the honest, fair-minded man, have done untold harm. People have concluded that if these are the best explanations, then there are really no explanations at all, and the Bible instead of being helped has been injured by the unintelligent zeal of foolish friends. If you are not really convinced that the Bible is the Word of God, you can far better afford to wait for an honest solution of a difficulty than you can afford to attempt a solution that is evasive and unsatisfactory.

Humbly

Recognize the limitations of your own mind and knowledge, and do not for a moment imagine that there is no solution just because you have found none. There is, in all probability, a very simple solution, even when you can find no solution at all.

Determinedly

Make up your mind that you will find the solution if you can by any amount of study and hard thinking. The difficulties of the Bible are our heavenly Father's challenge to us to set our brains to work. Do not give up searching for a solution because you cannot find it in five minutes or ten minutes. Ponder over it and work over it for days if necessary. The work will be more beneficial than the solution does. There is a solution somewhere, and you will find it if you will only search for it long enough and hard enough.

Fearlessly

Do not be frightened when you find a difficulty, no matter how unanswerable or how insurmountable it appears at first sight. Thousands of men have encountered just such difficulties, and still the old Book has withstood the test of time, being the bestseller that will never be touched, in the untold billions of copies. The Bible that has stood eighteen centuries of rigid examination, and of incessant and awful assault, is not likely to go down before your discoveries or before the discharges of any modern critical guns. To one who is at all familiar with the history of critical attacks on the Bible, the confidence of those modern critics who think they are going to annihilate the Bible at last is simply amusing.

Patiently

Do not be discouraged because you do not solve every problem in a day. If some difficulty persistently defies your very best efforts at a solution, lay it aside for a while. Later it will likely be resolved, and you will wonder how you were ever perplexed by it.

Scripturally

If you find a difficulty in one part of the Bible, look for another scripture to throw light upon it and dissolve it. Nothing explains scripture like scripture. Repeatedly people have come to me with some difficulty in the Bible that had greatly staggered them, and asked for a solution. I have been able to give a solution by simply asking them to read some other chapter and verse, and the simple reading of that scripture has thrown such light upon the passage in question that all the mists have disappeared and the truth has shone as clear as day.

Prayerfully

It is simply wonderful how difficulties dissolve when one looks at them on his knees. Not only does God open our eyes in answer to prayer to behold wonderful things out of His law, but He also opens our eyes to look straight through a difficulty that seemed impenetrable before we prayed. One great reason why many modern Bible scholars have learned to be destructive critics is that they have forgotten how to pray. Please see,

HOW TO PRAY: The Importance of Prayer [Updated and Expanded] by R. A. Torrey and Edward D. Andrews

CHAPTER 5 Bible Difficulties in the Book of Genesis

Genesis 1:1 Is the earth only 6,000 to 10,000 years old? Are the creative days literally, only 24 hours long?

There are over a dozen different interpretations concerning the creative days of Genesis. Herein we will consider the main four in an effort to make our point. First, there is the *young earth view* that asserts that all physical creation was produced in just six literal 24-hour days sometime between 6,000 and 10,000 years ago. Second, there is the *day-age view* that states that each creative day is to be understood figuratively as creative periods of unknown durations of time. According to this view, the earth is millions of years old, and the universe is billions of years old. Third, there is the *restoration view* (gap theory) that asserts that there is a large gap of time between Genesis 1:1 and 1:2. Fourth, there is the *literary framework view* that claims that God was not having Moses address how He created the world, nor the length of time in which to do such. This view holds that this account in Genesis one is merely a literary outline that summarizes a theology of creation. This so-called "seven-day framework" is not to be understood in a literal sense of order and chronology but is a literary device expressing God's involvement in the creation and the Sabbath. Different Evangelical Christian scholars hold all four of these views, but the authors of this book set aside three of these as being contrary to Scripture and science. We will discuss the first two views listed above in more detail below. [47]

We do not believe those who hold to the young-earth view of creationism have the evidence to support their case. Actually, we do not believe they even speak in terms of evidence. Why? Most of the young-earth commentators attempt to disprove the day-age view by using many words like "possibly," "could be," "may be," and so on. Also, we do not believe they look at the evidence without theological bias. Professor Kirk Wise writes:

> I am a young-age creationist because that is my understanding of the Scripture. As I shared with my professors years ago when I was in college, if all the evidence in the universe turns against creationism, I would be the first to admit it, but I would still be a

---

47. For a more in-depth understanding of these for creative views, see Gregory A. Boyd and Paul R. Eddy, *Across the Spectrum* (Grand Rapids, Baker Academic, 2002), 50–73.

creationist because that is what the Word of God seems
to indicate. Here I must stand. (Ashton, 2001)[48]

It shows theological bias when he states that no evidence will change his mind. Just as in the case of Galileo, theologians cast doubt on the Bible by ignoring scientific evidence. The Bible was not out of harmony with the truth that the earth revolves around the sun and not the other way. God's Word needed no revision. It was the Catholic Church's misinterpretation of the Bible that caused the problem. As one grows in understanding of physics, biology, and chemistry (as is also true with history, ancient languages, and manuscripts), one may need to revise conclusions derived from previous knowledge. When knowledge increases, it calls for humility to make adjustments in one's thinking.

To suggest, as do many conservative Christians, that one needs to read the Bible in a plain way (sensus plenoir) is quite misleading, as though one would never consider otherwise. Galileo's own words to a pupil said it well: "Even though Scripture cannot err, its interpreters and expositors can, in various ways. One of these, very serious and very frequent, would be when they always want to stop at the purely literal sense."[49] The professor argues that because Genesis chapter one was written as historical narrative, it disallows an interpretation that has millions of years involved. This is hardly the case, for he goes on to admit that other historical narratives contain imbedded material that is not to be taken literally. Moreover, it is implied that one who accepts long creative periods must also believe the Big Bang theory, and believe that fossils are millions of years old, and believe in other facets of Evolution. This is simply untrue.

Simply put, Genesis 1:1 says: "In the beginning God created the heavens and the earth." (ESV) This would include our home, the earth, and our solar system and galaxy that King David referred to when he looked into the night sky and wrote: "When I look at your heavens, the work of your fingers, the moon and the stars, which you have set in place, what is man that you are mindful of him, and the son of man that you care for him?" (Psalm 8:3, 4, ESV) It would also include all the billions of universes that David was unable to see with his naked eye. Therefore, all this came before the first day of creative preparation for life on the earth that starts in Genesis 1:3, as would also be the case with the description of the earth as found in verse 2. It is not until we get to Genesis 1:3–5 that Moses starts to expound on the first day of creation specifically in respect to the earth.

---

48. http://richarddawkins.net/articles/115.
49. Letter from Galileo to Benedetto Castelli, December 21, 1613.

What does this mean? It means that regardless of how long you may feel the creative days were, verses 1 and 2 are covering things that existed prior to the start of the events described in the successive creative days. Therefore, it takes nothing away from the Bible when geologists state that the earth is four billion years old, or astronomers who have calculated the age of the universe say it is at least 14–20 billion years old. For the Christian to argue with science is only history repeating itself, as you will see before this chapter closes. Again, Genesis chapter one, verses 1, 2, are outside the events of the creative days, which are simply a summary of the steps taken to transform the condition of verse 2 into the habitable earth in which the animals and Adam and Eve were created.

Now that we have settled the controversy between science and the *erroneous* interpretations of man's tradition that the universe and earth were created in only six literal days, we should clear the air over the age and origin of the sedimentary geological strata. Many have postulated that it was formed at the time of the flood of Noah. This answer is not to be found in God's Word. Those who hold to the young-earth view (6,000–10,000 years old), work very hard to try to reconcile the geologic column and the fossils of dinosaurs and such, in which they try to overcome evidence that shows the earth is millions of years old. What is now known and acknowledged by science is that the geological record does *not* contain a series of gradual and progressive stages of fossils from one species to another. Actually, the fossil record supports the creation account in that new species appear suddenly on the scene within this geological column, having absolutely no connection with any other species. The problem with young-earth proponents is that they are unable to use this information because it will not fit with their belief that all land and sea animals were created in two 24-hour days. This is not to say that this publication accepts the idea that the sea and land animals have existed for untold hundreds of millions of years, but it does not negate that the fifth and sixth creative days were possibly many thousands of years long, having flying and sea creatures, and land animals being created throughout, as well as dinosaurs.

What exactly does the Bible reveal? It says plainly that Jehovah God is the "fountain of life." (Psalm 36:9) In other words, life did not come from nothing and then develop gradually in some evolutionary process over billions of years. Additionally, God's Word says that everything was created according to its kind. (Genesis 1:11, 21, 24) And finally, the Bible does provide the time period of man's creation, some 6,000 years ago. On this, both archaeology and Biblical chronology are not far off from each other. Creation is clearly stated within God's Word, and can be understood in relation to the correct study and interpretation of its texts, in light of factual science, astronomy, physics, chemistry, geology, and biology. The evolutionary theory stands in opposition to the Bible and to the facts of paleontology and biology. The ideas of young-earth creationists are not supported by God's Word either, conflicting with astronomy, physics, and geology.

Back in the seventeenth century, the world-renowned scientist Galileo proved beyond any doubt that the earth was not the center of the universe, nor did the sun orbit the earth. In fact, he showed it to be the other way around (no pun intended), with the earth revolving around the sun. However, he was brought up on charges of heresy by the Catholic Church and ordered to recant his position. Why? From the viewpoint of the Catholic Church, Galileo was contradicting God's Word, the Bible. As it turned out, Galileo and science were correct, and the Church was wrong, for which it issued a formal apology in 1992. However, the point we wish to make here is that in all the controversy, the Bible was never in the wrong. It was a misinterpretation on the part of the Catholic Church and not a fault with the Bible. One will find no place in the Bible that claims the sun orbits the earth. So where would the Church get such an idea? From Ptolemy (b. about 85 C.E.), an ancient astronomer, who argued for such an idea.

A geocentric model that the earth is the center of the universe was long held by Ptolemy's predecessors like Aristotle and most of the ancient Greek philosophers. The idea of the earth being the center of the universe was held on to by the fact that the observer with his naked eye saw both the sun and moon appear to revolve around the earth each day, while the earth appeared to stand still. Now consider that the church fathers of the third to the fifth centuries C.E. were inundated by Greek thought, believing philosophical thinking was a means of interpreting God's Word. Commenting on such ones, Douglas T. Holden[50] stated, "Christian theology has become so fused with Greek philosophy that it has reared individuals who are a mixture of nine parts Greek thought to one part Christian thought." Couple this with a literal reading of some texts that should be understood figuratively and you have the makings for a conflict between the Church and the scientific world.

In interpretation, you may find one verse that appears to be in direct conflict with another (such as, fire will destroy the earth, or, the earth will last forever). We do not automatically assume that God's original Word is wrong. We must do some investigative work: (1) Is there a scribal error? (2) Is there an error in translation? (3) Is this a case of one verse using

---

50. Douglas T. Holden, *Death Shall Have no Dominion: A New Testament Study* (Bloomington: Bethany Press, 1971), 14.

"earth" in a literal sense, while another is using figurative language, speaking of mankind as the "earth?" This can be the case with science as well. One does not let the scientific world dictate our understanding of Scripture, but we should not be so dogmatic in the face of scientific facts that we will, like Professor Kirk Wise, set aside "all the evidence in the universe [that] turns against creationism," while still holding onto erroneous, unreasonable, and unscriptural interpretations.

We have many of conservative scholarship who still argues that the earth and all life on it were created in six literal 24-hour days. As you may know, this flatly contradicts modern-day science. Do we have another Galileo moment in time? Who is correct here, the scholars or science? One thing is for certain; there is no fault to be found in God's Word. The Bible does not explicitly say these creative days were literal 24-hour days. What many are failing to realize and quite a few refuse to accept is that in both the Hebrew and the Greek Scriptures, the word for "day" (Heb., *yohm*; Gr., *hemera*) is used both in a literal and in a figurative sense. Moreover, this is not a case of inerrancy. In other words, if one does not accept six literal 24 hour days, he has abandoned inerrancy. True inerrancy does not consider whether they are literal or figurative creative days, but rather is your interpretation in harmony with what the author meant by the words that he used.

These six creative days are representative of being like six successive days of a week. If we look at most modern translations, they read, "**the** first day," "**the** second day," "**the** third day," and so on. This is an error in translation and should read. "And there was evening and there was morning, **a** first day." (Gen. 1:5) There is no definite article in the Hebrew of these six creative days. It is the translators that choose to add it into their translations. (ESV, LEB, HCSB, NIV, etc.) However, the American Standard Version and the New American Standard Bible read, "And there was evening and there was morning, one day." (1:5) If we were talking about a definite period of time, generally there should be a definite article in the Hebrew, because it is written in the prose genre. It is only in Hebrew poetry that the definite article could be omitted. What we are looking at with these six creative days is simply a sequential pattern, as oppose to six literal units of definite time.

SIX CREATIVE DAYS		
DAY	**WORKS**	**GENESIS**
1	Light gradually came to be;[51] a separation between day and night	1:3–5
2	Expanse, a separation between the waters below from the waters above	1:6–8
3	Dry land appears; produces vegetation	1:9–13
4	Sources of light now become visible from earth [52]	1:14–19
5	Aquatic souls and flying creatures	1:20–23
6	Land animals; man and woman created	1:24–31

While the word "day" in Hebrew can mean a 24-hour period, clearly *yohm* and context allows for the creative days to be understood as a period of time, an age, or an era. For example, immediately after he mentions the six creative days, Moses uses the same word for "day" in a more general way, lumping *all six creative days together as one day:*

Genesis 2:4: These are the generations of the heavens and of the earth when they were created, in the day that Jehovah God made earth and heaven.

Here we are given the context of just how Moses is using *yohm*, which in this verse is referring to all six creative periods as "in the day." With this alone, it is difficult to argue that in chapter one *yohm* was being used to refer literally to a 24-hour period. Below are a few other examples where *yohm* is being used in the sense of an extended period of time, age, or era:

Proverbs 25:13: As the cold of snow *in the time* ["day" *yohm*] of harvest, So is a faithful messenger to them that send him; For he refresheth the soul of his masters.

---

51. Many believe that God said: "Let there be light" and it immediately appeared. No, this was a gradual process, taking such an enormous amount of time that speculation would be the result of any guess. J. W. Watt's translation reflects this gradual process: "And gradually light came into existence." (*A Distinctive Translation of Genesis*) This light from our sun was spread through the dark overcast, to the point that it was not at first observable but gradually became observable through time.

52. And God said, "Let there be light," and there was light, the first day. Hebrew has different words that distinguish their source and their quality. The Hebrew word used in verse one for "light" is *ohr*, which carries the general sense. However, by the fourth "day," or creative period, the Hebrew word changes to *maohr*, which is now referring to the source of the light.

Isaiah 4:2 (*ASV*): *In that day* [yohm] shall the branch of Jehovah be beautiful and glorious, and the fruit of the land shall be excellent and comely for them that are escaped of Israel.

Zechariah 14:1 (*ASV*): Behold, *a day* [yohm] *of* Jehovah cometh, when thy spoil shall be divided in the midst of thee.

You will have those who cling to the 24-hour creative day by informing you that *yohm*, "day, " is used 410 times outside of Genesis with a day and number and in all cases it is to be taken literally, meaning an ordinary day. First, let us point out that there is no absolute grammatical rule in Hebrew that would make this mandatory in every case. Young-earth proponents must support their proposition with their circular argument. For the sake of an argument, let us say that their claim is true. To have "day" used with an ordinal number in 410 places outside of Genesis chapter one would not negate *yohm* being used in a different setting (like creation) with ordinal numbers and still be referring to periods of time (epochs). One must keep in mind that those uses of a *yohm* outside the creation account are used in reference to humans and a human day. Because Genesis is the only place in Scripture where periods of time can be used with ordinal numbers, there is no problem with it being the exception to the rule. No other book has the setting of the creation of heaven and earth, so to equate uses of *yohm* in totally different settings with its use in Genesis is circular reasoning, as if to say: "*Yohm* is used with ordinals in 410 occurrences outside of Genesis and they are literal, so *yohm* must be literal in Genesis because it is used with ordinal numbers." You might as well say that "*yohm* is literal with ordinal numbers because *yohm* should be literal with ordinal numbers." The young-earth proponent's argument is circular by supporting a premise with a premise instead of a conclusion.

Exodus 20:11: For in six days Jehovah made heaven and earth, the sea, and all that in them is, and rested the seventh day: wherefore Jehovah blessed the sabbath day, and hallowed it.

Is Moses, the writer of Genesis, making reference here at Exodus 20:11 to the six creative days as a representative for the weekly Sabbath, thus suggesting that the six creative days were literal 24-hour days? No, this is not so. At Genesis 2:4, the same writer uses *yohm*, "day," figuratively to refer to the six creative days of Genesis chapter one and Exodus 20:11 as a whole, starting from the gradual appearance of light on the first day (Genesis 1:3, as it would appear to an earthly observer), but does not include the earth as it lay in its prior existence, in which it is described as being "without form and void, and darkness was over the face of the deep. And the Spirit of God was hovering over the face of the waters."

74

Another stumbling block for those who wish to take the creation account in a literal sense of 24-hour periods is that the context is really presented as events that take long periods of time to accomplish.

Genesis 1:11-12: And God said, Let the earth put forth grass, herbs yielding seed, and fruit-trees bearing fruit after their kind, wherein is the seed thereof, upon the earth: and it was so. [Resulting in] And the earth brought forth grass, herbs yielding seed after their kind, and trees bearing fruit, wherein is the seed thereof, after their kind: and God saw that it was good.

Obviously we are dealing with far more time than one 24-hour day would allow when speaking of grass, herbs, and fruit trees sprouting *and* growing to maturity *and* producing seed and fruit.

Genesis 2:18–20: And Jehovah God said, It is not good *that the man should be alone;* I will make him a help meet for him. And out of the ground Jehovah God formed every beast of the field and every bird of the heavens, and brought them unto the man to see what he would call them: and whatsoever the man called every living creature, that was the name thereof. And the man gave names to all cattle, and to the birds of the heavens, and to every beast of the field, but for man, there was not found a help meet for him.

At this point in the creation account, it was still the sixth creative day. However, as verse 27 of chapter 1 shows, it is the close of the sixth creation day. After all else had been created, after the animals had been fashioned, just before sundown of that day, "God created man in his own image, in the image of God he created him; male and female he created them." Taken literally, this means that Adam and Eve were created in the last hour of the sixth day. The question here is, if the sixth "day" was only going to be 24 hours, why would Adam be lonely? God would have known he was creating his helper in that sixth "day." Why the concern for loneliness if it were only moments before Eve was to be created? For this reader, the implication is that the sixth day is a long creative period.

Even more, activity would be impossibly crammed into the sixth creative day if it were only a 24-hour period. Adam is assigned the task of naming the different kinds of animals. This is not a simple task of just picking a name randomly. In the ancient culture, names carried even more meaning than in our modern Western culture. Names were chosen to be descriptive, to reflect something about the person, animal, or thing. From the descriptive forms of the names Adam chose, it is obvious that it took some time, for the account literally reads "whatever the man called *every living creature*, that was its name."[53] (Genesis 2:19) For example, the Hebrew word for the "ass" refers to the usual reddened color. The Hebrew word for stork is the feminine form of the word meaning "loyal one."[54] This name is certainly a perfect fit, as the stork is known for the loving care it gives its young, and the loyalty of staying with its mate for life, something that would have been impossible to observe within a mere 24-hour day.

Regardless, it has been estimated, even if Adam has taken just one minute to name each pair, it would have taken 40 days with no sleep. It was only after Adam completed this task that Eve was created. Yet, even conceding the possibility that the process of naming the animals went quicker, because Adam named only the basic kinds of animals, like what went in Noah's ark at the time of the flood, which did not involve thousands of creatures, it would have taken weeks, possibly months, not a literal 24-hour day. It is during the process of Adam's naming the animals that it is discovered that "for the man no helper was found who was like him." (Genesis 2:20) Thus, we now see where the concern from Genesis 2:18 comes from, with God's reference to Adam's getting lonely. If it took weeks, months, or decades for Adam to complete his assignment of naming the animals, he would have had the time to grow lonely, but not in a couple hours as would be the case with a 24-hour day. Thus, the context here is that over a long period of time of naming the animals, Adam took note that he was alone while all the animals had mates. Let us take an extensive look at this again with the leading Hebrew language scholar of the 20th century, Dr. Gleason L. Archer.

> It thus becomes clear in this present case, as we study the text of Genesis 1, that we must not short-circuit our responsibility of careful exegesis in order to ascertain as clearly as possible what the divine author meant by the language His inspired prophet (in this case probably Moses) was guided to employ. Is the true purpose of Genesis 1 to teach that all creation began just six twenty-four-hour days before Adam was "born"? Or is this just a mistaken inference that overlooks other biblical data having a direct bearing on this passage? To answer this question, we must take careful note of what is said in Genesis 1:27 concerning the creation of man as the closing act of the sixth creative day. There it is stated that on that sixth day (apparently toward the end of the day, after all the animals had been fashioned and placed on the earth—therefore not long

---

53. Walter A. Elwell and Barry J Beitzel, *Baker Encyclopedia of the Bible* (Grand Rapids, Mich.: Baker Book House, 1988), S. 93.
54. *Enhanced Brown-Driver-Briggs Hebrew and English Lexicon*. electronic ed. (Oak Harbor, WA : Logos Research Systems, 2000), S. 339.

before sundown at the end of that same day), "God created man in His own image; He created them male and female." This can only mean that Eve was created in the closing hour of Day Six, along with Adam.

As we turn to Genesis 2, however, we find that a considerable interval of time must have intervened between the creation of Adam and the creation of Eve. In Gen. 2:15 we are told that Yahweh Elohim (i.e., the LORD God) put Adam in the garden of Eden as the idle environment for his development, and there he was to cultivate and keep the enormous park, with all its goodly trees, abundant fruit crop, and four mighty rivers that flowed from Eden to other regions of the Near East. In Gen 2:18 we read, "Then the LORD God said, 'It is not good for the man to be alone; I will make him a helper suitable for him.' " This statement clearly implies that Adam had been diligently occupied in his responsible task of pruning, harvesting fruit, and keeping the ground free of brush and undergrowth for a long enough period to lose his initial excitement and sense of thrill at this wonderful occupation in the beautiful paradise of Eden. He had begun to feel a certain lonesomeness and inward dissatisfaction.

In order to compensate for this lonesomeness, God then gave Adam a major assignment in natural history. He was to classify every species of animal and bird found in the preserve. With its five mighty rivers and broad expanse, the garden must have had hundreds of species of mammal, reptile, insect, and bird, to say nothing of the flying insects that also are indicated by the basic Hebrew term ʿôp̄ ("bird") (2:19). It took the Swedish scientist Linnaeus several decades to classify all the species known to European scientists in the eighteenth century. Doubtless there were considerably more by that time than in Adam's day; and, of course, the range of fauna in Eden may have been more limited than those available to Linnaeus. But at the same time it must have taken a good deal of study for Adam to examine each specimen and decide on an appropriate name for it, especially in view of the fact that he had absolutely no human tradition behind him, so far as nomenclature was concerned. It must have required some years, or, at the very least, a considerable number of months for him to complete this comprehensive inventory of all the birds, beasts, and insects that populated the Garden of Eden.

Finally, after this assignment with all its absorbing interest had been completed, Adam felt a renewed sense of emptiness. Genesis 2:20 ends with the words "but for Adam no suitable helper was found." After this long and unsatisfying experience as a lonely bachelor, God saw that Adam was emotionally prepared for a wife—a "suitable helper." God, therefore, subjected him to a deep sleep, removed from his body the bone that was closest to his heart, and from that physical core of man fashioned the first woman. Finally God presented woman to Adam in all her fresh, unspoiled beauty, and Adam was ecstatic with joy.

As we have compared Scripture with Scripture (Gen. 1:27 with 2:15–22), it has become very apparent that Genesis 1 was never intended to teach that the sixth creative day, when Adam and Eve were both created, lasted a mere twenty-four hours. In view of the long interval of time between these two, it would seem to border on sheer irrationality to insist that all of Adam's experiences in Genesis 2:15–22 could have been crowded into the last hour or two of a literal twenty-four-hour day. The only reasonable conclusion to draw is that the purpose of Genesis 1 is not to tell how fast God performed His work of creation (though, of course, some of His acts, such as the creation of light on the first day, must have been instantaneous). Rather, its true purpose was to reveal that the Lord God who had revealed Himself to the Hebrew race and entered into personal covenant relationship with them was indeed the only true God, the Creator of all things that are. This stood in direct opposition to the religious notions of the heathen around them, who assumed the emergence of pantheon of gods in successive stages out of preexistent matter of unknown origin, actuated by forces for which there was no accounting.[55]

Below, we see more examples of accounts within creation that are not instantaneous. Those who favor literal 24-hour creation days really must ignore a lot of context that does not allow for a literal interpretation of the creation days.

Genesis 2:8-9 Updated American Standard Version (UASV)

8 And Jehovah God planted a garden toward the east, in Eden; and there he put the man whom he had formed. **9** And **out of the ground**

---

[55] Gleason L. Archer, New International Encyclopedia of Bible Difficulties, Zondervan's Understand the Bible Reference Series, 59-60 (Grand Rapids, MI: Zondervan Publishing House, 1982).

Jehovah God caused to grow every tree that is pleasing to the sight and good for food; the tree of life also in the midst of the garden, and the tree of the knowledge of good and evil.

The straightforward reading of this text is that it is not an instantaneous creation. It is that Jehovah God planted the trees, and they grew as we understand trees grow, in a normal fashion.

Genesis 1:11-12 Updated American Standard Version (UASV)

[11] And God said, "Let the earth sprout vegetation, plants yielding seed, and fruit trees bearing fruit in which is their seed, each according to its kind, on the earth." And it was so. [12] The earth **brought forth vegetation, plants yielding seed according to their own kinds**, and trees bearing fruit in which is their seed, each according to its kind. And God saw that it was good.

Here again, the straight-forward reading, we are seeing the natural process of all vegetation, as opposed to it being created instantly.

In addition, it should be noted that God's Word explicitly helps man to appreciate that a "day" to Jehovah God is not measured in the same way as man.

Psalm 90:4: For in Your sight a thousand years are like yesterday that passes by, like a few hours of the night.

2 Peter 3:8: Dear friends, don't let this one thing escape you: with the Lord one day is like 1,000 years, and 1,000 years like one day.

2 Peter 3:10: But the Day of the Lord will come like a thief; on that [day] the heavens will pass away with a loud noise, the elements will burn and be dissolved, and the earth and the works on it will be disclosed.

As we can see on the sixth creation day, we are introduced to the creation of both domestic and wild animals, these being in relation to what man could tame and use domestically, as opposed to what remain wild. Within this creation period was also the greatest of all creation, the creation of both man and woman. It with the creation of humans alone that it was said they were 'created in the image of God.'

Then there is the problem of the seventh day, as far as the young earth view is concerned: it never ended. There was no opening and closing, as occurred with the preceding six days; it is still in progress from the close of the sixth day, more than 6,000 years ago.

Hebrews 4:4, 5, 9–11: For somewhere He has spoken about the seventh day in this way: And on the seventh day God rested from all His works. Again, in that passage [He says], They will never enter My rest. A Sabbath rest remains, therefore, for God's people. For the person who has entered His rest has rested from his own works, just as God did from His. Let us then make every effort to enter that rest, so that no one will fall into the same pattern of disobedience.

Clearly, the context of God's Word as a whole shows the earth to be much older than 6,000+ years.

Habakkuk 3:6: He stood, and measured the earth; He beheld, and drove asunder the nations; And the *eternal mountains* were scattered; The *everlasting hills* did bow; His goings were as of old.

Micah 6:2: Hear, O ye mountains, Jehovah's controversy, and ye *enduring foundations of the earth*; for Jehovah hath a controversy with his people, and he will contend with Israel.

Proverbs 8:22, 23: Jehovah possessed me in the beginning of his way, Before his works of old. I was set up from everlasting, from the beginning, Before the earth was.

The writer of Proverbs is using the age of the earth to emphasize that wisdom is much older. But if one accepts the young-earth theory (4004 B.C.E. for the creation of man),[56] when Solomon, who died shortly after 1000 B.C.E., wrote this, the earth would have been only about 3,000 years old—so not much of an emphasis.

Science has established that light travels at 186,282 miles per second. We know that it takes 100,000 years for light to cross our galaxy. We also know that it has taken hundreds of millions of years for the light of the stars we now see to reach the earth. Let us not repeat the Galileo history once more. It takes humility to learn from past experience. The Galileo conflict between science and the Church should at the very least help Christendom to avoid taking "day" as a literal 24-hour day when Scripture itself allows for another understanding; context weighs in that direction and science has established that the earth and the universe are far older than 6,000–10,000 years. Regardless of whether some scholars will concede to the correct understanding, this would in no way put the Bible in the wrong, for it is its interpreters who have misunderstood it. We must keep in mind that science (or the scientist) has no quarrel with the Bible: the quarrel would be with the misinterpretation of the teachers of Christendom, Orthodox Jews, and others.

The website ChristianAnswers.Net concludes: "The lesson to be learned from Galileo, it appears, is not that the Church held too tightly to

---

56. Archbishop James Usher (1581–1656) developed a chronology of the Bible, and dated creation at 4004 B.C.E.

biblical truths; but rather that it did not hold tightly enough. It allowed Greek philosophy to influence its theology and held to tradition rather than to the teachings of the Bible. We must hold strongly to Biblical doctrine which has been achieved through sure methods of exegesis. We must never be satisfied with dogmas built upon philosophic traditions."[57] However, it is also true that science alone should not determine our interpretation, but it is to be used in a balanced way, as another source to consider.

The Copernican theory was, in fact, condemned by the theologians of the Inquisition and Pope Urban VIII. They argued that it contradicted the Bible: to be specific, Joshua's statement: "O sun, stand still . . . So the sun stood still, and the moon stopped." (Joshua 10:12, *ESV*) Of course, this is not meant to be taken literally. There are several reasonable explanations, one of which, I will give you here. Verse 13 says that "the sun stopped in the midst of heaven and did not hurry to set for about a whole day." This could simply allow for a slower movement of the earth, giving the appearance to an earthly observer that the sun and moon had stood still. As for another reasonable explanation, one Bible encyclopedia comments: "While this could mean a stopping of earth's rotation, it could have been accomplished by other means, such as a refraction of solar and lunar light rays to produce the same effect." Therefore, once more, it becomes obvious that the Bible does not contradict itself.

Let us take another look at this again with the leading apologist scholar of the 20th century, Dr. Norman L. Geisler.

PROBLEM: The Bible says that God created the world in six days (Ex. 20:11). But modern science declares that it took billions of years. Both cannot be true.

SOLUTION: There are basically two ways to reconcile this difficulty. First, some scholars argue that modern science is wrong. They insist that the universe is only thousands of years old and that God created everything in six literal 24-hour days (= 144 hours). In favor of this view they offer the following:

1. The days of Genesis each have "evening and the morning," (cf. Gen. 1:5, 8, 13, 19, 23, 31), something unique to 24-hour days in the Bible.

2. The days were numbered (first, second, third, etc.), a feature found only with 24-hour days in the Bible.

---

57. http://www.christiananswers.net/q-eden/edn-c007.html. (Accessed January 28, 2010.)

3. Exodus 20: 11 compares the six days of creation with the six days of a literal work week of 144 hours.

4. There is scientific evidence to support a young age (of thousands of years) for the earth.

5. There is no way life could survive millions of years from day three (1:11) today four (1:14) without light.

Other Bible scholars claim that the universe could be billions of years old without sacrificing a literal understanding of Genesis 1 and 2. They argue that:

1. The days of Genesis 1 could have a time lapse before the days began (before Gen. 1:3), or a time gap between the days. There are gaps elsewhere in the Bible (cf. Matt. 1:8, where three generations are omitted, with 1 Chron. 3:11-14).

2. The same Hebrew word "day" (yam) is used in Genesis 1-2 as a period of time longer than 24 hours. For example, Genesis 2:4 uses it of the whole six day period of creation.

3. Sometimes the Bible uses the word "day" for long periods of time: "One day is as a thousand years" (2 Peter 3:8; cf. Ps. 90:4).

4. There are some indications in Genesis 1-2 that days could be longer than 24 hours:

a) On the third "day" trees grew from seeds to maturity and they bore like seeds (1:11-12). This process normally takes months or years.

b) On the sixth "day" Adam was created, went to sleep, named all the (thousands of) animals, looked for a helpmeet, went to sleep, and Eve was created from his rib. This looks like more than 24 hours' worth of activity.

c) The Bible says God "rested" on the seventh day (2:2), and that He is still in His rest from creation (Heb. 4:4). Thus, the seventh day is thousands of years long already. If so, then other days could be thousands of years too.

5. Exodus 20:11 could be making a unit-for-unit comparison between the days of Genesis and a work week (of 144 hours), not a minute-by-minute comparison.

Conclusion: There is no demonstrated contradiction of fact between Genesis 1 and science. There is only a conflict of interpretation. Either, most modern scientists are wrong in insisting the world is billions of years old, or else some Bible interpreters are wrong in insisting on only 144 hours of creation some several thousand years before Christ with no gaps allowing millions of years. But, in either case it is not a question of inspiration of Scripture, but of the interpretation of Scripture (and of the scientific data).[58]

In Summary

- The Hebrew word for day that was used for the creation days of Genesis chapter 1 is the same word used at Genesis 2:4 as a reference to the whole of the creative period, six days, "in the day that . . ."

- The Bible uses the word for "day" as longer periods than a 24-hour day "one day is as a thousand years." (2 Peter 3:8; Psalm 90:4)

- There are indicators within the first two chapters that we are dealing with periods longer than 24-hour days.

(1) **Third Day**: At Genesis 1:11-12, we find that trees grew from seeds to maturity, and produced seeds of their kind. This takes months, even years.

(2) **Sixth day**: We find Adam was created, went to sleep, named thousands of animals (names that indicate observation of the animals), grew lonely (looking for a helper), went to sleep, Eve was produced out of Adam's rib. This is obviously longer than 24 hours.

(3) **Seventh Day**: Genesis 2:2 informs us that God "proceeded to rest."[59] The reader will note that Hebrews 4:4 shows that God is still in his rest from the ending of the six creative days. Therefore, the seventh day has been running for thousands if years thus far, which allows the other creative days to be thousands of years long.

As it usually turns out, the so-called contradiction between science and God's Word lies at the feet of those who are interpreting Scripture incorrectly. To repeat the sentiments of Galileo when writing to a pupil— Galileo expressed the same sentiments: "Even though Scripture cannot err, its interpreters and expositors can, in various ways. One of these, very serious and very frequent, would be when they always want to stop at the purely literal sense."[60] I believe that today's scholars, in hindsight, would have no problem agreeing.

---

[58] Thomas Howe; Norman L. Geisler. *The Big Book of Bible Difficulties: Clear and Concise Answers from Genesis to Revelation* (Kindle Locations 356-375). Kindle Edition.

[59] Why do I have it rendered as a continuous, "proceeded to rest", when most translations read "he rested"? Heb., waiyishboth (imperfect sequential): The verb is in the imperfect state denoting incomplete or continuous action, or action in progress.

60. Letter from Galileo to Benedetto Castelli, December 21, 1613.

Genesis 1:10 Is the Hebrew word for "earth" the same here as is used at Genesis 1:1, and do they mean the same thing?

The Hebrew word is erets in both verse 1 and verse 10. Erets refers to **(1)** earth, as contrasted to the heavens (Gen 1:1); **(2)** or more restricted to all the dry land of the earth (1:10); **(3)** or restricted even further by referring to just the land of a certain section of the earth (Gen 10:10); **(4)** or ground (Gen 1:26); **(5)** or people of the human race (Gen 18:25).

Many people do not realize that all words have more than one sense (meaning). The context will determine which sense belongs to the use under consideration. Even if we were to consider the word "mean," we cannot ascertain what we mean by "mean" outside its context. She says she is resigning, and I think this time she *means* it, would be an expression of intention. I do not know what half these words *mean*, is indicating a particular sense. That is not quite what I *meant*, is intent. Then, let us go to what the dictionary actually considers another word, but spelled the same way. You hurt her feelings, which was a *mean* thing to do. He plays a *mean* sax, which is used in the sense of being skillful. This is the *meanest* climate I have ever lived in, which means uncomfortable. Moreover, we could even look at another term, which is spelled the same, but considered a different word from the first two cases of "mean." We need to find the *mean* between these extremes.

According to A Hebrew and English Lexicon of the Old Testament (Gesenius, Brown, Driver, and Briggs; 1951) erets means: "1. a. earth, whole earth ([as opposed] to a part) . . . b. earth, [as opposed] to heaven, sky . . . c. earth=inhabitants of earth . . . 2. Land = a. country, territory . . . b. district, region . . . 3. a. ground, surface of ground . . . b. soil, as productive." Old Testament Word Studies by William Wilson says of erets, "The earth in the largest sense, both the habitable and uninhabitable parts; with some accompanying word of limitation, it is used of some portion of the earth's surface, a land or country." Therefore, the first and primary meaning of the Hebrew word is our planet, or globe, the earth.

(erets) in verses 10-12 is "land," while in verses 1-2 it was "earth." Recognizing this relieves us of the problems in Paul Seely, "The Geographical Meaning of `Earth' and `Seas' in Genesis 1:10," Westminster Theological Journal 59 (1997): 231-55, who takes [erets] as the entire earth, a flat disk of ancient conception.[61]

---

[61] C. John Collins. Genesis 1-4: A Linguistic, Literary, And Theological Commentary (Kindle Locations 3685-3687). Kindle Edition.

Genesis 1:16 Was light created or made, and was it on the first day or the fourth?

Genesis 1:3, 5 American Standard Version (ASV)	Genesis 1:3, 5 New American Standard Bible (NASB)	Genesis 1:3, 5 English Standard Version (ESV)	Genesis 1:3, 5 New International Version (NIV)
³And God said, **Let there be light**: and there was light. ⁵And God called the light Day, and the darkness he called Night. And there was evening and there was morning, **one day**.	³Then God said, "**Let there be light**"; and there was light. ⁵God called the light day, and the darkness He called night And there was evening and there was morning, **one day**.	³And God said, "**Let there be light**," and there was light. ⁵And there was evening and there was morning, **the first day**.	³And God said, "**Let there be light**," and there was light. ⁵God called the light "day," and the darkness he called "night." And there was evening, and there was morning—**the first day**.

Genesis 1:3, 5 Holman Christian Standard Bible (HCSB)

³ Then God said, "**Let there be light**," and there was light. ⁵ God called the light "day," and He called the darkness "night." Evening came, and then morning: **the first day**.

Genesis 1:3, 5 Updated American Standard Version (UASV)

³ And God said, "**Let there be light**," and there was light. ⁵ And God began calling the light Day, and the darkness he called Night. And there came to be evening and there came to be morning, **the first day**.

Genesis 1:16, 19 American Standard Version (ASV)	Genesis 1:16, 19 New American Standard Bible (NASB)	Genesis 1:16, 19 English Standard Version (ESV)	Genesis 1:16, 19 New International Version (NIV)
¹⁶And **God made the two great lights**; the greater light to rule the day, and the lesser light to rule the night: he made the stars also. ¹⁹And there was	¹⁶**God made the two great lights**, the greater light to govern the day, and the lesser light to govern the night; He made the stars	¹⁶And **God made the two great lights**— the greater light to rule the day and the lesser light to rule the night—and the stars. ¹⁹And there was	¹⁶**God made two great lights**—the greater light to govern the day and the lesser light to govern the night. He also made the stars. ¹⁹And

evening and there was morning, **a fourth day.**	also. ¹⁹There was evening and there was morning, **a fourth day.**	evening and there was morning, **the fourth day.**	there was evening, and there was morning—**the fourth day.**

Genesis 1:16, 19 Holman Christian Standard Bible (HCSB)

¹⁶**God made the two great lights**—the greater light to have dominion over the day and the lesser light to have dominion over the night—as well as the stars. ¹⁹Evening came, and then morning: **the fourth day**.

Genesis 1:16, 19 Updated American Standard Version (UASV)

¹⁶ And **God went on to make the two great lights**, the greater light to rule the day and the lesser light to rule the night, and the stars. ¹⁹ And there was evening and there was morning, **the fourth day**.

In the above there appears to be a difficulty, in that Genesis 1:3, 5 informs the reader that God brought about light during the first creation day, when he said: "'Let there be light,' and there was light." Then, Genesis 1:16, 19 informs the reader that "God made the two great lights" during the fourth creation day. Hence, did God create or make light on the first or fourth creation day? Before we begin to answer this difficulty, we must bear in mind that Genesis was written from a human perspective, as an earthly observer, as if he were there; not from a heavenly observation.

In looking at the fourth creation day first, we see that the "greater light" for ruling the day is our sun, and the "lesser light" for ruling the night is our moon. A further explanation of this is found at Psalm 136:7-9 (ASV): "To him that made great lights; for his loving-kindness endures forever: The sun to rule by day; for his loving-kindness endures forever; the moon and stars to rule by night; for his loving-kindness endures forever."

Returning to the first creation day, we find the expression: "let there be light." *Ohr* is the Hebrew word for light, which conveys the idea of light in a broad sense. However, for the fourth creation day, a different word is chosen, *maohr*, which refers to a source of light. Rotherham, in a footnote on "Luminaries" in the *Emphasised Bible*, says: "In ver. 3, 'ôr ['ohr], light diffused." Then he goes on to show that the Hebrew word *maohr* in verse 14 has the sense of something "affording light." In other words, on the first creation day *ohr* (light) was spread throughout the earth's atmosphere (being diffused). To an earthly observer, had he been there: he would not have been able to discern the source of light. However, by the fourth creation day, the observer would have been able to see the *maohr* (source) of that light, as the atmosphere would have changed.

It should also be noted that Genesis 1:16 does not use the Hebrew verb bara, meaning, "create." Instead, the Hebrew verb asah is used, meaning, "make." The reason being, Genesis 1:1 informs us "God created the heavens (which would include sun, moon and stars) and the earth." In other words, the "greater light" (sun) and the "lesser light" (moon) were created long before the fourth creation day. What we have on the fourth creation day is Jehovah God "making" the "greater light" and the "lesser light" to exist in a new way with the surface of the earth and the expanse that had now dissipated even further, allowing the source of light to be seen from earth. God said, "Let there be lights in the expanse of the heavens . . ." (Gen 1:14) This being a further indication of their discernibleness. In addition, they were "to separate the day from the night. And let them be for signs and for seasons, and for days and years." These were to evidence the existence of God and draw attention to His great power, as well as lead man in numerous ways.

Genesis 1-2 Is there a Different order of creation in Genesis 2 than Genesis 1?

Genesis 1:1-2 inform the reader of the creation of the heavens and the earth. **Genesis 1:3-31** gives the reader an outline of the six creative days and the basic events and creative activities on those days. **Genesis 2:1-3** is some basics on the seventh day, while **Genesis 2:4** is a summary verse of the whole six creative days. Genesis **chapter 2:5-25** is a parallel account that picks up the account, not on the first day, but the third day (after the land comes on the scene, but prior to the creation of land plants), adding details. **(2:5-6)** This chapter is used to give more details about the human creation. For example, there is no simple statement that Adam was created; it adds that he was formed out of the dust of the ground, with the breath of life being blown into him, his becoming a living soul. **(2:7)** It informs of the planting of the Garden of Eden and placing Adam in it. **(2:8)** We learn of the growth of many trees for food, tree of life, and the tree of knowledge of good and bad. **(2:9)** We are even given geographical sites that help the readers of Moses day, to know where the Garden of Eden was. **(2:10-14)** We are told of the work assignments given to Adam, to cultivate the Garden of Eden and to name the animals. **(2:15, 19-20)** We are informed of the prohibition of eating from the tree of knowledge of good and bad. **(2:16-17)** Then, we are informed that Adam grew lonely from his naming the animals, as he saw all of them had mates. **(2:18, 20)** From there the reader gets a detailed account of the creation of Eve **(2:21-22)**, and Adam's response, with the

Jehovah, in essence, performing the first marriage. **(2:23-25)** Therefore, as you can see, **chapter 1** is the barest of outlines, with **chapter 2** giving us details about the arrival of the humans. **Chapter 3:1-24** deals with the temptation of Eve by the serpent and the sinning of both Adam and Eve, with the terrible consequences of that willful rebellion.

Genesis 1:26 Who are the "us" and "our" of this verse

Genesis 1:26-27 Updated American Standard Version (UASV)

²⁶ And God went on to say, "Let us make man in our image, after our likeness. And let them have dominion over the fish of the sea and over the birds of the heavens and over the livestock and over all the earth and over every creeping thing that creeps on the earth."

²⁷ So God created man in his own image,
in the image of God he created him;
male and female he created them.

Different Bible scholars have offered up different interpretations over the last 2,000 years, one of which is that God is here referring to himself and the angels. However, this does not seem like a good option based on the context. If you will look at verse 26 again, you will see that God says, "Let us make man in our image" while verse 27 clearly states, "God created man in his own image," not the image of angels.

While it is true that the plural pronoun "us" is required because of the plural noun *elohim* (God): "And God [*elohim*, plural] went on to say, 'Let us [plural] make man in our image.' There are a couple points to keep in mind: **(1)** the plural ending "*im*" on *elohim* is majestic, expressing the majesty of God, not expressing multiple persons; **(2)** however, it is quite clear from Scripture that God's only-begotten Son was involved in the creation of man with his heavenly Father, as the Father's master worker. (John 1:3; 1:18; Col 1:15-16; Pro 8:21-22, 30-31, NASB) Therefore, the plural "us" and "our" simply means that two or more persons were involved. Therefore, when God used "us" and "our," he was merely addressing another person, the prehuman Jesus prior to his ascension to earth, the master workman of Proverbs 8:22-31, "the firstborn of all creation. For by him all things were created, in heaven and on earth, visible and invisible."—Colossians 1:15-16.

Genesis 1:27 Were Adam and Eve Allegorical or Historical Persons?

Critical Scholars either consider Adam and Eve as a myth or symbolic persons, representing humankind. The evidence from the Bible, on the other hand, is that they are real historical persons. Before looking at the biblical evidence, let us note that Hebrew manuscripts are archaeological evidence that gives us the historicity of humanity. The oldest manuscripts date to the 3rd century B.C.E. In addition, Greek New Testament manuscripts give us how Jewish Christians from the first century, as well as the Son of God, views the Hebrew Old Testament and the historicity of Adam and Eve, and these NT MSS are archaeological evidence, some even dating as early as the second-century C.E.[62]

Scriptural Evidence

(1) Genesis 1-2 is a historical narrative that expounds on Adam and Eve's creation and events within their lives. **(2)** They are recorded as giving birth to children, as do the others mentioned in the early genealogies. (Gen 4:1, 25; 5:1) **(3)** The Hebrew word toledoth, often translated "generations," should be translated "history" at Genesis 2:4; 5:1; 6:9; 10:1; 11:10; as well as five other places in Genesis. Regardless, it shows that toledoth is used all throughout Genesis, in speaking of descendants of so-and-so, and has the same meaning in its use with Adam and Eve at Genesis 5:1. **(4)** If we look at the chronologies throughout the Old Testament, Adam starts the list. (1 Ch 1:1) **(5)** All early humankind did not father Seth. No, Adam fathered him at the specific age of 130 years. (Gen 5:3) **(6)** Luke places Adam at the start of human history. (Lu 3:38) **(7)** Jesus viewed Adam and Eve as real historical persons. (Matt 19:24-25) **(8)** The inheritance of sin and death came from a literal Adam. (Rom 5:12-14) **(9)** Jesus is contrasted with Adam, which means if we deny Adam as a historical person, we deny Jesus Christ and his sacrifice as well. (1 Cor. 15:45-47) **(10)** Again, Paul comes to the stage as a witness, when he informs us that Adam was created first and then Eve. (1 Tim 2:13-14) **(11)** Was Enoch the seventh in line from all early humankind? (Jude14) Reasonably, humankind had to of started from just two people at some time. The fact is that the Bible, as a reliable book and archaeological evidence of human history, gives us those two individuals, Adam and Eve.

Has Science Now Caught Up With the Fact That All of Us Descended from the Same Original Parents?

---

[62] **Common Era**: B.C.E. means "before the Common Era," which is more accurate than B.C. ("before Christ"). C.E. denotes "Common Era," often called A.D., for *anno Domini*, meaning "in the year of our Lord."

Dr. Purdom explains:

The genetic evidence is consistent with human DNA being "young" and the human race beginning with a very small starting population (the Bible tells us the starting population was two people!).

The International HapMap project endeavors to study a select group of DNA similarities and differences between humans known as single nucleotide polymorphisms (SNPs).[63] The SNPs are believed to be representative of the genome (total human DNA) such that what is true for them would be true for the whole genome. These studies and others have shown that the difference in DNA between any two humans is amazingly low . . . only 0.1 percent.[64]

Reflecting on this very low percentage, some scientists posited, "This proportion is low compared with those of many other species, from fruit flies to chimpanzees, reflecting the recent origins of our species from a small founding population" (emphases mine).[65] They also stated, "[Certain genetic estimates] tell us that humans vary only slightly at the DNA level and that only a small proportion of this variation separates continental populations."[66]

These findings are consistent with the Bible's history that humans were created several thousand years ago; in other words, a short amount of time has passed, so there is little genetic variation.

The Bible Concurs

Acts 17:26 Updated American Standard Version (UASV)

and he [God] made from one man every nation of mankind to live on all the face of the earth, having determined their appointed times and the boundaries of their habitation,

---

[63] HapMap Homepage

[64] Lynn B. Jorde and Stephen P. Wooding, "Genetic Variation, Classification and 'Race'," Nature Genetics 36 (2004):S28–S33. Quoted in "Were Adam and Eve Real People," chapter 20 of How We Know the Bible is True volume 2, Green Forest, Arkansas: Master Books, 2012.

[65] IBID

[66] IBID

How does the Bible View Adam?

Jude 14 Updated American Standard Version (UASV)

[14] It was also about these men that Enoch, the seventh one in line from Adam,[67] prophesied, saying, "Behold, the Lord came with tens of thousands of his holy ones,

Note here that Jude makes a historical reference to Enoch being the seventh in line from Adam, not all, early mankind.

Luke 3:23-38 Updated American Standard Version (UASV)

[23] Jesus, when he began his ministry, was about thirty years of age, being the son (as was supposed) of Joseph, the son of Heli, . . . [31] son of David . . . [34] son of Abraham . . . [37] son of Adam."

Both David and Abraham are well-known historical persons, so why would Luke go through the genealogy of all many historical persons to get back to an allegorical person? Would not the Jews know if Adam were an allegorical person? Would it not make a genealogical list look quite silly if one took it back to an allegorical person?

Genesis 5:3 Updated American Standard Version (UASV)

[3] When Adam had lived one hundred and thirty years, he became[68] the father of a son in his own likeness, according to his image, and named him Seth.

So, if Adam is allegorical, standing for early mankind, how do we reason that early mankind fathered Seth, specifically at 130 years of age?

Can the fact that we have a serpent speaking to Eve be used to argue for an allegorical story?

Genesis 3:1-4 Updated American Standard Version (UASV)

3 Now the serpent was more crafty than any beast of the field which Jehovah God had made. And he said to the woman, "Did God actually say, 'You[69] shall not eat of any tree in the garden'?" [2] And the woman said to the serpent, "From the fruit of the trees of the garden we may eat, [3] but from the tree that is in the midst of the garden, God said, 'You

---

[67] Following the genealogy of Genesis 5:1–24; 1 Chronicles 1:1–3, Enoch was the seventh in the line of Adam. – MacArthur, John (2005-05-09). *The MacArthur Bible Commentary* (Kindle Locations 66202-66203). Thomas Nelson. Kindle Edition.

[68] Lit *begot*

[69] In Hebrew *you* is plural in verses 1–5

shall not eat from it, nor shall you touch it, lest you die.'" ⁴ And the **serpent said to the woman**, "You shall not surely die.

John 8:44 Updated American Standard Version (UASV)

⁴⁴ You are of your father the devil, and your will is to do your father's desires. That one was a manslayer from the beginning, and does not stand in the truth, because there is no truth in him. When he lies, he speaks out of his own character, for he is a liar and the father of lies.

We see here that Jesus, whose historicity is settled states unambiguously that Satan the Devil was the one behind the first lie in the Garden of Eden. Satan, a powerful angel (specifically a Cherub), spoke through the serpent, just as a ventriloquist can make his voice come through a dummy.

Revelation 12:9 Updated American Standard Version (UASV)

⁹ And the great dragon was thrown down, the serpent of old who is called the devil and Satan, who deceives the whole inhabited earth; he was thrown down to the earth, and his angels were thrown down with him.

If we say the first man Adam was allegorical, what does that mean for Jesus Christ, as we know he is not allegorical, making the contrast in Corinthians meaningless.

1 Corinthians 15:45, 47 Updated American Standard Version (UASV)

⁴⁵ So also it is written, "The first man, Adam, became a living soul." The last Adam became a life-giving spirit ... ⁴⁷ The first man is from the earth and made of dust; the second man is from heaven.

If we deny the historicity of Adam and his sin, a rebellion against God, it would mean the denial of the purpose of Jesus Christ's coming. Such a rejection is a motive for the anti-miracle Bible critics, activist atheists, who want such a rejection to be a repudiation of the Christian faith.

How did Jesus himself view the Genesis?

Matthew 19:4-5 Updated American Standard Version (UASV)

⁴ And he answered and said, "Have you not read that he who created them from the beginning made them male and female, ⁵ and said, 'For this reason a man shall leave his father and mother and be joined to his wife, and the two shall become one flesh'?

Clearly, Jesus viewed the Genesis account to be factual and historical. If we look at the entire sixty-six books of the Bible, which covered 1,600 years of the history of the Israelite nation, written by forty+ men, all of which a belief in a historical Adam, it would seem that while we do not have archaeological evidence for the historicity of Adam, we have archaeological evidence that references him as being a historical person that goes back to the third century B.C.E. up unto the sixteenth century C.E., i.e., well over 33,000 manuscripts. The irony is, those same secularists would not reject a real historical person, with far less evidence.

Sumeria

The first recorded name given in an actual writing system can be found on clay tablets dating from the Jemdet Nasr period in Sumeria between 3200 and 3101 BC.[70]

Example of Jemdet Nasr cuneiform (Credit: Metropolitan Museum of Art

The tablets are not profound treatises on human thinking, but accounting ledgers for tallying up goods and possessions! Some of the first names are those of the slave owner Gal-Sal and his two slaves Enpap-x and Sukkalgir (3200-3100 BC). Another

---

[70] Who Was the First Named Human? - The Huffington Post, http://www.huffingtonpost.com/dr-sten-odenwald/who-was-the-first-named-h_b_56798 (accessed February 17, 2016).

name is that of Turgunu Sanga (3100 BC) who seems to have been an accountant for the Turgunu family. There are many more names from this period but none that appear much before 3200 BC.[71]

What Is Recorded History?

Recorded history or written history is a historical narrative based on a written record or other documented communication. Recorded history can be contrasted with other narratives of the past such as mythological or oral traditions.

Historical Method

The historical method comprises the techniques and guidelines by which historians use primary sources and other evidence to research and then to write history. Primary sources are firsthand evidence of history (usually written, but sometimes captured in other mediums) made at the time of an event by a present person. Historians think of those sources as the closest to the origin of the information or idea under study.[72] These types of sources can provide researchers with, as Dalton and Charnigo put it, "direct, unmediated information about the object of study."[73]

Historians use other types of sources to understand history as well. Secondary sources are written accounts of history based upon the evidence from primary sources. These are sources which, usually, are accounts, works, or research that analyze, assimilate, evaluate, interpret, and/or synthesize primary sources. Tertiary sources are compilations based upon primary and secondary sources and often tell a more generalized

[71] Who Was the First Named Human?
Who Was the First Named Human? - The Huffington Post, http://www.huffingtonpost.com/dr-sten-odenwald/who-was-the-first-named-h_b_56798 (accessed February 17, 2016).
[72] User Education Services. "Primary, Secondary and Tertiary Sources". University of Maryland Libraries. Retrieved 10 Jul 2013.
"Library Guides: Primary, secondary and tertiary sources"
[73] Dalton, Margaret Steig; Charnigo, Laurie (2004). "Historians and Their Information Sources" (PDF). College & Research Libraries. September: 400–25, at 416 n.3, citing U.S. Dept. of Labor, Bureau of Labor Statistics (2003),Occupational Outlook Handbook; Lorenz, C. (2001). "History: Theories and Methods". In Smelser, Neil J.; Bates. International Encyclopedia of Social and Behavior Sciences

account built on the more specific research found in the first two types of sources.[74]

It should be mentioned again that the Hebrew manuscripts that date to the 3rd, 2nd and 1st centuries B.C.E. are copies of what came down from the originals, which date to as early as middle of the 16th century B.C.E. Moreover, the Dead Sea community believed and wrote that Adam was a real historical person, based on their earliest manuscripts.

Manuscript 4QMMT (also known as the Halakhic Letter or the Sectarian Manifesto, later called Some Precepts of the Law) states, "We have written to you so that you should understand the Book of Moses and the Books of the Prophets and David."

This is one of if not the earliest reference to the custom of subdividing the Scriptures into three parts—'the law of Moses, the Prophets, and the Psalms.' It supports Jesus words, "These are My words which I spoke to you while I was still with you, that all things which are written about Me in the Law of Moses and the Prophets and the Psalms must be fulfilled." (Lu 24:44) The Jewish historian Josephus is in harmony with this text as well (I, 38-40 [8]) around the year 100 C.E., as he confirms the close of the Hebrew Scriptures cannon at the time of Malachi. He wrote, "We do not possess myriads of inconsistent books, conflicting with each other. Our books, those which are justly accredited, are but two and twenty [counted as thirty-nine today], and contain the record of all time. Of these, five are the books of Moses, comprising the laws and the traditional history from the birth of man down to the death of the lawgiver. . . . From the death of Moses until Artaxerxes [i.e., 475-424 B.C.E., who succeeded Xerxes as king of Persia, the prophets subsequent to Moses wrote the history of the events of their own times in thirteen books. The remaining four books contain hymns to God and precepts for the conduct of human life."

Genesis 2:4 "God" is used in Genesis chapter 1, while chapter 2 changes to Jehovah God. Does this mean that there are two different authors?

The higher critics argue that every Bible verse that contains the Hebrew word for God, (Elohim), set off by itself has its own writer, designated by the capital "E" ("Elohist"). On the other hand, any verse that contains the Tetragrammaton, (Jehovah, Yahweh), God's personal name, is attributed to yet another writer, "J" ("Jawist"). (Cassuto, 18-21)

---

[74] User Education Services. "Primary, Secondary and Tertiary Sources". University of Maryland Libraries. Retrieved 10 Jul 2013.
Amsterdam: Elsevier. p. 6871
"Library Guides: Primary, secondary and tertiary sources"

Let us see how they explain this. The critics argue that "God" (*Elohim*) is restricted in use exclusively in the first chapter of Genesis (1:1–31) in relation to God's creation activity, and that starting in Genesis 2:4 through the end of the second chapter we find God's personal name.

R. E. Friedman speaks of a discovery by three men: "One was a minister, one was a physician, and one was a professor. The discovery that they made ultimately came down to the combination of two pieces of evidence: doublets and the names of God. They saw that there were apparently two versions each of a large number of Biblical stories: two accounts of the creation, two accounts each of several stories about the patriarchs Abraham and Jacob, and so on. Then, they noticed that, quite often, one of the two versions of a story would refer to God by one name and the other version would refer to God by a different name." (R. E. Friedman, 50)

Different settings, however, require different uses. This principle holds true throughout the whole of the entire Old Testament. Moses may choose to use (*Elohim*) in a setting in which he wants to show a particular quality clearly, like power, creative activity, and so on. On the other hand, Moses may choose to use God's personal name (Jehovah, Yahweh) when the setting begs for that personal relationship between the Father and his children, the Israelites, or even more personable, a one-on-one conversation between Jehovah God and a faithful servant.

The Divine Names: The weakness of claiming multiple authors because of the different names used for God is quite evident when we look at just one small portion of the book of Genesis in the *American Standard Version* (1901). God is called "God Most High," "possessor (or maker) of heaven and earth," "O Lord Jehovah," "a God that seeth," "God Almighty," "God," "[the] God,"[75] and "the Judge of all the earth." (Genesis 14:18, 19; 15:2; 16:13; 17:1, 3; 18:25) It is difficult to believe that different authors wrote these verses. Moreover, let us take a look at Genesis 28:13, which says: "And, behold, Jehovah stood above it, and said, I am Jehovah, the God ["Elohim"] of Abraham thy father, and the God of Isaac: the land whereon thou liest, to thee will I give it, and to thy seed." Another scripture, Psalm 47:5, says: "God is gone up with a shout, Jehovah with the sound of a trumpet."[76] (*ASV*) In applying their documentary analysis, we would have to accept the idea that two authors worked together on each of these two verses.

Many conservative scholars have come to realize that in a narrative format one will often find a ruler being referred to not only by name, but also by a title, such as "king." M. H. Segal observes: "Just as those

---

[75] The title Elohim preceded by the definite article ha, giving the expression ha Elohim.

76. See also Psalm 46:11; 48:1, 8.

interchanges of human proper names and their respective appellative common nouns cannot by any stretch of the imagination be ascribed to a change of author or source of document, so also the corresponding interchanges of the divine names in the Pentateuch must not be attributed to such a literary cause."* If one were to look up "Adolf Hitler" using Academic American Encyclopedia, within three paragraphs he will find the terms "Führer," "Adolf Hitler," and simply "Hitler." Who is so bold as to suggest that there are three different authors for these three paragraphs?

Dr. John J. Davis[77] helps us to appreciate that there is "no other religious document from the ancient Near East [that] was compiled in such a manner; a documentary analysis of the Gilgamesh Epic or Enuma Elis would be complete folly. The author of Genesis may have selected divine names on the basis of theological emphasis rather than dogmatic preference. Many divine names were probably interchangeable; Baal and Hadad were used interchangeably in the Hadad Tablet from Ugarit[78] and similar examples could be cited from Egyptian texts."[79]

In fact, we now know that there were many deities in the ancient Near East that had multiple names. As stated above with the Babylonian Creation account, the Enuma Elish, the god Marduk (Merodach), chief deity of Babylon, also had some 50 different names.[80] It would not even be thinkable to apply any of the Documentary Hypothesis analysis to any of these works. Why? Not only because we can see that ancient writers are no different than modern writers and are able to use different names and titles interchangeably within their work, but they were written on stone, so to speak. If one has one clay tablet that has both a personal name, and two different titles for the same king, it would be difficult to argue that there were two or three different authors for the one tablet. Bible scholar Mark F. Rooker has the following to say about the use of Elohim and Yahweh in the Old Testament:

> Moreover, it is clear that throughout the Old Testament that the occurrence of the names of God as Elohim or Yahweh is to be attributed to contextual and semantic issues, not the existence of sources. This conclusion is borne out by the fact that the names consistently occur in predictable genre. In the legal and prophetic texts the name Yahweh always appears, while in wisdom literature the name for God is invariably

77. John J. Davis, *Paradise to Prison: Studies in Genesis* (Salem: Sheffield, 1975), 22–23.

78 . G. R. Driver, *Canaanite Myths and Legends* (New York: T. & T. Clark, 1971), 70-72.

79. For example, see the "Stele of Ikhernofret" in James B. Pritchard, ed., *Ancient Near Eastern Texts*, 2nd ed. Princeton: Princeton University Press, 1955, pp. 329–30.

80. K. A. Kitchen, *On the Reliability of the Old Testament* (Grand Rapids: Eerdmans, 2003), 424–5.

Elohim. In narrative literature, which includes much of the Pentateuch, both Yahweh and Elohim are used.[81]* Yet consistently the names do not indicate different sources but were chosen by design. The name Elohim was used in passages to express the abstract idea of Deity as evident in God's role as Creator of the universe and the Ruler of nature. Yahweh, on the other hand, is the special covenant name of God who has entered into a relationship with the Israelites since the name reflects God's ethical character. (Cassuto, 31) Given the understanding of the meaning of these names for God, it is no wonder that the source which contains the name Yahweh would appear to reflect a different theology from a selected group of texts which contained the name Elohim."[82]

Let us, on a small scale, do our own analysis of the divine names in the first two chapters of Genesis. The Hebrew word (*elohim*) is most often agreed upon to be from a root meaning "be strong," "mighty," or "power."[83] It should be said too that by far, most Hebrew scholars recognize the plural form (*im*) of this title *elohim* to be used as a plural of "majesty," "greatness," or "excellence." The Hebrew word (*elohim*) is used for the Creator 35 times from Genesis 1:1 to 2:4a. Exactly what is the context of this use? It is used in a setting that deals with God's power, his greatness, his excellence, his creation activity, all of which seems appropriate, does it not?

Moving on to Genesis 2:4b–25, we find God now being referred to by his personal name, the Tetragrammaton (YHWH, JHVH), which is translated "Jehovah" (*KJV, ASV, NW, NEB*, etc.) or "Yahweh" (*AT, NAB, JB, HCSB*, etc.). It is found in verses 4b–25 a total of 11 times; however, it comes before his title (*elohim*).[84] Why the switch, and what is the context of this use? This personal name of God is used in a setting that deals with his personal relationship with man and woman. This is not a second creation account; it is a more detailed account of the creation of man, which was only briefly mentioned in chapter one in passing, as each feature of creation was ticked off. In chapter two, the Creator becomes a person as he speaks to his intelligent creation, giving them the prospect of an eternal perfect life in a paradise garden, which is to be cultivated earth wide, to be filled with perfect offspring. Therefore, we see a personal

---

[81] Similarly, Livingston has pointed out that the cognate West Semitic divine names il and ya(w) appear to be interchangeable in the Eblaite tablets. (The Pentateuch in Its Cultural Environment, 224.)

82. Mark F. Rooker, *Leviticus: The New American Commentary* (Nashville: Broadman & Holman, 2001), 26–27.

[83]. Ibid., 27.

[84] "Jehovah God." Heb., Yehwah Elohim.

interchange between God and man as He lays out His plans to Adam, which seems very appropriate, does it not, when switching from using a title in chapter one to using a personal name in chapter two? In chapter two, we have the coupling of the personal name "Jehovah" with the title "God," to show that we are still talking about this 'great,' 'majestic,' 'all powerful' Creator, but personalized as he introduces himself to his new earthly creation.

Thus, there is no reason to assume that we are talking about two different writers. No, it is two different settings in which a skilled writer would make the transition just as Moses did. It would be no different from if a modern-day news commentator were giving as a report about the United States President visiting Russia to meet with Dmitry Anatolyevich Medvedev, in which he used the title President predominately. The following week the same news commentator may be covering the President visiting a hospital with injured children who had survived a tornado, and refer to the President as President Obama. It isn't difficult to see that one is an official setting where the President needs to be portrayed as powerful, while in the other setting; he needs to be portrayed as personable. The same principles used herein apply to the rest of the Pentateuch and the Old Testament as a whole.

Genesis 2:8 Was the Garden of Eden a real historical place?

The search for the Garden of Eden has gone on since Noah stepped of the ark. The exact location is speculative at best. Nevertheless, we can infer some things, without going beyond Scripture.

Genesis 2:10-14 Updated American Standard Version (UASV)

[10] Now a river flowed out[85] of Eden to water the garden; and from there it divided and became <u>four rivers</u>.[86] [11] The name of the first is <u>Pishon</u>; it flows around the whole land of Havilah, where there is gold. [12] And the gold of that land is good; bdellium and onyx stone are there. [13] The name of the second river is <u>Gihon</u>; it flows around the whole land of Cush. [14] The name of the third river is <u>Tigris</u>; it flows east of Assyria.[87] And the fourth river is the <u>Euphrates</u>.

The Euphrates has long been known, as is also true of the Tigris. However, the identity of the Pishon and Gihon has never been identified. In addition, the topography today does not have the Euphrates and Tigris Rivers proceeding from a single source. The earth-wide flood that Noah

---

[85] Lit., *was going out*; Hebrew participle refers to a continuous stream

[86] Lit *became four heads*

[87] *Assyria* Heb., *Ashshur*

and his family survived in the ark would explain the change in topography. Some rivers would have been filled in and others would have had their courses changed. Even a tremendous local flood can change the course of a river, such as the Mississippi in the United States.

The long accepted location of the Garden of Eden has been the mountainous area about 140 miles Southwest on Mount Ararat, in the Eastern part of Modern-day Turkey. Again, the mountains could be a result of the flood, or it could be that a mountainous range surrounded the Garden of Eden, giving us the reason why cherubs protected only the East of Eden.—Genesis 3:24.

Genesis 2:10-14 Was the mention of Assyria an inaccurate statement?

The account at Genesis 2:10-14 gives geographical details about the Garden of Eden. Moses wrote that one river was "the one going to the east of Assyria." However, the land of Assyria received its name from Asshur, the son of Shem born after the Flood. (Genesis 10:8-11, 22; Ezekiel 27:23; Micah 5:6) Clearly, in his accurate, inspired description, Moses merely used the term "Assyria" to denote to a region that his readers would have been aware of.

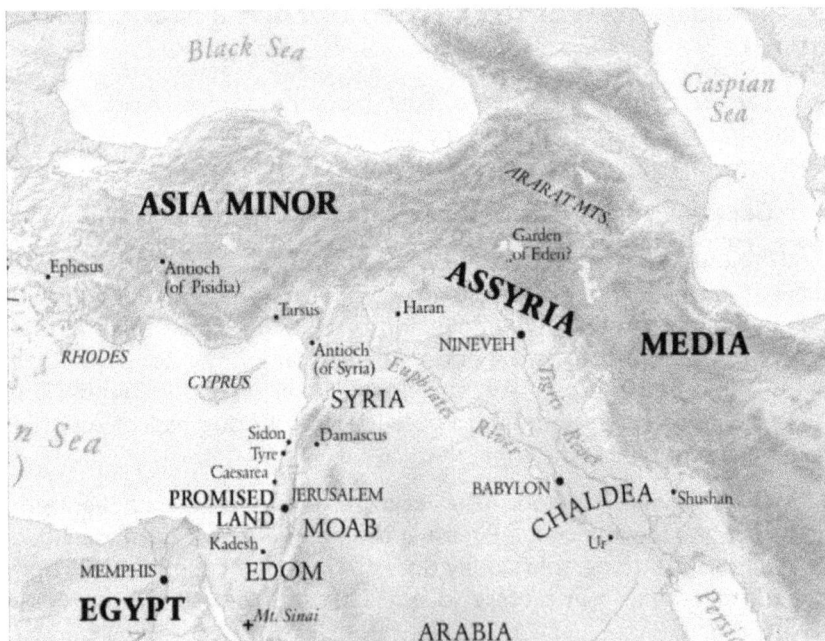

Sadly, it is true that most modern scholars dismiss the Garden of Eden as a legend or a myth, not being a real historical account. Nevertheless, this writer, as well as many other conservative scholars,

100

accept the historical reality of the whole of Genesis. The account itself is highly detailed, giving the sense of a historical narrative, not a myth or legend. Moreover, we do have geographical evidence, as two of the four rivers identified, are still in existence today. In addition verse 14 says, "The name of the third river is the Tigris, which flows east of Assyria. And the fourth river is the Euphrates." This location is present day Iraq.

Genesis 2:17 Why did Adam and Eve not die in the day that they ate of the fruit from the forbidden tree?

God at Genesis 2:17 warned Adam of "the tree of the knowledge of good and evil you shall not eat, for in the day that you eat of it you shall surely die." It would seem that when Adam passed that warning on to Eve, she took it very seriously, because she expanded on and emphasized the warning when speaking with the serpent. The woman said to the serpent, God said, 'You shall not eat of the fruit of the tree that is in the midst of the garden, neither shall you touch it, lest you die.'" (Gen 3:3) You will notice that she added, "neither shall you touch it." "But the serpent said to the woman, "'You will not surely die.'" (Gen 3:4) Was the serpent (i.e., Satan), telling the truth, as Adam would go on to live for another 930-years? (Gen. 5:5) No, Satan lied! In the day of their eating the fruit of the forbidden tree, they died spiritually.

If we look at the context of Adam when he received the command at Genesis 2:17, how would have Adam understood the expression, "in the day that you eat of it"? It is true, that Moses said to God, "For a thousand years in your sight are but as yesterday." (Ps 90:4) In addition, while addressing the extent of Jehovah God's patience, the apostle Peter said, "that with the Lord one day is as a thousand years, and a thousand years as one day." (2 Pet 3:8) However, Adam lived and died long before both of these statements, and would have had no knowledge of such. It was not as though Adam was thinking of his great love for Eve, and saying to himself, "If I eat of the forbidden tree, I will have one of Jehovah's days to live, a thousand years to spend with Eve. Yes, Adam would have no knowledge with which to reason in such a way. In other words, he would have understood the word "day" to be a literal twenty-four-hour day. God does not speak ambiguously, and he would have expressed himself in order to be understood, according to what Adam would know as to the terms that were used. Thus, God meant exactly what Adam would have understood it to mean, a twenty-four-hour day. God did not mean, "the tree of the knowledge of good and evil you shall not eat, for in the [thousand-year-long day] that you eat of it you shall surely die." Such a statement as that would have had no force in the mind of Adam; it would have lost all intended force of Jehovah's warning.

Adam would have received the Genesis 2:17 warning directly from God, even if a representative, his only-begotten Son, "the Word", delivered that warning.[88] This of course, begs the question, why then did Adam and Eve not die 'in a twenty-four-hour day?' Well, we must ask another question first. As to the Bible, what is death? The World Book Encyclopedia (1987, Vol. 5, p. 52b) pointed out: "A person whose heart and lungs stop working may be considered clinically dead, but somatic death may not yet have occurred. The individual cells of the body continue to live for several minutes. The person may be revived if the heart and lungs start working again and give the cells the oxygen they need. After about three minutes, the brain cells, which are most sensitive to a lack of oxygen, begin to die. The person is soon dead beyond any possibility of revival. Gradually, other cells of the body also die. The last ones to perish are the bone, hair, and skin cells, which may continue to grow for several hours." We know that the breathing and the active life force (Heb., ruach chaiyim) maintained in the cells by the blood is very important. From this, we can see that it is not the termination of breathing and the heartbeat alone, but also includes the loss of the life force from the body's cells that brings the sort of physical death as spoken of in the Scriptures. Ps 104:29; 146:4; Eccl 8:8.

However, the Scriptures speak of another kind of death, a spiritual death, which is illustrated by the death spoken of above as the condition of humankind at present, but is also relative to our discussion as well. In other words, Adam died spiritually in the very day of eating from the forbidden tree, and this would result in old age and eventually death. A man was begging off from following Jesus, saying, "Lord, let me first go and bury my father." Jesus responded, "Leave the dead to bury their own dead. . ." (Lu 9:59-60) The man's father was not dead yet, the son simply wanted to hold off following Jesus until his father died, and was simply looking for a way out. However, Jesus' response, "Leave the dead to bury their own dead," illustrated that spiritually dead and being dead are, in essence, one and the same unless there is some sort of intervention (more on that later) because physical death is the eventuality of those that are spiritually dead.

In addition, we have the apostle Paul referring to the woman living for sensual indulgence as "dead even while she lives." (Lu 9:60; 1Ti 5:6; Eph 2:1) Physical death was the sentence handed down to Adam and thus his descendants as well. However, this was brought about by way of the spiritual death, which affected Adam and Eve the very moment they ate from the forbidden tree. They were now alienated from God, and removed from the symbolic tree of life, being sent out from the Garden

---

[88] See question on Genesis 3:8 as to who had spoken directly with Adam.

of Eden. This alienation is self-evident as the two vainly tried to hide from God, their guilt ridden conscious affecting them. (Gen 3:8) The apostle Paul expressed it as being "dead in the trespasses and sins," becoming "children of wrath." (Eph. 2:1–3)

Romans 6:7 says, "one who has died has been set free from sin." However, Roman 6:2, 11 informs us that a Christian can 'consider themselves dead to sin and alive to God in Christ Jesus." Romans 7:2-6 helps us to appreciate that Christians "are released from the law, having died to that which held us captive, so that we serve in the new way of the Spirit and not in the old way of the written code. Jesus said that he came to earth "to give his life as a ransom for many." (Matthew 20:28).

Adam and Eve were guilty before God and then stood before him in an unrighteous condition. Within this unrighteous condition came a defilement and pollution of a new state of being, fallen flesh (Gr., sarx), which placed Adam and his descendants in an alienated position toward God and in enmity toward him (Rom 8:5-8) Hence, the mindset of imperfect man is mentally bent and geared toward evil. Because of Adam, we are born into sin (missing the mark of perfection) and are looking at the sentence of death. (Ps 51:5; Rom 5:12; Eph 2:3). This was the condition of Adam and Eve, the very moment they willfully chose to rebel against God, and commit that awful transgression. Instantly, they were thrown into the condition of a spiritual death. At that moment there was no hope for the human race, regardless of what any would do in life, the sentence would be death. However, Jehovah is a God of mercy, and while the human race merited death, we received undeserved kindness, which can be found in Genesis 3:15.

As has been stated and is obvious from Scripture, the physical death did not come immediately. God had created them perfectly after all; therefore, they would take far longer to grow older and die. Regardless, they were no longer going to be perfect but had taken on imperfection. God had removed his blessing of them as being good, and, eventually, their imperfection would show signs of growing old and impending death

The penalty was unavoidable. As to justice, from the viewpoint of God, Adam and Eve died that day. (Compare Luke 20:37-38.) However, to fulfill his own will and purpose regarding the inhabiting of the earth, Jehovah permitted them to produce a family before they were to grow old, get sick and die. All the same, while Adam and Eve may not have been aware of God's viewpoint of time, they both did die within one of his days, a thousand years. While there may be no absolute connection between Moses or Peter's statement about the way God views time, it seems a bit too much, to be a mere coincidence that Adam lived to be 930-years, and Methuselah lived to be 969-years, with not one preflood person living beyond a thousand years old.—Genesis 5:3-5; Psalm 90:4; 2 Peter 3:8.

Genesis 2:17; 3:3 What was the fruit of the tree of the knowledge of good and evil?

Genesis 2:17 Updated American Standard Version (UASV)

[17] but from the tree of the knowledge of good and evil you shall not eat,[89] for in the day that you eat from it you shall surely die."[90]

There were plenty of trees to eat from in the Garden of Eden, more than enough to satisfy the desires of the first human couple. However, there was the tree that they were forbidden to eat from, "the tree of the knowledge of good and evil." (Gen 2:17) This probation to not eat from that tree was so severe that Adam must have been very emphatic when he told Eve. How do we know that? We can infer it from Eve's Response to the Serpent when he was tempting her. Eve not only said 'you cannot eat from it,' but also added, "neither shall you touch it, lest you die."—Genesis 3:3.

Some have suggested that the prohibition against the fruit of this tree is symbolic, the fruit standing for sexual intercourse. Others have suggested that it stood for having a knowledge of or an awareness of right and wrong. Still, others have suggested that it stood for the knowledge that they would have attained upon reaching maturity, by way of experience, which could be used for good or bad. The sexual intercourse can immediately be dismissed, as they were commanded to, "be fruitful, multiply, and fill the earth." (Gen. 1:28) The awareness of good and bad must be dismissed as well, because both had that capacity already, as it was good not to eat from the tree, and bad to eat from the tree. Lastly, the idea of it being a sin to acquire knowledge upon reaching maturity, as this would contradict the whole of the rest of God's Word, not to mention the idea of expecting the human creation, He designed to grow and mature, to remain in an immature state, is illogical.

The Bible is silent as to the type of tree. However, the idea of the tree being symbolic is correct. The fruit had no intrinsic power to give knowledge, as was evidenced after their eating from it. It did symbolize God's right of sovereignty, His right to set a standard of what is good and bad. To eat from the tree would have been a rejection of that sovereignty, a rebellion that said that could set their own standard of

---

[89] Lit *eat from it*

[90] Lit *dying you* [singular] *shall die.* Heb. *moth tamuth*; the first reference to death in the Scriptures

good and bad, independence from their creator. This was a simple test, for a couple that was to serve as the father and mother of a perfect human race. A footnote on Genesis 2:17, in The Jerusalem Bible (1966):

> This knowledge is a privilege, which God reserves to himself and which man, by sinning, is to lay hands on, 3:5, 22. Hence it does not mean omniscience, which fallen man does not possess; nor is it moral discrimination, for unfallen man already had it and God could not refuse it to a rational being. It is the power of deciding for himself what is good and what is evil and of acting accordingly, a claim to complete moral independence by which man refuses to recognize his status as a created being. The first sin was an attack on God's sovereignty, a sin of pride.

Genesis 2:17; 3:3 what did the tree of the knowledge of good and evil symbolize?

There is more involved in Adam and Eve's choice to eat from the "tree of knowledge of good and evil," as being a sin. It is not like the act of a child stealing a piece of fruit off a fruit stand. This was a rebellion against their Creator, Jehovah God. What escapes most humans is that they were created, and there is a Creator. The desire for absolute independence runs contrary to this, and is hard for him to accept. Jehovah God had every right in setting a tree that would establish the point of his sovereignty (right to rule). Adam and Eve were created, and did not have absolute independence and freedom, it was relative to their environment, as created persons, which is a lesson that they needed to understand through more than mere words.

If perfect humankind were to do as Jehovah had requested, multiply and fill the earth, it would have resulted in a paradise wide planet, filled with perfect human creation. If there was to be universal peace, man needed to appreciate that he had been created and that he was designed to walk with God, not walk on his own. This would have been established if the first two, especially Adam, were to refrain from eating from the "tree of knowledge of good and evil." Adam was to become the father to all of perfect humankind, and he needed to be loyal to his Creator, proving his obedience, by this one small act of refraining from eating from the forbidden tree.

Luke 16:10 Updated American Standard Version (UASV)

[10] "The one who is faithful in the least thing is also faithful in much, and the one who is unrighteous in what is least is also unrighteous in much.

Both Adam and Eve were able to choose not to eat from the tree. In fact, they were designed in such a way that to do bad would be going against their natural inclinations. Of course, they knew the difference between good and bad. It was bad to eat from the forbidden tree, and it was good not to eat from it. Therefore, it was not a matter of their being ignorant of good and bad, as though God were trying to keep such knowledge from them. Thus, the tree or its fruit had no intrinsic substance, which would wake them up to the idea of what is good and what is bad. The good and bad was the ability to choose what is good and bad. The right and wrong of life belonged under the umbrella of the sovereignty of their Creator, not man. If man lived under the standard of right and wrong of his Creator, all would remain perfect.

A footnote on Genesis 2:17, in The Jerusalem Bible represents well what the tree stood for (1966):

> This knowledge is a privilege which God reserves to himself and which man, by sinning, is to lay hands on, 3:5, 22. Hence it does not mean omniscience, which fallen man does not possess; nor is it moral discrimination, for unfallen man already had it and God could not refuse it to a rational being. It is the power of deciding for himself what is good and what is evil and of acting accordingly, a claim to complete moral independence by which man refuses to recognize his status as a created being. The first sin was an attack on God's sovereignty, a sin of pride.

Genesis 3:5 Is man made in the image of God or does he become like God?

We are told at Genesis 1:27 that "God created man in his own image." However, Genesis 3:22 tells us "the man has become like one of us." It seems that Genesis 1:27 is saying that humans *were made* like God, while Genesis 3:22 is saying that humans *became* like God.

The answer lies in the fact that we are dealing with two different subject matters, and to look at the two together isolated from their individual sections is to take them out of context. Genesis 1 is dealing with the creation of humanity, and that we were *made in* the image of God, something we were given. Genesis 3 is dealing with man's fall into sin, and his willful rebellion against God, rejecting God's sovereignty, God's standard of right and wrong. In this, Adam and Eve had acquired the right to *become* like God in determining for themselves what is right and what is wrong. Genesis 1 is prior to the fall, refers to the nature of Adam and Eve, while Genesis 3 is after the fall, and refers to their state of being.

Genesis 3:6 She also gave some to her husband who was with her?

Almost all translations translate Genesis 3:6 as follows.

Genesis 3:6	Genesis 3:6	Genesis 3:6	Genesis 3:6
English Standard Version (ESV)	Lexham English Bible (LEB)	American Standard Version (ASV)	New American Standard Bible (NASB)
⁶ So when the woman saw that the tree was good for food, and that it was a delight to the eyes, and that the tree was to be desired to make one wise, **she took of its fruit and ate, and she also gave some to her husband who was with her**, and he ate.	⁶ When the woman saw that the tree was good for food and that it was a delight to the eyes, and the tree was desirable to make one wise, then **she took from its fruit and she ate. And she gave it also to her husband with her**, and he ate.	⁶ And when the woman saw that the tree was good for food, and that it was a delight to the eyes, and that the tree was to be desired to make one wise, **she took of the fruit thereof, and did eat; and she gave also unto her husband with her**, and he did eat.	⁶ When the woman saw that the tree was good for food, and that it was a delight to the eyes, and that the tree was desirable to make one wise, **she took from its fruit and ate; and she gave also to her husband with her**, and he ate.

As you can see from these English translations, the plain sense of the text is, Adam was with her. This creates a real Bible difficulty. Before I delve into why, I will say that if almost all of the translations are in agreement, generally, this should be respected, and accepted. It is very unlikely that the very best Hebrew and Greek scholars of the past 100 years are all mistaken. Now, the difficulty arises because, if Eve and Adam were standing there before the tree of knowledge, as the serpent spoke to Eve, it means that Adam, the head, was very much involved in this process. Think as you read this commentary below, trying to rationalize how the situation played out, with the both being there.

Eve "was indeed deceived," but Adam "was not deceived." Of course, this cannot be taken absolutely. It must mean something on this order: Adam was not deceived in the manner in which Eve was deceived. See Gen. 3:4–6. She listened directly to Satan; he did not. She sinned before he did. She was the leader. He was the follower. She led when she should have followed; that is, she led in the way of sin, when she should have followed in the path of righteousness.[91]

The reason for the difficulty is this; they are taking it as though Adam and Eve are standing before the tree of knowledge of good and evil, and the serpent, Satan, starts to speak to Eve. They carry on a conversation, with Adam only passively listening. Satan deceives Eve, but Adam is not deceived, yet he does not argue with the serpent, snatch the fruit from Eve, but rather just stands there letting Eve eat the fruit, knowing she will die. Really? I just cannot see how that can rationally be the case. I would argue that Eve was alone before Adam joined her.

Was Adam standing beside Eve when she had the conversation with the serpent, was deceived and chose to rebel against God? The Bible shows no indication that this is the case. The translations above make it appear as though that is the case, "she took of its fruit and ate, and she also **gave** some to **her husband who was with her**, and he ate."

The Hebrew verb translated "gave" is in the imperfect waw consecutive, as a result, it points to a temporal or logical sequence (usually called an "imperfect sequential"). Hence, a Bible translator or committee can translate the several occurrences of the waw, which tie together the chain of events in verse 6, with "and" as well as other transitional words, such as "subsequently," "then," "after that," afterward," and "so."

Genesis 3:6 English Standard Version (ESV)	Genesis 3:6 Updated American Standard Version (UASV)
6 So when the woman saw that the tree was good for food, **and** that it was a delight to the eyes, **and** that the tree was to be desired to make one wise, she took of its fruit **and** ate, **and** she also gave some to her husband who was with her, **and** he ate.	6 So when the woman saw that the tree was good for food, **and** that it was a delight to the eyes, **and** that the tree was to be desirable to make one wise, **and** she took of its fruit **and** ate, *then* she also gave some to her husband when with her, **and** he ate.

One has to ask themselves, would Adam have passively stood beside his wife Eve, listening to the conversation, between her and the serpent, as Satan spewed forth lies and malicious talk through this serpent,

---

[91] William Hendriksen and Simon J. Kistemaker, vol. 4, Exposition of the Pastoral Epistles, New Testament Commentary, 110 (Grand Rapids: Baker Book House, 1953-2001).

especially, especially, when Paul tells us explicitly that he was not deceived by the serpent? Supposedly, Adam just stood there and remained silent? Adam just chose not to interrupt the peddling of lies. Listen to the Bible scholar below; he actually believes this is reasonable.

Genesis 3:6 makes it clear that he was "with her" during the interchange with the serpent, but he remained silent. He should have interrupted. He should have chased the serpent off. And when it comes down to it, when he is offered the fruit himself, he eats it--no questions asked, no protests given. Adam and Eve together rebelled against their Creator, so they both suffer the horrible consequences.[92]

The conversation with the serpent reveals that Adam had previously carried out his responsibilities as the head, informing her of the command not to eat from the tree. (Gen. 3:3) It seems far more likely that Satan, through the serpent ignored this headship, going after the newer person in the Garden of Eden, Eve, when she was alone. Eve later replied, "The serpent deceived me, and I ate."

Let us assume that I am just mistaken, and it should be translated, "and she also gave some to her husband who was with her." Adam need not be clear on the other side of the Garden; he could have just been out of hearing range, and still have been with her. Suppose he was across the field, visually in sight, but still, out of hearing range, it could still be said he was with her. Husbands have you ever been in a huge store with your wife, like Wal-Mart, and at the same time you are on one side of the store (lawn-garden or automotive), and she is on the other side of the store. If you were to say you were **with your wife** at Wal-Mart, would that mean that you were necessarily standing right beside her? Say an issue came up in the store, so you walked over. The Garden of Eden was no small place, like a city park, but more like the size of a state park, possibly 18,000 acres of land and 3,000 acres of water. If Adam were in eyesight, but out of hearing range, it could still be said that he was with her. She could have called him over after her transgression, at which point, he demonstrated that his love for her was greater than that of his Creator, and so he ate.

Genesis 3:8 Did God speak directly to Adam?

Generally, in the Bible, when God had dealings with the human family, it was by means of an angel. (Gen. 16:7-11; 18:1-3, 22-26; 19:1; Judges 2:1-4; 6:11-16, 22; 13:15-22) The primary person in Scripture, who

---

[92] Longman III, Tremper (2005-05-12). How to Read Genesis (How to Read Series How to Read) (p. 111). Intervarsity Press - A. Kindle Edition.

spoke and had dealings with humans, as a representative of the Father, Jehovah God, was his only only-begotten Son, appropriately called "the Word." (John 1:1) Therefore, while the Bible does not explicitly say, it was very likely that God spoke with Adam and Eve by means of "the Word."—Genesis 1:26-28; 2:16; 3:8-13.

Genesis 3:17 How is it that the ground would be cursed for Adam, and for how long?

The curse that Jehovah God had placed on the ground meant that cultivation was going to be a far greater task than it would have been had Adam not sinned. Lamech, Noah's father, in connection with the thorns and thistles, expresses this level of the curse, "the painful toil of our hands." (Gen 5:29) The curse was lifted after the flood, at which time God blessed his faithful servants Noah and his sons. (Gen 9:1) Jehovah gave Noah and his family a good start, reissued the command to multiply and fill the earth (Gen 13:10), and placed under man's power the animal and plant realms, with no handicapping curse on the earth: "I will never again curse the soil because of man." However, take note that the work of cultivating the entire earth given to Adam was not contained within that given to Noah. This suggests that there would not be an earth wide paradise accomplished by imperfect man, just because the curse was lifted. (Gen. 1:28; 6:17; 8:21; 9:1-17)

Genesis 3:19-21 Will Adam and Eve be among those receiving a resurrection?

The conclusion below will be drawn from silence, and cannot be taken dogmatically. It is inferential only, and the final answer will have to be one that we seldom like, 'we will have to wait and see.' However, just because something is drawn from silence does not necessarily mean it is not true. We have absolutely no record that Jesus ever bathed, but we can be most certain that he did. It is certainly true that both Adam and Eve attempted to sidestep their responsibility of eating from the forbidden tree. Adam blamed Eve, while Eve blamed the serpent. However, both did not deny that they had actually violated the command.

Jehovah has said that if you eat from this tree, "you shall surely die." (Gen. 2:17) That was the explicit punishment, death. Their sentence was to "suffer the punishment of eternal destruction." (2 Thess. 1:9) The reason that this could be said is, justice required death, with no provision for anything else at the time that they were given the command. It does not seem fair that a Just God, in his command, would not include additional punishments of Eve's difficulty in childbirth and Adam's

110

struggle to get the earth to respond to his care if they were a part of the original provision. It seems that the extra penalty for Eve ("I will greatly multiply thy pain and thy conception; in pain thou shalt bring forth children"), and for Adam ("cursed is the ground for thy sake; in toil shalt thou eat of it all the days of thy life"); where a means to move the two to repentance. Do the extra penalties, which were not part of the original punishment, for eating the forbidden fruit, mean that Jehovah was going to forgive them after they paid the price that he had laid down? The Apostle Paul said at Romans 6:7, "he that hath died is justified from sin."

Just as humankind are under the condemnation of death, because we are sinners; as Romans 5:12 informs us, "Therefore, as through one man sin entered into the world, and death through sin; and so death passed unto all men, for that all sinned." Thus, it would seem that Adam and Eve could be afforded this as well, being chastised beyond the original punishment, because of Jehovah's love for them. In fact, he did not give them this additional punishment, until after he informed them of the hope held out to all of the humankind, the hope of a coming seed. (Gen. 3:15) Discipline by God is because of his love, and it always starts as a means of correction, this extra chastisement was a constructive reminder of their unfaithfulness to him and their need to return and repent. We have no knowledge that they ever returned to God, or that they did not for that matter.

It is very much possible that when Jehovah God clothed and protected the first human couple, he informed them, of the coming seed, Jesus Christ (Gen. 3:15), who would crush the head of the serpent (Satan), and "give his life as a ransom for many." (Matt 20:28) It would seem that God must have informed Adam of the atoning value of the blood sacrifice as well. Otherwise, we are in a difficulty, as to how Abel, Adam's second son, acquired this knowledge.—Genesis 4:4.

Both Cain and Abel brought their offering to the altar individually. This means that Adam had no priestly function. The vegetable offering of Cain would have been displeasing to Adam because it was displeasing to Jehovah. Cain's offering lacked the atoning blood. (Gen. 4:5) On the other hand, Jehovah was well pleased with Abel's blood atoning sacrifice of "the firstborn of his flock and of their fat portions."—Genesis 4:4.

Some may argue that Adam and Eve were perfect, and this would indicate that they had no excuse for their rebellious act, which means that they willfully and knowingly sinned against God under perfection, like the blasphemy against the "Spirit" that Jesus spoke of, forfeiting any hope of a resurrection. (Matt. 12:32; Heb. 6:4-6) They would point out maybe that we in our imperfection are prone, inclined, leaned toward sin, while Adam and Eve were prone, inclined and leaned toward good. However, the Christian can find himself, because of the ransom sacrifice of Christ, in an approved standing before God. There are allowances made for his imperfection, which means, he has a righteous standing before God. (Ps 103:8-14) Thus, if we were to put them on a scale, Adam would not have needed any allowance for his standing before Jehovah, while God graciously gives imperfect man that exercises faith in Christ some counter weights undeservedly so, to offset and give him his standing before Jehovah.

In the end, we must say that there is no conclusive answer to this question. One should offer both arguments, and allow the listener to decide for themselves where they stand. The other option is to be neutral and not commit to either position, choosing to wait and see, as God is a God of mercy, love, and justice, and will do the right thing. In conclusion, it is difficult for this writer to believe that Adam and Eve spent 930 years and did not repair their relationship with their Father.

Genesis 3:24 Was Jehovah God the inventor of swords?

After Adam and Eve sinned and were ejected from the garden, Jehovah banned them from returning. How? Genesis 3:24 says: "So he drove the man out, and placed cherubim east of the garden of Eden, and a flaming, turning sword to guard the way to the tree of life." Notice, "a flaming, turning sword." Was Jehovah God the inventor of swords?

The idea that the God that we know as being the epitome of love, while at the same time, being the inventor of what we know as the sword, is not a necessary logical conclusion. All Adam and Eve saw turning in front of the angel that was guarding the entrance to the Garden of Eden was a blazing object. What it was specifically, we do not know. At the time Moses penned Genesis, the sword was a common weapon of warfare, and as a means of defending oneself. (Gen. 31:26; 34:26; 48:22; Ex. 5:21; 17:13) Therefore, Moses' words "a flaming, turning sword" allowed his readers to visualize to a certain point what existed at the entrance of the Garden of Eden. We have a common saying today that 'a picture is worth a thousand words,' which is certainly true, and would have been no less true for Bible writers. By Moses giving a visual aid, he would have helped his readers better appreciate and have a better understanding.

Genesis 3:24 Why Has God Permitted Wickedness and Suffering?

"God has morally sufficient reasons for permitting the evil and suffering in the world."—William Lane Craig

That *morally sufficient reason* lies below.

"The significant issue that drove me to Agnosticism [Bible Scholar Dr. Bart D. Ehrman is now an Agnostic] has to do not with the Bible, but with the pain and suffering in the world." He writes, "I eventually found it impossible to explain the evil so rampant among us—whether in terms of genocides (which continue), unspeakable human cruelty, war, disease, hurricanes, tsunamis, mudslides, the starvation of millions of innocent children, you name it—if there was a good and loving God who was actively involved in this world." *Misquoting Jesus* (p. 248)

As you will see below, Ehrman's issue is simply a matter of starting with the wrong assumption. **Point One**: He starts with 'if God is a God of love, who has the power to fix anything, how can there have been such horrific pain and suffering in imperfection over the last 6,000 years?' **Point Two**: He also likely begins with the premise that 'God is responsible for everything that happens.' If one starts with the wrong assumption, there is no doubt that he will reach the wrong conclusion(s). **Point One** is dealt with below, but let it be said that Ehrman is looking through the binoculars from the opposite end, the big side through the small. When we do that, we get a narrow, focused outlook. God looks through the binoculars the correct way, and can see the big picture. Ehrman can only see but a fraction and a moment of time, 70 – 80 years, while God has seen everything that has happened over these past 6,000 plus years in the greatest of detail, and can see what the outcome would be if he had handled things in a variety of ways.

Point Two is certainly one reason suffering and evil is often misunderstood. God is responsible for everything, but not always directly. If he started the human race, and we end up with what we now have, in essence, he is responsible. Just as parents, who have a child are similarly responsible for the child committing murder 21 years into his life, because they procreated and gave birth to the child. The mother and father are indirectly responsible. King David commits adultery with Bathsheba and has her husband Uriah killed to cover things up, and impregnates Bathsheba, but the adulterine child, who remains nameless, died. Is God responsible for the death of that child? We can answer yes and no to that question. He is responsible in two ways: **(1)** He created humankind, so there would have been no affair, murder, adulterine child if he had not. **(2)** He did not step in and save the child when he had the power to

113

do so. However, he is not directly responsible, because he did not make King David and Bathsheba commit the acts that led to the child being born, nor did he bring an illness on the adulterine child, he just did not move in to protect the child, in a time that had a high rate of infant deaths.

The reason people think that God does not care about us is the words of some religious leaders, which have made them, feel this way. When tragedy strikes, what do some pastors and Bible scholars often say? When 9/11 took place, with thousands dying in the twin towers of New York, many ministers said: "It was God's will. God must have had some good reason for doing this." When religious leaders make such comments or similar ones, they are actually blaming God for the bad things that happened. Yet, the disciple James wrote, "Let no one say when he is tempted, 'I am being tempted by God,' for God cannot be tempted with evil, and he himself tempts no one." (James 1:13) God never directly causes what is bad. Indeed, "far be it from God that he should do wickedness, and from the Almighty that he should do wrong." Job 34:10.

The history of humans has been inundated with pain and suffering on an unprecedented scale, much of which they have brought on themselves. The problem/question that has plagued many persons is, 'why if there is a loving God, would he allow it to start with, and worse still, why allow it to go on for over 6,000 years?' Some apologist scholars have struggled to answer this question, because they are over analyzing, as opposed to just looking for the answer in God's Word. Therefore, if we are to answer this question, we must go back to Adam and Eve at the time of the first sin. Many have read this account, but I will list the texts as a refresher.

Genesis 2:17 Updated American Standard Version (UASV)

[17] but from the tree of the knowledge of good and evil you shall not eat,[93] for in the day that you eat from it you shall surely die."[94]

Genesis 3:1-5 Updated American Standard Version (UASV)

[1] Now the serpent was more crafty than any beast of the field which Jehovah God had made. And he said to the woman, "Did God actually say, 'You[95] shall not eat of any tree in the garden'?" [2] And the woman said to the serpent, "From the fruit of the trees of the garden we may eat, [3] but from the tree that is in the midst of the garden, God said, 'You shall

---

[93] Lit *eat from it*

[94] Lit *dying you* [singular] *shall die.* Heb *moth tamuth*; the first reference to death in the Scriptures

[95] In Hebrew *you* is plural in verses 1–5

not eat from it, nor shall you touch it, lest you die.'" **4** And the serpent said to the woman, "You shall not surely die. **5** For God knows that when you eat of it your eyes will be opened, and you will be like God, knowing good and evil." knowing good and evil.

Later Bible texts establish Satan the Devil as the one using a serpent as his mouthpiece like a ventriloquist would a dummy. Anyway, take note that Satan contradicts the clear statement that God made to Adam at Genesis 2:17, "you will not surely die." Backing up a little, we see Satan asking an inferential question, "Did God actually say, 'You shall not eat of any tree in the garden'?" First, he is overstating what he knows to be true, not "any tree," just one tree. Second, Satan is inferring, 'I can't believe that God would say . . . how dare he say such.' Notice too that Eve has been told so thoroughly about the tree that she even goes beyond what Adam told her, not just that you 'do not eat from it,' no, 'you do not even touch it!' Then, Satan out and out lied and slandered God as a liar, saying that 'they would not die.' To make matters much worse, he infers that God is withholding good from them, and by rebelling they would be better off, being like God, 'knowing good and bad.' This latter point is not knowledge of; it is the self-sovereignty of choosing good and bad for oneself and act of rebellion for created creatures. What was symbolized by the tree is well expressed in a footnote on Genesis 2:17, in The Jerusalem Bible (1966):

> This knowledge is a privilege which God reserves to himself and which man, by sinning, is to lay hands on, 3:5, 22. Hence it does not mean omniscience, which fallen man does not possess; nor is it moral discrimination, for unfallen man already had it and God could not refuse it to a rational being. It is the power of deciding for himself what is good and what is evil and of acting accordingly, a claim to complete moral independence by which man refuses to recognize his status as a created being. The first sin was an attack on God's sovereignty, a sin of pride.

The Issues at Hand

(1) Satan called God a liar and said he was not to be trusted, as to the life or death issue.

(2) Satan's challenge, therefore, took into question the right and legitimacy of God's rightful place as the Universal Sovereign.

(3) Satan also suggested that people would remain obedient to God only as long as their submitting to God was to their benefit.

(4) Satan all but said that humankind was able to walk on his own, there being no need for dependence on God.

(5) Satan argued that man could be like God, choosing for himself what is right and wrong.

(6) Satan claimed that God's way of ruling was not in the best interests of humans, and they could do better without God.

Job 1:6-11 Updated American Standard Version (UASV)

⁶ Now there was a day when the sons of God came to present themselves before Jehovah, and Satan also came among them. ⁷ Jehovah said to Satan, "From where do you come?" Then Satan answered Jehovah and said, "From roaming about on the earth and walking around on it." ⁸ Jehovah said to Satan, "Have you considered my servant Job? For there is no one like him on the earth, a blameless and upright man, fearing God and turning away from evil." ⁹ Then Satan answered Jehovah, "Does Job fear God for nothing? ¹⁰ Have you not made a hedge about him and his house and all that he has, on every side? You have blessed the work of his hands, and his possessions have increased in the land. ¹¹ But put forth your hand now and touch all that he has; he will surely curse you to your face."

Job 2:4-5 Updated American Standard Version (UASV)

⁴ Satan answered Jehovah and said, "Skin for skin! Yes, all that a man has he will give for his life. ⁵ However, put forth your hand now, and touch his bone and his flesh; he will curse you to your face."

This general reference to "a man," as opposed to explicitly naming Job, is suggesting that all men [and women] will only obey God when things are good, but when the slightest difficulty arises, he will not obey. If you were put to the test, would you prove your love for your heavenly Father and show that you preferred His rule to that of any other?

God Settles the Issues

There is one thing that Satan did not challenge, namely, the power of God. Satan did not suggest that God was unable to destroy him as an opposer. However, he did challenge God's way of ruling, not His right to rule. Therefore, a moral issue must be settled.

An illustration of how God chose to deal with the issue can be demonstrated in human terms. A neighbor down the street slandered a man, who had a son and daughter. The slanderer said that he was not a good father, i.e., he withheld good from his children and was so overbearing, to the point of being abusive. The slanderer stated that the children would be better off without their father. He further argued that the children had no real love for their father and only obeyed him because of the food and shelter. How should the father deal with these false, i.e., slanderous accusations? If he were to go down the road and pummel the slanderer, it would only validate the lies, making the neighbors believe the accuser is telling the truth.

The answer lies within his family as they can serve as his witnesses. (Pro 27:11; Isa 43:10) If the children stay obedient and grow to be successful adults, turning out to be loving, caring, honest people with spotless character, it proves the accusations false. If the children accept the lies and rebel and grow up to be despicable people, it just further validates that they would have been better off by staying with the father. This is how God chose to deal with the issues. The issues that were raised must be settled beyond all reasonable doubt.

If God had destroyed the rebellious three: Satan, Adam, and Eve; he would not have resolved the issues of

(1) Whether man could walk on his own,

(2) if he would be better off without his Creator,

(3) if God's rulership were not best, and

(4) if God were hiding good from man.

(5) In addition, there was an audience of untold billions of angelic spirit creatures looking on.

If God destroyed without settling things, these spirit persons would be following God out of dreadful fear, not love, fear of displeasing God. Moreover, say He did kill them, and start over, and ten thousand years down the road (with billions of humans now on earth), the issues were raised again, He would have to destroy billions of people again, and again, and again all throughout time, until these issues were laid to rest.

What God has done is, allow time to pass, and the issues to be resolved. Man thought he was better off without God, and could walk on his own. In addition, man has attempted every kind of rulership imaginable, and one must ask, 'have they proven themselves better than rulership under the sovereignty of their Creator?' (Proverbs 1:30-33; Isaiah 59:4, 8) Sadly, the issues must be taken up to the brink of destroying man. (Rev 11:18) Otherwise, the argument would be that if given enough time, they could have turned things around. If man goes up to the point of destroying himself and Armageddon comes at the last minute, it will have set a case law, solved the issue, and the Bible can serve as the example forever. If the issues of God's sovereignty or the loyalty of His created creatures, angelic or human, is ever questioned again, we would have the Holy Bible that will serve as a law established based on previous verdicts of not guilty, please see below.

What Have the Results Been?

(1) God does not cause evil and suffering. Romans 9:14.

(2) The fact that God has allowed evil, pain and suffering has shown that independence from God has not brought about a better world. Jeremiah 8:5, 6, 9.

(3) God's permission of evil, pain, and suffering has also proved that Satan has not been able to turn all humans away from God. Exodus 9:16; 1 Samuel 12:22; Hebrews 12:1.

(4) The fact that God has permitted evil, pain, and suffering to continue has provided proof that only God, the Creator, has the capability and the right to rule over humankind for their eternal blessing and happiness. Ecclesiastes 8:9.

(5) Satan has been the god of this world since the sin in Eden (over 6,000 years), and how has that worked out for man, and what has been the result of man's course of independence from God and his rule? Matthew 4:8-9; John 16:11; 2 Corinthians 4:3-4; 1 John 5:19; Psalm 127:1.

Satan's impact on the earth's activities has carried with it conflict, evil and death, and his rulership has been by means of deception, power and his own self-interest. He has demonstrated himself an unfit ruler of everything. Therefore, God is now completely vindicated in putting an end to this corrupted rebel along with all who have shared in his evil deeds.—Romans 16:20.

God has tolerated evil, sickness, pain, suffering and death until our day in order to resolve all the issues raised by Satan. We are self-centered in thinking that this has only pained us. Imagine that you are holding a rope on a sinking ship that 20 other men, women, and children are clinging to, when your child loses her grip and falls into the ocean. You can hold the rope, saving 20 people, or you can let go and attempt to rescue your daughter. God has been watching the suffering of billions from the day of Adam and Eve's sin. Moreover, it has been His great love for us, which causes Him to cling to the rope of issues, saving us from a future of repeated issues. Nevertheless, he will not allow this evil to remain forever. He has set a fixed time when He will end this wicked system of Satan's rule.

Daniel 11:27 Updated American Standard Version (UASV)

²⁷ As for both kings, their heart will be inclined to do what is evil, and they will speak lies to each other at the same table; but it will not succeed, for the end is still to come <u>at the appointed time</u>.

Unlike what many people of the world may think (the world that lies in the hands of Satan), being obedient to God is not difficult. We simply must set our pride aside and accept that the wisdom of God is so far greater than our own, and accept that He has worked for the good of obedient humankind, as He loves each one of us.

Matthew 7:21 Updated American Standard Version (UASV)

²¹ "Not everyone who says to me, 'Lord, Lord,' will enter the kingdom of heaven, but <u>the one who does the will of my Father</u> who is in heaven.

1 John 2:15-17 Updated American Standard Version (UASV)

¹⁵ Do not love the world or the things in the world. If anyone loves the world, the love of the Father is not in him. ¹⁶ For all that is in the world, the lust of the flesh and the lust of the eyes and the boastful pride of life, is not from the Father, but is from the world. ¹⁷ The world is passing away, and its lusts; but the one who does the will of God remains forever.

As Christians, there is a love we must not have. We must 'not love the world or anything in it.' Instead, we need to keep from becoming infected by the corruption of unrighteous human society that is alienated from God and must not breathe in its mental disposition or be moved by its sinful dominant attitude. (Ephesians 2:1, 2; James 1:27) If we were to have the views of those in the world that are in opposition to God, "the love of the Father" would not be in us. (James 4:4)

Was Satan Punished?

Yes.

COMMON QUESTION: Why did God not destroy the Satan, Adam, and Eve right away?

I would follow up with what would have happened if God had chosen that path. Hundreds of billions of angels with free will were watching, and they knew of the issues raised. What would their love of God have been like if God did not address the issues raised? Was Satan right? Was God lying? Would free will creatures, spirit and humans, be better off? Will God just destroy us over anything? First, the spirit creatures would have followed God out of dreadful fear, rather than fear of displeasing the one they loved so much up to that point, like a child to a parent. Second, what happens if the issue is raised a hundred thousand years after a restart and there are 30 billion perfect humans on the planet? Would God simply destroy everyone again and start over. Do we think it wise that he does this reboot every time or was it not better that he settled the issue once and for all?

POINT: Satan raised Issues of sovereignty in the Garden of Eden.

POINT: Can humans walk on their own; do they really need their Creator? Are they better off without God?

POINT: Was God lying and withholding?

When a teenager becomes a rebel in our house, we have a choice: (1) severe punishment or (2) teach them an object lesson.

HUMANS AND ANGELS are a created product no different than a car coming off of an assembly line, i.e., (1) they owe their existence to their creator and (2) they were created to function based on the design of the creator. If we take a ford escort and treat it like a heavy duty four-wheel drive truck and go off roading (not what the car was designed to do), what will happen?

God wisely chose to teach both angels and humans an object lesson. Neither was designed to walk on their own. Both angel and human were given relative freedom (under the sovereignty of God), not absolute freedom. They were not designed to choose what is right and what is wrong on their own. They were given God's moral standards by way of an internal conscience. How can we tell a rebel that we do not have absolute freedom, we are better off under the umbrella of our creator's sovereignty, we cannot walk on our own? They will just reject it as a rebel teenager would.

OBJECT LESSON: We let them learn from their choice, no matter how painful it is, and hard love means that we do not step in until the lesson is fully learned. Humankind was essentially told, "Oh, you think you can walk on your own, well go ahead, we will see how that works out." After six-thousand-years, God could actually use a common saying among young people today: "How is that absolute freedom working out for you?"

When will the lesson fully be learned? Humankind will walk right up to the very edge of the cliff of killing themselves, actually falling over, when God will step in and stop the object lesson. To stop it anytime before, will cause doubts. If it had been stopped a century ago, the argument would have been; God simply stepped in before we got to the scientific age because he knew we were going to find true peace and

120

security, along with something to give us eternal life. However, if humanity has actually fallen over the edge of the cliff and the destruction of us is definite, and God steps in, no argument can be raised, the object lesson is learned.

Why Was Satan Not Kicked Out of Heaven Right Away?

Satan stayed in his realm, just as humans stayed in theirs. God changed nothing right away because he would have been accused of adjusting the pieces on the chessboard to get the desired outcome, i.e., cheating. When will Satan be kicked out of heaven? Satan and the Demons lost access to the person of God long age, and they lost some of their powers, such as being able to materialize in human form, like they did when they took human women for themselves at the flood, producing the Nephilim.

Satan would be thrown to the earth very shortly before the end of his age of rulership, when "he knows that his time is short." (Rev 12:9-12) This, then, means that Satan will be thrown from heaven likely sometime before the Great Tribulation and Christ's return. Revelation 12:12 says, "'Therefore, rejoice, O heavens and you who dwell in them! But woe to you, O earth and sea, for the devil has come down to you in great wrath because he knows that his time is short!'"

Notice that it is at a time, when "Satan knows that his time is short!" What comes next for Satan? He will be abyssed, thrown into a super-maximum-security prison for a thousand years (for lack of a better way to explain it) while Jesus fixes all that Satan done. After the thousand years, he will be let loose for a little while, and he will tempt perfect humans, and sadly some will fall away. In the end, Satan and those humans will be destroyed, and Jesus will hand the kingdom back over to the father.

Genesis 4:3 Why was Cain's offering unacceptable to God?

There are two aspects of Cain's offering, which found him unapproved before God: **(1)** his attitude and **(2)** the type of offering.

Eventually, Cain and Abel came before God with their offerings. "Cain brought to Jehovah an offering of the fruit of the ground." (Gen. 4:3) "Also brought of the firstlings of his flock and of their fat portions." (Gen. 4:4) It is likely that both Cain and Abel were close to 100 years old at the time, as Adam was 130 years old when he fathered his third son, Seth.—Genesis 4:25; 5:3.

We can establish that the two sons became aware of their sinful state, and sought our God's favor. How they garnered this knowledge is

121

guesswork, but it is likely by way of the father, Adam. Adam likely informed them about the coming seed and the hope that lie before humankind.[96] Therefore, it seems that they had given some thought to their condition and stand before God, and realized that they needed to try to atone for their sinful condition. The Bible does not inform us just how much time they had given to this need before they started to offer a sacrifice. Rather, God chose to convey the more important aspect, each one's heart attitude, which gives us an inside look at their thinking.

Some scholars have suggested that Eve felt that Cain was the "seed" of the Genesis 3:15 prophecy that would destroy the serpent, "she conceived and bore Cain, and said, 'I have gotten a man with the help of Jehovah.'" (Gen. 4:1) It might be that Cain shared in this belief and had begun to think too much of himself, and thus the haughty spirit. If this is the case, he was very mistaken. His brother Abel had a whole other spirit, as he offered his sacrifice in faith, "By faith Abel offered to God a more acceptable sacrifice than Cain, through which he was commended as righteous, God commending him by accepting his gifts."—Hebrews 11:4.

It seems that Abel was capable of discerning the need for blood to be involved in the atoning sacrifice, while Cain was not, or simply did not care. Therefore, it was the heart attitude of Cain as well. Consequently, "but on Cain and his offering he did not look with favor. So Cain was very angry, and his face was downcast." (Gen 4:5, NIV) It may well be that Cain had little regard for the atoning sacrifice, giving it little thought, going through the motions of the act only. However, as later biblical history would show, Jehovah God is not one to be satisfied with formal worship. Cain had developed a bad heart attitude, and Jehovah well knew that his motives were not sincere. The way Cain reacted to the evaluation of his sacrifice only evidenced what Jehovah already knew. Instead of seeking to improve the situation, "Cain was very angry, and his face fell."[97] (Gen. 4:5) As you read the rest of the account, it will become clearer as to the type of temperament Cain had before Jehovah God.

Genesis 4:6-16 Updated American Standard Version (USV)

6 Then Jehovah said to Cain, "Why are you angry, and why has your face fallen? **7** If you do well, will there not be a lifting up?[98] And if you do

---

[96] Adam's family must have received God's revelation about the necessity of sacrifice to create and maintain fellowship with God. The background to this was probably the sacrifice that God performed to provide the clothing to cover Adam and Eve's shame (see Gen. 3:21). Anders, Max; Gangel, Kenneth; Bramer, Stephen J. (2003-04-01). Holman Old Testament Commentary - Genesis: 1 (p. 56). Holman Reference. Kindle Edition.

[97] Or, his countenance fell

[98] This is a shortening of the Hebrew idiom "to lift up the face," which means "to accept" favorably

not do well, sin is crouching at the door. Its desire is for you, but you must rule over it."

⁸ Cain said to Abel his brother. And it came about when they were in the field, that Cain rose up against Abel his brother and killed him.

⁹ Then Jehovah⁹⁹ said to Cain, "Where is Abel your brother?" And he said, "I do not know. Am I my brother's keeper?" ¹⁰ He said, "What have you done? The voice of your brother's blood is crying to me from the ground. ¹¹ Now you are cursed from the ground, which has opened its mouth to receive your brother's blood from your hand. ¹² When you cultivate the ground, it will no longer yield its strength to you; you will be a fugitive and a wanderer on the earth." ¹³ Cain said to Jehovah, "My punishment is greater than I can bear! ¹⁴ Behold, you have driven me today away from the ground, and from your face I shall be hidden. I shall be a fugitive and a wanderer on the earth, and whoever finds me will kill me." ¹⁵ So Jehovah said to him, "Therefore whoever kills Cain, vengeance will be taken on him sevenfold." And Jehovah put a mark on Cain, so that no one finding him would slay him.

¹⁶ Then Cain went out from the presence of Jehovah, and dwelt in the land of Nod,¹⁰⁰ east of Eden.

Genesis 4:5 Does God have respect for mankind?

Genesis 4:5 King James Version (KJV)	Romans 2:11 King James Version (KJV)	Deuteronomy 10:17 King James Version (KJV)
⁵ But unto Cain and to his offering he had not respect. And Cain was very wroth, and his countenance fell.	¹¹ For there is no respect of persons with God.	¹⁷ For the LORD your God is God of gods, and Lord of lords, a great God, a mighty, and a terrible, which regardeth not persons, nor taketh reward:

First, it is immediately evident from Scripture that we were created in the image of God, and even in our imperfection, we carry a measure of that. Therefore, God does have respect for his creation, to do otherwise would be to disrespect himself.

---

⁹⁹ The Tetragrammaton, God's personal name, יהוה (JHVH/YHWH), which is found in the Hebrew Old Testament 6,828 times.
¹⁰⁰ I.e. wandering

Second, we need to appreciate that literal translation can be a little harder to understand, and this is actually a good thing because it forces us to pause and ponder.

Third, you will find as we work our way through this publication that the King James Version has been improved upon, and many of the Bible difficulties will be better understood by simply looking to a modern literal translation. If you look at Deuteronomy 10:17 in the King James Version, it reads that God, "regardeth no persons." This can be better grasped by looking at the English Standard Version, which reads, "God, who is not partial." Moses is telling his readers that God is not partial in his justice that he meets out to man. In other words, as the text goes on to say, he "takes no bribe."

However, it is the type of person that Jehovah God has no respect for, such as Cain, who slew his brother, because he had a wicked heart. Moreover, he lacked respect for Cain even prior to that, because Cain lacked faith when he came before Jehovah with his offering. (Heb. 11:4)

At Malachi 1:2-3 God says, "I loved Jacob," then he states, "Esau I have hated." What brought on this contrast between these two brothers? First, it must be noted, this "love" and "hate" contrast in the Bible is understood to mean, not that he literally "hated," but that he loved less. Even still, it is the fact that Jacob loved God and magnified him, while Esau failed to do so. Genesis 25:34 tells the reader "Esau despised his birthright." It is not that Jehovah hates the person; it is their willfulness sinning and practice of sin that he hates.

Genesis 4:7 Why would the language, 'sin is crouching at the door, its desire is for you,' be used if before the Flood, animals ate only vegetation?

God warned Cain that 'sin is crouching at the door, and its desire is for you,' which appears to refer to a wild beast and its prey. (Gen. 4:7) If animals only age vegetation before the flood, why would that language be used?

First, one interpretation principle is never to expect more out of a book than its intended purpose. The was not written to be a science textbook, a history book, a book on geography, yet it touches on these subjects in passing along the message that Jehovah God want mankind to receive. In Genesis, there are some verses that reveal facts or historical information that might seem oddly out of place in their historical setting. Please see other examples of Moses informing his readers by updating the information (Gen. 2:10-14), or using visual aids.—Genesis 3:24.

At Genesis 4:7 God warned Cain: "If you do well will I not accept you? But if you do not do well, sin is crouching at the door. And its desire is for you, but you must rule over it." The language appears to depict the image of a hungry wild beast crouched to jump on and devour prey.

Nevertheless, The Bible seems to indicate that Adam and Eve were at peace with all the animals, and had no reason to fear them. It is quite possible that some of the animals were more comfortable around them than others; while others were wild beasts that dwelt outside of the human family. (Gen. 1:25, 30; 2:19) However, the Bible seems to be quite clear that none of the animals preyed upon the other animals or humans. In the beginning, God precisely assigned vegetation as the food for both animals and humans. (Gen. 1:29, 30; 7:14-16) There is no indication of a change in this until after the Flood, as Genesis 9:2-5 indicates.

How then are we to explain God's warning to Cain, as we read in Genesis 4:7? Surely, the visual of a vicious beast crouched and ready to jump on prey would have been effortlessly understood in Moses' day, as well as for generations after that, and we also understand it. Here, again, we see Moses using language adjusted to readers familiar with the post-Flood world. While it is quite likely, that Cain never saw such a creature in such a position, the point of a desire consuming him, like the wild animals that roamed outside of the human population, would not have been misunderstood.

Our focus on the text should not be like the Bible critic, who looks for chinks in the armor, but to appreciate that the Creator of all things, was very kind in giving Cain a warning, and our need to not be like Cain, but to humbly accept the counsel from God's Word. We do not want to allow jealousy to corrupt and of our relationships. Moreover, we need to heed the divine warnings that we find within Scripture.—Exodus 18:20; Ecclesiastes 12:12; Ezekiel 3:17-21; 1 Corinthians 10:11; Hebrews 12:11; James 1:14, 15; Jude 7, 11.

Genesis 4:12-13 Why did Cain not receive capital punishment for the murder he committed?

Genesis 9:6 Updated American Standard Version (USV)

[6] "Whoever sheds man's blood,
By man his blood shall be shed,
For in the image of God
he made man.

Exodus 21:12 Updated American Standard Version (USV)

[12] "He who strikes a man so that he dies shall be put to death.

As can be seen from the above, the penalty for willfully taking the life of another is the death penalty. We see from the account concerning Cain that he not only did not receive the death penalty for murdering his brother Abel, but he was given protection from anyone seeking to avenge that murder.—Genesis 4:15.

At first glance, this may seem like an inconsistency on the part of Jehovah's justice, but it is not. There are multiple reasons as to why Cain did not receive the death penalty. At the time of this murder, God had not established the death penalty for the murder of another. (Rom 13:1-4) It was only after, "the LORD saw that the wickedness of man was great in the earth, and that every intention of the thoughts of his heart was only evil continually." (Gen 6:5) After the destruction of the Nephilim and wicked man by means of the flood, did God say, ""Whoever sheds the blood of man, by man shall his blood be shed . . ."—Genesis 9:6.

Jehovah is the giver of life and death, and he rightly chose to give Cain a life sentence of banishment. (Deut. 32:39) However, God did express his thoughts that Cain was worthy of death. Jehovah said, "What have you done? The voice of your brother's blood is crying to me from the ground." (Gen. 4:10) Even Cain himself knew that death was the possibility, and asked Jehovah for protection. Cain said to the Jehovah, "My punishment is greater than I can bear. Behold, you have driven me today away from the ground, and from your face, I shall be hidden. I shall be a fugitive and a wanderer on the earth, and whoever finds me will kill me." (Gen. 4:13-14) In addition, the death penalty then was made known as an option, for the taking of a life, as Jehovah said, "If anyone kills Cain, vengeance shall be taken on him sevenfold." (Gen. 4:15) Therefore, due to mitigating circumstances, Cain is the exception to the rule, and cannot be used against the justice of the death penalty that was to become a part of human law after the flood.

Genesis 4:15 How did God "put a mark on Cain"?

The Bible does not say exactly what this mark was, but it is highly unlikely that it was a physical mark on his person. Such a mark would be meaningless centuries later when thousands of people were living before the flood. The sign was likely a verbal decree made by Jehovah to Adam and Eve, which would have become an oral tradition that would have been passed down from generation to generation, avoiding the murder of Cain for the sake of revenge.

Genesis 4:17 Where did Cain get his wife?

Genesis 4:17 Updated American Standard Version (UASV)

[17] Cain had sexual relations[101] with his wife and she conceived, and gave birth to Enoch; and he built a city, and called the name of the city Enoch, after the name of his son, Enoch.

Genesis 3:20 Updated American Standard Version (UASV)

[20] Now the man called his wife's name Eve, because she was the mother of all living.

Here we are just setting up the situation, and as you can see, all humans came to be the offspring of Adam and Eve.

Genesis 5:3-4 Updated American Standard Version (UASV)

[3] When Adam had lived one hundred and thirty years, he became[102] the father of a son in his own likeness, according to his image, and named him Seth. [4] Then the days of Adam after he became the father of Seth were eight hundred years, and he had other sons and daughters.

As you can see, aside from Cain and Abel, there was Seth, as well as "other sons and daughters." Therefore, one of Adam's daughters must have married Cain. In fact, they lived for centuries; it could have even been his niece. We must keep in mind that these are the immediate descendants of Adam and Eve; therefore, they would have been closer to perfection. Their condition of good health would be far beyond the healthiest person living today; so, there would have been no chance of passing on defects, as would be the case even in the Time of Abraham, when they were still living almost 200 years. This is reason you find Jehovah God forbidding incest 2.500 years later in the Mosaic Law.

Genesis 4:16-17 Updated American Standard Version (USV)

[16] Then Cain went out from the presence of Jehovah, and dwelt in the land of Nod,[103] east of Eden.

[17] Cain had sexual relations[104] with his wife and she conceived, and gave birth to Enoch; and he built a city, and called the name of the city Enoch, after the name of his son, Enoch.

---

[101] Lit *knew*

[102] Lit *begot*

[103] I.e. wandering

[104] Lit *knew*

Please note that Cain met his wife before he fled to another land. She was not from some other family. However, it was there that they had relations, and fathered a son.

Genesis 4:26 Exactly when did the worship of God begin?

It is here that we are expressly told, "To Seth, to him also a son was born, and he called his name Enosh. At that time men began to call upon the name of Jehovah." (Gen. 4:26) This is in the days of Enosh, the son of Seth, the third son of Adam and Eve. However, over 105 years earlier before the birth of Enosh, you have Abel offering sacrifices to God in faithful worship. (Gen. 4:3-4) Is this not a historical error? No.

Obviously, in the days of Enosh, we are not talking about calling on the name of Jehovah in faith and pure worship as Abel had done. Some Hebrew scholars have offered that it should read, "began profanely," or "then profanation began." In reference to Enosh's day, the Targum of Onkelos says, "then in his days the sons of men desisted from praying in the Name of the Lord." The Targum[105] of Jonathan says, "That was the generation in whose days they began to err, and to make themselves idols, and surnamed their idols by the Name of the Word of the Lord." Rashi an influential Jewish Bible Commentator from the twelfth century C.E. says, "Then was there profanation in calling on the Name of the Lord." Furthermore, if the purity of worship was begun in the days of Enosh, instead of profanation in calling on the Name of Jehovah, what "ungodliness" did Enoch; "the seventh from Adam" have to prophesy about in Jude 14-15? It could be that men misused the name of Jehovah by applying it to themselves, or other men, approaching God through these ones in worship. Alternatively, it could be that they applied Jehovah's name on idol objects.

Genesis 5:1 Can we trust Bible chronology?

Many of the archaeologist and anthropologists date modern man back to at least 10,000 years ago. How are we to reconcile this when Bible Chronology takes us back to just a little over 6,000 years?

It seems that some scholars that call themselves conservative or fundamentalist, who are supposed to believe that the original texts that contribute to our modern Bibles are "God breathed" and fully inerrant, are not so conservative at times. As a result, it seems that some of these

---

[105] The Targum is an Aramaic translation of part of the Bible.

scholars tend to have secular history as the advantage over biblical history. The Bible scholar and especially the secular scholar tend to view Bible chronology as inferior to that of pagan nations. It is true; one would like to harmonize the biblical account with secular history. However, there is no demonstration that secular chronology is exact or reliable, leaving us a standard by which to judge.

However, no serious Bible student should ever doubt Bile chronology merely because certain secular records are in disagreement with it. Quite the reverse, for the careful Bible student, it is only when secular chronology lines up with biblical chronology that we are to draw confidence in secular dating. Why? There is extensive evidence of certain sloppiness and impreciseness or even of intentional falsification on the part of the pagan historians and their chronologies.

There is no doubt that there are some gaps in the genealogies within Genesis. Looking at the Gospel of Matthew, we find a gap of three generations. Matthew 1:8 reads "**Joram** the father of **Uzziah**" also called Azariah, while 1 Chronicles 3:11-14 reads

1 Chronicles 3:10-14 Updated American Standard Version (UASV)

[10] The son of Solomon was Rehoboam, Abijah his son, Asa his son, Jehoshaphat his son, [11] **Joram** his son, **Ahaziah** his son, **Joash** his son, [12] **Amaziah** his son, **Azariah** his son, Jotham his son, [13] Ahaz his son, Hezekiah his son, Manasseh his son, [14] Amon his son, Josiah his son.

Matthew	1 Chronicles
Joram	Joram
-	Ahaziah
-	Joash
-	Amaziah
Uzziah	Azariah also call Uzziah

As you can see, Matthew leaves out three generations: Ahaziah, Joash, and Amaziah. Why would Matthew omit these persons from the genealogy list? Joram was married to the wicked Athaliah of the house of Ahab, who was the daughter of Jezebel, in so doing; this brought a God condemned strain into the lineage of the Judean kings. (1 Ki 21:20-26; 2 Ki 8:25-27) Matthew only mentions Joram, omitting the fruits of this alliance to the fourth generation. In addition, we have at least one omission from the genealogy of Genesis. Below you will note that Luke has Cainan between Shelah and Arphaxad, while Genesis omits Cainan.

Luke 3:35-36 Updated American Standard Version (UASV)

35 the son of Serug, the son of Reu, the son of Peleg, the son of Eber, the son of **Shelah**, **36** the son of **Cainan**, the son of **Arphaxad**, the son of Shem, the son of Noah, the son of Lamech,

Genesis 10:22-24 Updated American Standard Version (UASV)

22 The sons of Shem: Elam, Asshur, Arpachshad, Lud, and Aram. **23** The sons of Aram: Uz, Hul, Gether, and Mash. **24** Arpachshad fathered Shelah; and Shelah fathered Eber.

Again, Cainan is listed in Luke's genealogy of Jesus Christ as the son of Arpachshad, while his name is missing from Genesis. (Lu 3:36; Gen. 10:22-24) If one were to look to our present copies of the Greek Septuagint, they would find that the name Cainan appears in the genealogical lists, such as the Alexandrine Manuscript of the fifth century C.E.—Genesis 10:24; 11:12, 13; 1 Chronicles 1:18 but not 1 Chronicles 1:24.

However, the same search in the Hebrew manuscripts, as well as the Samaritan texts or the Targums or versions would find "Cainan" missing. In addition, P[75], which dates to about 175 – 200 C.E. and Bezae Codices of the fifth and sixth centuries C.E. omit "son of Cainan," in harmony with Gen 10:24; Gen 11:12, 15; 1Ch 1:18. In these latter texts, it is Shelah, not Cainan, who is the son of Arpachshad.

Moreover, "Cainan" was likely missing from the earlier copies of the Septuagint, because the first-century Jewish historian Josephus, who generally follows the Septuagint, list Shelah next as the son of Arpachshad.[106] Some of the early Church Fathers Irenaeus, Africanus, Eusebius, and Jerome rejected the second "Cainan" in copies of Luke's account as an interpolation. Many scholars take the second "Cainan" in Luke to be a copyist's error. Dr. Stephen J. Bramer discusses this question in his Holman Old Testament Commentary of Genesis, where he writes,

> The numbers must be given for a reason. Later genealogies, essentially from after the time of Abraham, do not contain ages for the people in the genealogies. After Abraham we are able to date the biblical history and correlate it with secular history. It is true that when the Bible refers back to pre-Abraham events or people, it never adds up these numbers. But this does not mean

---

[106] Jewish Antiquities, I, 146 [vi, 4]

that they can't be added up. Perhaps they were not added up for the very reason that people could if they desired to do so.[107]

Genesis 5:5 – How is it possible for the preflood people to live over 900 years?

Genesis 5:5 Updated American Standard Version (UASV)

[5] So all the days that Adam lived were **nine hundred and thirty years**, and he died.

Genesis 5:27 Updated American Standard Version (UASV)

[27] So all the days of Methuselah were **nine hundred and sixty-nine years**, and he died.

Psalm 90:10 Updated American Standard Version (UASV)

[10] As for the days of our years,[108] within them are seventy years,
 or even by reason of strength, eighty years;
yet their pride[109] is but toil and trouble;
 for soon it is gone and we fly away.

The first things that we need to note is that (1) all people who lived to 900 years or more, were preflood, (2) those immediately after the flood started to drop in years, (3) with those living 700 years later, the time of Moses is what Psalm 90:10 is referring to. In addition, he Psalm is not to be taken literally in an absolute sense, it is meant in a generally speaking sense. Generally speaking, "The years of our life are **seventy**, or even by reason of strength **eighty**." Because God used Moses, he was blessed with a lengthy life in comparison to most other Israelites at that time. Even today, people are alive that are over 120 years of age, but that is a handful among more than seven billion people.

Some scholars, who do not believe the Bible to be the Word of God, who are always looking for a natural angle, argue that the "years" are months. This would mean Methuselah really died at a little over 80 years old. However, this is simply impossible, because there is no other example of taking a year to mean a month. Moreover,

Genesis 5:12 Updated American Standard Version (UASV)

[12] Kenan lived **seventy years**, and became the father of Mahalalel.

---

[107] Anders, Max; Gangel, Kenneth; Bramer, Stephen J. (2003-04-01). Holman Old Testament Commentary - Genesis: 1 (p. 67). Holman Reference. Kindle Edition.
[108] I.e. *life*
[109] Or *span*

Genesis 5:15 Updated American Standard Version (UASV)

¹⁵ Mahalalel lived **sixty-five years**, and became the father of Jared.

This would mean that Kenan would have only been five years and eight months old when he fathered Mahalalel. In addition, Mahalalel would have been 5 years and four months old when he fathered Jared. This is biologically impossible.

Then, there are other naturalist scholars arguing that these names are not persons, but family lines. Again, this is illogical reasoning and grasping at straws. The first obstacle is that persons such as Adam, Seth, Enoch, Noah are undoubtedly individuals, as their lives are spelled out in the text. (Gen. 1-9) In addition, one family line does not father another family line, which is just nonsensical. Moreover, family lines do not die, as each of these persons did. (See 5:5, 8, and 11) Finally, the texts say that they were having sons and daughters (5:4), which does not the family line argument either.

There is no other alternative but, to take the text at its word, as these were individuals, who lived literally 900 years or more. Remember, the lifespan dropped dramatically after the flood, from 900s to 600s to 200s, and eventually under 80 as a norm. We must remember that the genetically closer one was to Adam; the closer he was to perfection. Alternatively, the further removed from Adam; the genetics would be more affected by imperfection. In addition, science has stated that they are baffled as to why we die at all, they say under the right conditions, our bodies should go on forever.

Genesis 5:24 Did Enoch Go to Heaven?

Hebrews 11:5 Updated American Standard Version (UASV)

⁵ By faith Enoch was transferred¹¹⁰ so as not to see death, and he was not to be found because God had transferred him; for before he was transferred he obtained the witness that he was pleasing to God.

Some translators have chosen to go beyond the Scripture, being more in the realms of an interpretative translation. The Message Bible reads, "By an act of faith, Enoch skipped death completely." Worse still the James Moffatt translation states, "It was by faith that Enoch was taken to heaven so that he never died." All the original says is that "Enoch was taken away;" (why), "so that he did not experience death." We need to

---

¹¹⁰ **to convey from one place to another, *put in another place, transfer* –** BDAG, p. 642.

work within what was written and no subject the text to our preconceived doctrinal ideas. Let us look at what Jesus adds to this . . .

John 3:13 Updated American Standard Version (UASV)

[13] And no one has ascended into heaven except the one who descended from heaven, the Son of man.

This is stated by the Son of God, who exited in heaven at the very time "Enoch was taken away so that he did not experience death." We know two primary point from Jesus' exchange with Nicodemus: (1) Jesus had been in heaven before coming to the earth, and (2) no one was to ever ascend to heaven but those who were 'born again.' It is only by faith in Jesus ransom sacrifice that ones can be born again.

Since only Jesus himself had been in heaven before coming to earth, he speaks with authority. Tenney offers a great line here: "Revelation, not discovery, is the basis for faith" (Tenney, EBC, p. 48). Some Jews of Nicodemus's day taught that great saints would attain heaven by their godliness and righteous living. But no one ever sees heaven apart from the new birth.[111]

Here again, digging deeper we look to another New Testament writer, the Apostle Paul, who wrote . . .

Hebrews 11:13, 39 Updated American Standard Version (UASV)

[13] These all died in faith, not having received the things promised, but having seen them and greeted them from afar, and having acknowledged that they were strangers and temporary residents in the land.[112] [39] And all these, having obtained a testimony through their faith, did not receive the promise,

All prior true followers of God prior to Jesus' ransom sacrifice would "died in faith."

The promises for which believers eagerly waited appeared only in Christ. Old Testament saints did not experience the eternal inheritance. Their faith earned for them a remarkable reputation and favor with God. They lived and died in the hope of a fulfillment which none of them saw on earth. The

---

[111] Kenneth O. Gangel, vol. 4, John, Holman New Testament Commentary; Holman Reference (Nashville, TN: Broadman & Holman Publishers, 2000), 53.

[112] Lit on the earth; the Greek (ges) literally means "earth, land, region, humanity," and it is the context that determines our word choice. The Greek here means the surface of the earth as the habitation of humanity. (BDAG) Dods and Lane, take it in reference to the land of Canaan. (Dods, "Hebrews," 357; Lane, Hebrews 9–13, 357) See vs 16 note

reaping of the benefits did not occur until Christ opened the box of spiritual treasures.[113]

Why would these ones not receive a heavenly inheritance at death, prior to Jesus' ransom sacrifice? All of humankind has inherited sin from Adam, including Enoch. (Ps 51:5; Rom. 5:12) As man would come to find out in the era of the New Testament, the only means of salvation is by means of Jesus' ransom sacrifice. (Ac 4:12; 1 John 2:1, 2) Enoch lived three thousand years before Jesus' days on the earth, and that ransom had not been paid at that time. Therefore, Enoch was simply asleep in death, awaiting a future resurrection.—John 5:28-29

How then are we understand the phrase, "he did not experience death"? Enoch was an outstanding example of faith. "Enoch walked with God, and he was not there because God took him." (Gen. 5:18, 21-24; Heb. 11:5; 12:1) He was a prophet of God, prophesying of God's coming "with thousands of His holy ones to execute judgment on all, and to convict them of all their ungodly deeds that they have done in an ungodly way, and of all the harsh things ungodly sinners have said against Him."—Jude 14-15.

Enoch only lived 365 years in an era where everyone lived over 900 years, because God "God took him." Why would God take the only man walking with Him at the time? There is no doubt that this evil world was about to persecute Enoch for his prophecies, to the point of executing him. Instead of letting Satan and the wicked men of that day torture and kill this one faithful follower, God chose to take him in such a way, so as to not experience death. While we do not know how God did this, it is possible that he could have given Enoch a vision, and while in that vision, Jehovah took him so that he would not experience the pains of death. God had chosen to do a similar thing with Moses as well, disposing of his body. (Deut. 34:5-6; Jude 9) Like some other Bible details, we cannot be dogmatic. However, we can be certain of the following: (1) God took Enoch, (2) so he would not experience death, (3) but he did enter the sleep of death in such a way as to not experience that entry, (4) and had the hope of a future resurrection, (5) based on Jesus' ransom sacrifice.

Genesis 6:2: Who were the "sons of God"?

Who were the "sons of God" that fathered the Nephilim? Some have suggested that they were worshipers of God, as opposed to the other wicked men. This could hardly be the case if we follow the context. The account says that their marriage to "the daughters of man" caused the

---

[113] Thomas D. Lea, vol. 10, Hebrews, James, Holman New Testament Commentary; Holman Reference (Nashville, TN: Broadman & Holman Publishers, 1999), 206.

wickedness to increase substantially. Noah and his family of a wife, three sons and their wives were the only ones walking with God at that time.—Genesis 6:9; 8:15, 16; 1Pe 3:20.

Therefore, if we were to suggest that these "sons of God" were merely men, this would beg the question, why would their offspring be referred to as "the mighty men who were of old, the men of renown," more so than the other wicked men, or especially Noah and his family? Moreover, the question arise as to what would be so special, if they were just men, for the account to mention their marriage to "the daughters of man" as though that was special in some way? Men had been marrying women and having children for some 1,500 years at this point.

The understanding that these "sons of God" were disobedient angels, an interpretation that has been around since the beginning is the best choice. The same expression "sons of God" is found at Job 1:6 and Job 38:7, and is applied to angels. This interpretation is supported by the apostle Peter as well, for he writes, "he [Jesus] went and proclaimed to the spirits in prison, because they formerly did not obey, when God's patience waited in the days of Noah, while the ark was being prepared." (1 Pet. 3:19-20) Moreover, Jude adds weight to this position as well, when he writes, "the angels who did not stay within their own position of authority, but left their proper dwelling, he has kept in eternal chains under gloomy darkness until the judgment of the great day." (Jude 6)

These rebel angels had the power at one time to material in human form, just like the ones that remain faithful to Jehovah God, as they delivered messages for Him. (Gen. 18:1, 2, 8, 20-22; 19:1-11; Josh. 5:13-15) The "proper dwelling" that Jude speaks of is heaven, to which these angels abandoned, to take on human form, and have relations that were contrary to nature with the "the daughters of man." (Dan. 7:9-10) The Bible intimates that these rebel angels were stripped of their power to take on human form, as you never hear of it taking place again after the flood, only spirit possession after that. These disobedient angels are now "spirits in prison," who had been thrown into "eternal chains under gloomy darkness," which is more of a condition of limited powers, not so much a place, like a maximum-security prison.—1 Peter 3:19; 2 Peter 2:4; Jude 6.

Genesis 6:3 Does this text contradict what Moses said about the length of human life in Psalm 90:10?

No, it does not, for at least two reasons. First, the text here is not dealing with human longevity, but the amount of time before the global flood was to come. However, for the sake of argument, say it was a reference to the longevity of humans; this reference is back at the time when man was living longer because they were not so far removed genetically from Adam and Eve's human perfection.

At that time, man lived for hundreds of years, and Noah was almost 500 years old at the time. In fact, he was 600 years old when the flood came, and continued to live after the flood. Abraham live to be 175 years old, and Moses lived to be 120 years old. Even today, there are exceptions to the norm, some people live to be over 120 years. However, that is the exception in the extreme today. You are talking about a few people out of seven billion.

In summary, then, you are mixing one context with another context thousands of years apart. Genesis is referring to the time remaining before the flood; Psalm was using a general statement. In other words, generally speaking, The years of our life are 70, or even by reason of strength 80. The psalm is of the poetic type of writing and is not to be taken in a literal sense.

Genesis 6:4 Who were the Nephilim?

Some scholars have argued that the Nephilim are simply wicked men like Cain, but worse, nothing more. They base their argument on the statement of "and also afterward" in verse 4, as they say, the Nephilim "were **on the earth in those days, and also afterward,** when the sons of God came into the daughters of man and they bore children to them." In other words, the Nephilim were on the earth before the "sons of God had relations with "the daughters of man."

This position does not outweigh the correct interpretation that the "sons of God", who were rebel angels, took on human form, had relations with the "daughters of man," and produced a mighty offspring of half-man, half-angelic. There are some translations, which have moved the phrase "and also afterward" closer to the beginning of verse 4, which would identify the Nephilim with the "mighty men." For example: "In those days, as well as afterward, there were giants [Heb., hannephilim] on the earth, who were born to the sons of the gods whenever they had intercourse with the daughters of men; these were the heroes [Heb., haggibborim] who were men of note in days of old."—Genesis 6:4, AT, NIV, and TEV.

The Greek Septuagint, a Greek translation of the Hebrew Old Testament made between 280 and 150 B.C.E., also agrees that both the "Nephilim" and "mighty men" are one and the same, using the word gigantes (giants) to translate both expressions. If we look at the context, we will see that in verses 1 through 3, the "sons of God" were taking wives for themselves and that God had tired of this rebellious behavior and said of man, "his days shall be 120 years." Thus, in verse 4, we see that the Nephilim was in the earth "in those days." "In those days" was obvious referring to when God made the statement. Therefore, it showed that this ongoing situation continued, "also afterward, when the sons of God came into the daughters of man and they bore children to them."

Genesis 6:6 In what sense can it be said that God "regretted" that he had made man?

Genesis 6:6 Holman Christian Standard Bible (HCSB)

⁶ the LORD **regretted that He had made man** on the earth, and He was grieved in His heart. ⁷ Then the LORD said, "I will wipe off the face of the earth: **man**, whom I created, together with **the animals**, creatures that crawl, and birds of the sky, for **I regret** that **I made them**."

Feel regret over: (*nacham*) Or *feel regret over*. The Hebrew word (*nacham*) translated "be sorry," "repent," "regret," "be comforted," "comfort," "reconsider" and "change one's mind" can pertain to a change of attitude or intention. God is perfect and therefore does not make mistakes in his dealings with his creation. However, he can have a change of attitude or intention as regards how humans react to his warnings. God can go from the Creator of humans to that of a destroyer of them because of his unrepentant wickedness and failure to heed his warnings. On the other hand, if they repent and turn from their wicked ways, he can be compassionate and merciful, slow to anger, and abounding in loyal love; and he will "reconsider" the calamity that he may have intended.—Joel 2:13.

The English word "regret" means 'to feel sorry and sad about something previously done or said that **now appears wrong, mistaken, or hurtful to others**.' The Hebrew word (*nacham* here translated "regretted" in the HCSB) relates to a change of attitude or intention. This could not be used to suggest that God felt **that he had made a mistake** in creating man.

However, returning to our Hebrew word behind the English word, we find that Jehovah had changed his attitude or intention toward the pre-flood generation of which he said, "the wickedness of man was great in the earth, and that every intention of the thoughts of his heart was only evil continually. (Gen 6:5) Since they had willfully rejected and disobeyed Him, it was now obligatory for Him to reject them in return. The change in their attitude mandated a resultant change in His attitude toward them. It is this change or altered situation that is conveyed by the Hebrew *nicham* ("repent," "be sorry about," "change one's mind about"). The Theological Wordbook of the Old Testament had this to say,

> Unlike man, who under the conviction of sin feels genuine remorse and sorrow, God is free from sin. Yet the Scriptures inform us that God repents (Gen 6:6–7: Ex 32:14; Jud 2:18; I Sam 15:11 et al.), i.e. he relents or changes his dealings with men according to his sovereign purposes. On the surface, such language seems inconsistent, if not contradictory, with certain passages which affirm God's immutability: "God is not a man ... that he should repent" (I Sam 15:29 contra v. 11); "The lord has sworn and will not change his mind" (Ps 110:4). When nāham is used of God, however, the expression is anthropopathic and there is not ultimate tension. From man's limited, earthly, finite perspective it only appears that God's purposes have changed. Thus the OT states that God "repented" of the judgments or "evil" which he had planned to carry out (I Chr 21:15; Jer 18:8; 26:3, 19; Amos 7:3, 6; Jon 3:10). Certainly, Jer 18:7–10 is a striking reminder that from God's perspective, most prophecy (excluding messianic predictions) is conditional upon the response of men. In this regard, A. J. Heschel (The Prophets, p. 194) has said, "No word is God's final word. Judgment, far from being absolute, is conditional. A change in man's conduct brings about a change in God's judgment."[114]

The change in attitude and intention was going from the Creator of humanity to that of destroying them by means of an earth-wide flood. He was very displeased with their wicked heart condition, but saved Noah and his family to continue with his plan of offering a future seed that would ransom humankind. (Gen 3:15' Matt 20:28) The evidence is that he only "regretted" those that had chosen to become so evil in their ways that they forced him to the course of destroying them. (2 Peter 2:5, 9) However, his choice to all some to survive means that his words are not applicable to His creation of mankind itself.

As a final thought, some may conclude that the "them" at the end of verse 7 is in reference to both animals and wicked mankind, but this is not the case. There is nothing in the text that would suggest that the animals had done anything to displease God. Therefore, it would be inappropriate to suggest that "them" is in reference to the animals as well. They were simply victims of man's sin, and the flood would result in their destruction as well. The antecedent of "them" need not be the immediate

---

[114] Marvin R. Wilson, "1344 נחם" In , in Theological Wordbook of the Old Testament, ed. R. Laird Harris, Gleason L. Archer, Jr. and Bruce K. Waltke, electronic ed. (Chicago: Moody Press, 1999), 571.

referent, but was to the preceding reference to "man" (Heb., ha adam), wicked mankind.

Genesis 6:14 How could the ark have held all those kinds of animals?

The "kinds" of animals that were chosen are not the same as the modern day term "species." The account says they were chosen "according to their kinds." In fact, over a million species can be reduced to a few "kinds." You have the dog "kind", the horse "kind" and the cow "kind", to mention just a few. With this in mind, it is estimated that there were 43 kinds of mammals, 74 kinds of birds, and 10 kinds of reptiles, which over the last 4,400 years has produced the variety of species that we now have. Moreover, the sea animals could have stayed in the sea. Finally, Noah could have taken most of the larger "kinds" in when they were small, and there would have been plenty of room.

Genesis 7:2 What was used to determine the distinction between clean and unclean animals?

The distinction between *clean* and *unclean* animals came about by the use of sacrifices in worship, and not by what was permitted to be eaten and what was not permitted. The flesh of the animals was not permissible to be eaten by man prior to the flood. The *clean* and *unclean* designation were applied to the human diet at the receiving of the Mosaic Law, which also ended when the Law of Moses was abolished. (Acts 10:9-16; Ephesians 2:15) Apparently, Adam had informed future generations of what God had found acceptable as a sacrifice in the worship of Jehovah, just as he had informed Abel. (Gen 4:4) As Noah and his family came out of the ark on Mount Ararat, Noah "built an altar to Jehovah, and took of every clean beast, and of every clean bird, and offered burnt-offerings on the altar." (Gen 8:2) Thus, it is obvious that Noah knew was pleasing and acceptable as a sacrifice in the worship of his God.

Genesis 7:11 Where did the water come from that cause the flood in Noah's day?

Genesis 1:6-8 Updated American Standard Version (UASV)

⁶ And God went on to say, "Let there be an **expanse** in the middle of the waters, and let there be a separation between the waters and the waters." ⁷And God went on to make the expanse, and make a separation between the waters, which were <u>**under** the expanse</u> and between the

waters, which were **above the expanse**: and it came to be so. ⁸ And God called the expanse Heaven. And there was evening and there was morning, **the second day.**

You will notice that on the second creative "day" or period, when the expanse (or sky, the atmosphere above the earth), was formed, there were **waters that were under the expanse** and **waters that were above the expanse.** Therefore, there was a body of water above the sky, our atmosphere and water under our sky on the earth.

Genesis 6:17 Updated American Standard Version (UASV)

¹⁷ Behold, I, even I am bringing **the flood of waters** ["the **heavenly ocean**" (Heb., ham**mabbul**)] **upon the earth,** to destroy all flesh in which is the breath of life, from under heaven; everything that is on the earth shall perish.

Genesis 7:11 Updated American Standard Version (UASV)

¹¹ In the six hundredth year of Noah's life, in the second month, on the seventeenth day of the month, on the same day **all the fountains of the great deep burst open, and the windows of heaven were opened.**

There was a "surging waters; water canopy" (Heb., *tehohm*), a "heavenly ocean" (Heb., *hammabbul*),¹¹⁵ above the atmosphere. This water fell to the earth in the six hundredth year of Noah's life, in the second month, on the seventeenth day of the month.

Genesis 7:24 Did the flood rains last forty days or one hundred fifty days?

Genesis 7:24 and 8:3 say the floodwaters lasted for 150 days, yet; Genesis 7:4, 12 and 17 say it was only forty days. The difference is solved with a simple explanation. Each is referring to two different periods of time. Let us look at these verses again (italics mine):

Genesis 7:12 Updated American Standard Version (UASV)

¹² And the rain fell upon the earth for forty days and forty nights.

Notice that the 40-days refer to how long the rain fell—"the rain fell."

---

¹¹⁵ William Lee Holladay, Ludwig Köhler and Ludwig Köhler, *A Concise Hebrew and Aramaic Lexicon of the Old Testament.* (Leiden: Brill, 1971), 181.

Genesis 7:24 Updated American Standard Version (UASV)

²⁴ The waters prevailed on the earth one hundred and fifty days.

Notice that the one hundred and fifty days refer to how long the flood lasted—"waters prevailed."

Genesis 8:3 Updated American Standard Version (UASV)

³ and the waters receded from the earth continually, and at the end of one hundred and fifty days the waters had abated.

Genesis 8:4 Updated American Standard Version (UASV)

⁴ And in the seventh month, on the seventeenth day of the month, the ark came to rest on the mountains of Ararat.

Genesis 7:11; 8:13-14 Updated American Standard Version (UASV)

¹¹ In the six hundredth year of Noah's life, in the second month, on the seventeenth day of the month, on the same day all the fountains of the great deep burst open, and the windows of heaven were opened. ¹³ In the six hundred and first year, in the first month, the first day of the month, the waters were dried up from upon the earth. And Noah removed the covering of the ark and looked, and behold, the face of the ground was dried up. ¹⁴ In the second month, on the twenty-seventh day of the month, the earth was dry.

By the end of the one hundred and fifty days, the water had gone down [Gen 8:3]. Five months from the beginning of the rain, the ark comes to rest on Mount Ararat [8:4]. Eleven months later the waters dried up [7:11; 8:13]. Exactly 370 days from the start (lunar months), Noah and his family left the ark and were on dry ground.

Genesis 8:1 How are we to understand the thought that "after that God remembered Noah," is it possible that God forgot Noah?

This would seem to conflict with other texts that say God knows everything. (Ps. 139:2-4; Jer. 17:10; Heb. 4:13) Moreover, Isaiah 49:15 has God Himself saying that He will not forget his holy ones. Therefore, how are we to reconcile what appears to be God temporarily forgetting Noah? God never forgot Noah. "Remembered" is being used in a way that is an idiomatic expression and does not literally mean that God forgot Noah. A husband will use a similar expression when he remembers his wife on their anniversary. This does not mean the husband forgot their mate existed. In Scripture, to 'remember' is not always to recall to mind, but can be used to express interest, care and concern for another.

Genesis 8:11 If the trees were destroyed by the floodwaters, where did the dove get the olive leaf?

The olive is a very strong and resistant tree, so it is possible that it could have remained alive under water for many months of the flood. After the flood waters had gone down, leaving the tree on dry ground once more, it could then have put forth leaves once more. Another alternative is that the dove was carrying the leaf of a very young sprout that came up after the flood waters had gone down.

Genesis 8:21 God had herein promised to never destroy the world again, did he change his mind?

At 2 Peter 3:10 we are told "the heavens will pass away with a great noise, and the elements will melt with fervent heat; both **the earth** and the works that are in it **will be burned up**." There are multiple things going on in 2 Peter 2:10, so let us take Genesis 8:21 first. There God was saying that he would never destroy the world in the *same way* again, in other words, by means of floodwaters. 2 Peter 3:10 is talking about fire, a whole other means.

According to 2 Peter 3:10 in the King James Version, "the earth also and the works that are therein **shall be burned up**." However, other modern translations read, "the earth and the works that are done on it **will be exposed [or discovered]**." This comes about because there is a textual problem, The Codex Sinaiticus and Vatican MS 1209, both of the 4th century C.E., and other manuscripts, read (*huerethesetai*) "be discovered." Later manuscripts, the 5th-century Codex Alexandrinus and the 16th-century Clementine recension of the Vulgate, read (*katakaesetai*) "be burned up."

Now looking to the context in 2 Peter, are we talking about the literal earth anyway. Verses 5 and 6 speak of the flood in Noah's day, likening it to "the day of judgment and destruction of the ungodly" (3:7). First, what was destroyed by the floodwaters? It was not the earth itself that was to be destroyed; it was ungodly men. This is exactly what Peter is talking about as well. The planet earth is not going to be destroyed on judgment day, it will be ungodly men. What is to be "discovered" on the earth in those days after judgment is righteousness.

Genesis 9:3 Did God permit the eating of meat or only plants?

After the creation of Adam, God had informed him "And God went on to say, "Behold, I have given you every plant yielding seed that is on the face of all the earth, and every tree with seed in its fruit. You shall have them for food." (Gen 1:29) However, meat was not on the human diet. Therefore, some are confused at God's words to Noah after he came out of the ark, "Every moving thing that lives shall be food for you; as I gave you the green plants, I give you everything." (Gen. 9:3) Is this a contradiction of God's earlier command to Adam?

No, it is not. We must remember that the human family was like a child, growing and maturing, as they adapted to life as a creation. This was progressive revelation where the latter supersedes the former, as a parent would give a child. Norman L. Geisler offers a human example to what progressive revelation is. When you have a toddler, you would let him eat with their fingers. When they get a little older, you may instruct them to eat with a spoon. Older still, and you might instruct them to use a fork to eat certain foods. It would only be a contradiction if one of the two were in opposition to God's standards. Therefore, God has the right to alter a command as he pleases, being that he is the Creator.

Genesis 9:6 The Death Penalty: Is It Biblical?

Three Views on Capital Punishment

> There are three basic views on capital punishment: reconstructionism, which insists on the death sentence for all serious crimes; rehabilitationism, which would not allow it for any crime; and retributionism, which recommends death for some (capital) crimes. Forms of all three views are held by Christians. (Geisler 1989, 199)

Is the death Penalty God's Law? The objective of this paper will be to determine if the death penalty, as imposed by modern day countries is biblical. What is the Bible's point of view? Undeniably, this is an ethical issue overflowing with passion, for we are talking about a human life, both that of the victim and the offender, the greatest gift from God. Are modern day nations qualified and authorized to determine such issues as life and death? Should Christians support the death penalty of imperfect nations? If not, should they protest and oppose them? Lastly, if neither of those choices is optional, should Christians simply remain neutral over the death penalty?

The issues of capital punishment are not an island within itself, as other issues will be interrelated, such as pacifism and war, abortion, legislating morality, really all areas related to life. If one is going to be consistent as a pro-life person in an absolute sense or stance, she or he could not be a pacifist toward war, and yet support capital punishment, or be for abortion, and yet against capital punishment. However, seldom will you find a person that will be absolute pro-life in all areas that involve the loss of life. It should be said before moving on that a person can be neutral to war, but not a pacifist. If one defends family and friends, she or he knows the moral reasons as to why, and can judge accordingly. If they are in a military, they may be called on to take lives for a country that is making the moral decisions as to why. (Nash 2007)

Biblical Evaluation

Many Christians of the last 50-years has felt that the death penalty is not biblical and that Christians should not support it. In fact, a number of Christian groups work toward the abolition of the death penalty. The primary argument against capital punishment (execution as punishment), has been that it is cruel and inhumane. However, some advocates do accept the statistics that seem to show it deters crime if effectively carried out.

Of course, this is written by a Christian for Christians, so the perspective of who is best qualified to determine the matter will be quite obvious, and likely carry little merit with the non-Christian. Of course, for the Christian, Jehovah God is the authority on life, 'for with you is the source of life of all who live on earth, the Creator of heaven and earth.' (Ps. 36:9; Isa. 42:5) Therefore, he has the right to enact any laws that affect the life that he produced. Moreover, 'his thoughts and ways are far superior to ours.' (Isa. 33:22; 55:8) Of course, it may be difficult for our finite minds to appreciate and understand the laws that he has established. Nevertheless, his rules and regulations that he has laid out within Scripture, are done so with 'loving-kindness, justice, and mercy to everyone on earth.'—Jer. 9:24.

If we were to consider the Bible from Genesis to Revelation, we would discover that Jehovah God does not approve of all executions that take place therein, but he is not against executing someone as a means of punishment either. In fact, all of humankind has received the death penalty for Adam's rebellious disobedience to the divine law in the Garden of Eden. (Gen. 2:16, 17; 3:17-19; 5:5) Then, there is the execution of every human, with the exception of Noah and his family at the flood in Genesis, as well as the wicked in Sodom and Gomorrah. (2 Pet. 2:5, 6) Moreover, Jehovah used human authorities to carry out capital punishment throughout the history of ancient Israel. (Ex. 32:27, 28; Num.

25:1-11) In fact, there are 18 offenses in the Mosaic Law that brought capital punishment. (Nash 2007) Moreover, Jesus and his angelic army are set to bring wicked humankind to an end at Armageddon.—2 Thess. 1:6-9.

Murder, taking the life of a person by a dangerous animal, raping a married woman, adultery, incest, homosexuality, bestiality, breaking the Sabbath, striking one's parents, rebel children, cursing God, kidnapping, to mention just a few offenses that were punishable by death. First, we must acknowledge that the Israelites were under a theocratic government, meaning they were God-ruled, and had a means of getting God's decision on things by way of the Urim and the Thummim, among other ways to get the direction of divine will. However, this all came to an end after the destruction of Jerusalem by the Babylonians in the Old Testament, because you never hear of the Urim and the Thummim after that. The issue that we must address as Christians is would we find it acceptable to allow governmental authorities to legislate morality? Would we accept the death penalty for a person that commits adultery, or a person caught in a homosexual act? One way to deal with this would be to **separate** what God said to Noah after the flood, which applied to humankind as a whole, from what was said to the Israelite nation, and primarily applicable to them. One of the directives of God to Noah was, "Whoever sheds the blood of man, by man shall his blood be shed, for God made man in his own image." (Gen 9:6) This does not mean that the Old Testament and the Mosaic Law is not applicable to Christians, as the principles behind it are, as well as our discovering how God feels about things, not to mention, the ability to get to know him, and draw close to him as a person by means of that information. Then, there is the prophetic value of the Old Testament as well.

Exodus 19:5-6 Updated American Standard Version (UASV)

[5] Now therefore, if you [*Natural Jews, Sons of Jacob*] will indeed obey my voice and keep my covenant, you shall be my treasured possession among all peoples, for all the earth is mine; [6] and you shall be to me a kingdom of priests and a holy nation. These are the words that you shall speak to the sons of Israel." (See 24:3; 1 Ki 8:53; Ps 135:4)

Matthew 21:43-44 Updated American Standard Version (UASV)

[43] Therefore I say to you [*Natural Jews, Sons of Jacob (vs 23)*], **the kingdom of God will be taken away from you** [*Natural Jews, Sons of Jacob (vs 23)*] and given to a nation,[116] producing the fruit of it. [44] And the person falling on this stone will be shattered. As for anyone on whom it falls, it will crush him."

---

[116] Or *people*

Matthew 23:37-39 Updated American Standard Version (UASV)

37 "Jerusalem, Jerusalem, who kills the prophets and stones those who are sent to her! How often I wanted to gather your children together, the way a hen gathers her chicks under her wings, and you were unwilling.

38 Look, **your house is being left to you desolate!**

39 For I say to you, from now on you will not see me until you say, 'Blessed is he who comes in the name of the Lord.'"

Tutor Leading to Christ

Galatians 3:19-25 Updated American Standard Version (UASV)

19 Why, then, the Law? It was added because of transgressions, until the seed should arrive to whom the promise had been made; and it was transmitted through angels by the hand of a mediator. **20** Now a mediator is not a mediator of one; but God is one. **21** Is the law then contrary to the promises of God? May it never be! For if a law had been given that was able to give life, then righteousness would indeed have been from the law. **22** But the scriptures shut up all things under sin, so that the promise by faith in Jesus Christ might be given to them who believe.

23 But before faith came, we were kept in custody under the law, being shut up to the faith which was later to be revealed. **24** Therefore the Law has become our tutor[117] to lead us to Christ, so that we may be justified by faith. **25** But now that faith has come, we are no longer under a tutor. (See 1 Pet. 2:9-10)

Jesus came to fulfill the Law, to bring it to a close. The purpose of the Law was that it was a tutor leading to Christ, once Christ was here; we no longer needed the tutor for its intended purpose, the protection of the Israelites and the seed of Genesis 3:15. A tutor in the first century was not the teacher, but was a bodyguard that protected the child to and from school, and along the way, he instilled values. The Law served as a protection along the way; it also taught principles. Now, even having said this, one is not saying that the Old Testament is not applicable to the Christian. It is. The Jewish system of things made way to the new system of things, Christianity. If a natural Jew wanted to be right with God, he had to leave the Jewish system and become as Christian. Let us look at Jesus words found at Matthew 9:14-17, which is indicative of Jesus position on the Law.

---

[117] Lit *pedagogue*; Gr *paidagogos*. The tutor in Bible times was not the teacher but rather a guardian who led the student to the teacher.

Matthew 9:14-17 Updated American Standard Version (UASV)

[14] Then the disciples of John came to him, saying, "Why do we and the Pharisees fast,[118] but your disciples do not fast?" [15] And Jesus said to them, "The sons of the bridal chamber[119] are not able to mourn as long as the bridegroom is with them, can they? The days will come when the bridegroom is taken away from them, and then they will fast. [16] But **no one puts a patch of unshrunk cloth on an old garment**; for the patch pulls away from the garment, and the tear becomes worse. [17] **Nor do they put new wine into old wineskins**. If they do, then the wineskins burst and the wine spills out and the wineskins are ruined. But they do put new wine into new wineskins, and both are preserved."

Jesus was saying that no one should get the idea that his disciples and the coming Christianity of the first century were going to conform to the old practices of the former Jewish system of things of the last 1,500 years prior to him, such as the ritual of fasting. Jesus did not come to patch up the old and worn-out Jewish system of things that was soon to be nailed to the cross. Christianity was not going to be made to conform to the Judaism that Jesus walked through in his ministry, nor the past Jewish history with its traditions that they had handed down. No, this was not going to be any new patch on an old garment or new wine in an old wineskin.

This is not a shift from Jew to Gentile, but a shift from the Jewish system of things, to the Christian system of things, from a natural Jew, to a spiritual Jew. There are two basic positions, and then, there is a less held position. **(1)** Some see the church as the direct continuation of Israel in the Old Testament. **(2)** Others, although acknowledging similarities and parallels between the two, view Israel and the church as entirely distinct. These ones also teach that God has a distinct program for Israel and a distinct program for the church. **(3)** This writer's position is that the church completely replaced Israel, and if natural Israel wants to be in a good standing with God, they must become a Christian, and have an active faith in Christ. They are no longer God's chosen people.

Department of Rehabilitation and Corrections

Many states have had this within their title for the state department of prison systems. The **rehabilitation** aspect of the title would suggest that they are there to help the inmate return to a normal life, given the skills to be able to cope and live within society. While we do not have the

---

[118] Some mss add *much*, or *often*

[119] That is, *wedding guests*

time to argue whether they do a good job of this, let it be said that they make a valiant effort, but like many government run programs, it is not effective, because about seventy percent of those released from prison return. However, before moving on, we must consider whether the Creator of heaven and earth is in the rehabilitative business as well.

Let us take just one example, the Assyrians, which was the second world power of Bible history from about 780 B.C. E. to about 630 B.C.E. Nineveh, the capital of Assyria, with a population that numbered more than 120,000 men, not to mention women and children, was sent the prophet Jonah, who proclaimed a judgment against Nineveh, saying that they were to be destroyed by Jehovah God, because of their evil ways. (Jonah 1:1-2) Why? The historical image left of Assyria's abuses is one of enormous inhumane and merciless conquering of one territory after another, making even the most notorious modern-day serial killer pale in comparison. They are listed number three out of the five most terrifying civilizations in world history. The great warrior monarch, Ashurnasirpal, refers to his treatment of several disobedient cities this way:

> I built a pillar over against his city gate, and I flayed all the chief men who had revolted, and I covered the pillar with their skins; some I walled up within the pillar, some I impaled upon the pillar on stakes ... and I cut off the limbs of the officers, of the royal officers who had rebelled. ... Many captives from among them I burned with fire, and many I took as living captives. From some I cut off their hands and their fingers, and from others I cut off their noses, their ears, and their fingers(?), of many I put out the eyes. I made one pillar of the living, and another of heads, and I bound their heads to posts (tree trunks) round about the city. Their young men and maidens I burned in the fire ... Twenty men I captured alive and I immured them in the wall of his palace. ... The rest of them [their warriors] I consumed with thirst in the desert of the Euphrates. (Luckenbill 1989, 145, 147, 153, 162)

Because of Assyria's evil ways, Nineveh was given the death penalty, subject for destruction. However, Jehovah has a judgment policy that most are not aware of, but the Jonah's original audience would have been aware. Judgment by Jehovah God is **conditional** whether one is going from condemnation to restoration because he has turned from his sin and does what is right, as well makes restitution; or he goes from an approved condition to condemnation, because he turns toward evil with an unrepentant heart.

148

Jeremiah 18:7-8 Updated American Standard Version (UASV)

[7] At one moment I might speak concerning a nation or concerning a kingdom to uproot, to tear down, and to destroy it; [8] and if that nation which I have spoken against **turns from its evil, I will also feel regret over**[120] **the calamity that I intended to bring against it.**

Ezekiel 18:23 Updated American Standard Version (UASV)

[23] Have I any pleasure in the death of the wicked, declares the Sovereign Lord Jehovah, and not rather that he should turn from his way and live?

Ezekiel 33:13-15 Updated American Standard Version (UASV)

[13] When I say to the righteous one: "You will surely keep living," and he trusts in his own righteousness and does injustice, none of his righteous acts will be remembered, but he will die for the wrong that he has done. [14] "'And when I say to the wicked one: "You will surely die," **and he turns away from his sin and does what is just and righteous,** [15] and the wicked one returns what was taken in pledge and pays back what was taken by robbery, and he walks in the statutes of life by not doing what is wrong, **he will surely keep living. He will not die**.

Corrective not Punitive

Further, we find that there are occasions when God's actions toward a sinner are for the sole purpose of correcting the person, not so much for the purpose of punishing him. Consider a Scriptural example of expulsion. Below is a case of a man in the first century Corinthian Christian congregation, who is committing fornication with his father's wife. When expelled from the congregation at the direction of the Apostle Paul, and as a result handed over to Satan, this many was again a part of Satan's world, and alienated from God. His being expelled removed the fleshly component from the Christian congregation and preserved the "spirit," or principal mindset.

1 Corinthians 5:5 Updated American Standard Version (UASV)

[5] you must hand such a man over to Satan for the destruction of the flesh,[121] so that the spirit may be saved in the day of the Lord.

---

[120] Lit *repent of*; .e., *I will change my mind concerning*; or *I will think better of*, or *I will relent concerning*

[121] In this context, "the flesh" is referring to the sinful state of human beings, often described as a power in opposition to the spirit, i.e. mental disposition.

An understanding of the preposition εἰς [eis] can shed some light on this verse. The NIV reads as if there were two equally balanced purposes behind Paul's command: one punitive and one remedial [corrective]. But the Greek prefaces the first with an εἰς [eis] and the second with the conjunction ἵνα [hina]. εἰς [eis] can denote either result or purpose; ἵνα [hina] far more commonly denotes purpose. Paul's change of language is likely deliberate to point out that his purpose in discipline is entirely rehabilitative, even if one of the results of his action is temporary exclusion and ostracism of the persistently rebellious sinner. Or in Gordon Fee's words, "What the grammar suggests, then, is that the 'destruction of the flesh' is the anticipated result of the man's being put back out into Satan's domain, while the express purpose of the action is his redemption." (Mounce 2009, 55)

In other words, the punishment's purpose is to rehabilitate, to correct the person's thinking, which is in essence, a correction of his behavior. We can also consider the fact that humankind received the death penalty, and out of his great love God chose to offer a sacrifice to cover that sin, giving humans yet another chance. (Gen. 3:15; Rom. 5:12-18) In this, he placed humans in an objective lesson, to learn from the error of his ways? What was the error of his ways that he needs to learn from, was it anywhere near what a serial killer might accomplish, or a mass murderer? Yes, one man, in extension, all of humankind brought about the pain and suffering, old age, and death of untold billions of people. What was God's greatest tool that he gave to billions of people sitting on death row?

2 Timothy 3:16-17 Updated American Standard Version (UASV)

¹⁶ All Scripture is inspired by God and profitable for **teaching**, for **reproof**, for **correction**, for **training** in righteousness; ¹⁷ so that the man of God may be fully competent, equipped for every good work.

Before moving on, let us revisit what we spoke of earlier: would we find it acceptable to allow governmental authorities to legislate morality? Would we accept the death penalty for a person that commits adultery, or a person caught in a homosexual act? One way to deal with this would be to **separate** what God said to Noah after the flood, which applied to humankind as a whole, from what was said to the Israelite nation, and primarily applicable to them. One of the directives of God to Noah was, "Whoever sheds the blood of man, by man shall his blood be shed, for God made man in his own image."—Genesis 9:6.

Thus, another argument might be made that we are under Mosaic Law in that we follow the do's and don'ts of what might be considered criminal behavior, but Jesus changed the landscape, and now the Christian is not stoned to death, but is removed from the Christian congregation, handed over to Satan, going from life to death spiritually that is. Now, the people must face secular authority for criminal offenses, and the church for moral and criminal ones.

Beyond Repentance

However, there are times that God has chosen to destroy those that were beyond repentance. A Christian can pass from death to life by choosing Christ. However, he can also pass from life to death if he stumbles to the point of spiritual shipwreck. There are times when these ones can be recovered. (Gal 6:1) However, if he rejects the help from spiritual leaders within the congregation because his heart has grown callused, he can go to the point of being beyond repentance. He would come to the point of having no desire to be restored. (Heb. 6:4-8; 10:26-29)

Certainly, the same principle would hold true for those in the world, who are beyond rehabilitation. We speak of 'hardened criminals.' They are sadistic, and have absolutely no remorse in the pain and suffering they cause. Their heart has grown callused, meaning they cannot feel regret for what they do. They passed from the life of this system to death when they stumbled into a life of crime, deviant behavior. Along the way, many have tried to recover these ones, but the help has been rejected until the person has become a hardened criminal, and he is beyond rehabilitation. These are the ones housed in maximum and supermax prisons.

Success of Department of Rehabilitation and Corrections

There is neither the time, nor the space to deal with this to the fullest extent. The inadequacies of the prison system are many, and all cannot be covered. The recidivism rate (return rate) of inmates is and has been for 80 years about 70 percent. In other words, seven out of every ten inmates released will offend again, and go back to prison. Generally, each time they are released their crimes escalates in seriousness, because they are becoming more and more hardened with each trip to prison. One of the reasons for lack of success is the combining of repentant inmates with unrepentant inmates.

For example, the state of Ohio has about forty prisons: one supermax, one maximum and the rest are close (close means just short of max), medium and minimum security prisons, each housing about 2,500 inmates. Every one of these prisons has educational, vocational and rehabilitative programs, which means the money is stretched thin, and ineffective. The best solution is to have 2-3 prisons that are specifically designed to rehabilitate and correct, and sink all of the money into those, with the inmates that are repentant working their way to these places. When you have an inmate taking a rehabilitative program class in a prison with 39 other inmates, and 28 of them are hardened, unrepentant criminals, it is fruitless for the one who is looking to better himself.

Life for a Life

Most countries have classified aggravated or first-degree murder as being worthy of capital punishment. For example, in the state of Ohio, where this writer lives, it must be premeditative, and there must be any one of eight aggravating factors, such as it being committed in the commission of a felony. What does God's Word say? The most notable would be the tenth commandment, "You shall not murder." (Deut. 5:17) The apostle John wrote, "Everyone who hates his brother is a murderer, and you know that no murderer has eternal life abiding in him." (1 John 3:15; Rev. 21:8) Many, who are influenced by the United States' liberal news media, would argue that the execution of a malicious killer is cruel punishment. However, the conservative element of the same country would argue that the willful and purposeful slaughter of an innocent life by the offender is cruel punishment for the victim and his family. Therefore, the anti-death penalty element has their focus on the offender's well-being, while the pro-death penalty element has their focus on the victim of the offender. At times, there has been a case where a person, who protests out in front of prisons where death row inmates are executed, who has then had a close family member taken from them in some hideous way by a killer, and they then change their position on the cruelty of the death penalty. By and large, those that battle the inappropriateness of the death penalty have never been a victim of a violent crime. However, to be fair, there are those that have had their children end up on death row, and have gone from supporters of the death penalty to ones who oppose it.

As was already stated in the above, the creator of heaven and earth, as well as humankind, stated the following on capital punishment, "your lifeblood I will require a reckoning: from every beast I will require it ... Whoever sheds the blood of man, by man shall his blood be shed, for God made man in his own image." (Gen. 9:1, 5-6) It was at this stage in human history that the ultimate lawgiver gave human authorities the right to execute those found guilty shedding the blood of man. When a governmental authority executes a person for capital murder, it is, in essence, acting as "God's servant for your good ... For he is the servant of God, an avenger who carries out God's wrath on the wrongdoer. (Rom.

13:1, 3-4) Of course, this does not give governmental authorities the right to perform vigilantly justice on someone who is believed to have murdered another.

Scripture applicable to the Christian community clearly shows that premeditative murder of another is a capital offense; however, the same Scriptures had exceptions for someone who took another's life **un**intentionally. He was given refuge within certain cities at the time. Still, this was only after the leaders of the community ascertained that the murder was not intentional, as it was a case of manslaughter. The Israelite's did not have jails or prisons, so he or she would not have been imprisoned, but would have been required to live in the city of refuge until the death of the high priest He would also be required to work to benefit himself, as well as the community he lived within.—Num. 35:9-34.

Murder was not the only capital offense for the nation of Israel either. As was already stated, an Israelite could receive the death penalty for criminal negligence and certain wrongful actions that were exceptionally harmful physically, mentally and spiritually. This makes evident that God was far more concerned for the victim of a crime than the offender. If followed as laid out in the Law, this raised the Israelite nature morally above the pagan nations that surrounded them, who saw nothing wrong with such deviant practices as incest, sodomy, and bestiality. (Ex. 21:29; Lev. 18:6-30; 20:10-23) Capital punishment was imposed for gross immoral acts, which kept the nation of Israel pure and clean if obeyed, as well as having a society, whose perverse (and really criminal) behavior, was not allowed to influence others into this ruination.

Is Capital Punishment A Deterrent?

Some would be so bold to state that no punishment ever deters any wrongful actions. Others would argue that the one, who receives capital punishment for aggravated murder, receives justice, but that this is a deterrent for others who may be considering such a crime.

A heinous crime against state is worthy of capital punishment, such as one who commits treason, a violation of the allegiance owed to his or her own country. Thus, treason against the Creator is worthy of capital punishment. However, in relation to violating one's allegiance owed to God, it would not be known as treason, but as apostasy. 'In classical Greek, apostasia is a technical term for political revolt or defection. In LXX it always relates to rebellion against God (Josh. 22:22; 2 Ch.

29:19).'[122] "If your brother, the son of your mother, or your son or your daughter or the wife you embrace or your friend who is as your own soul entices you secretly, saying, 'Let us go and serve other gods,' which neither you nor your fathers have known, ... you shall not yield to him or listen to him, nor shall your eye pity him, nor shall you spare him, nor shall you conceal him. But you shall kill him. Your hand shall be first against him to put him to death, and afterward the hand of all the people. You shall stone him to death with stones, **because he sought to draw you away** from the Lord your God, ... And **all Israel shall hear and fear and never again do any such wickedness as this among you**." (Deut. 13:6-11) Two points are to be made here, **(1)** this is not a revolt against God, because this one no longer wanted to follow him, it is 'because the Israelite sought to draw others away.' **(2)** The penalty of capital punishment for apostasy (treason) was to deter people from committing such an offense. If the Creator Himself knows that appropriate penalties will serve as a deterrent, we should accept that as fact.

There is little doubt that the death penalty will deter the offender who received it from committing murder again. Moreover, if the death penalty deters so small a number of murders each year that are not going to get caught in statistics, say 100 in the United States, and there was no death penalty, who can rationalize this to the innocent victims that would have never been. Then again, if the death penalty is in place, and those 100 lives are saved, it is the lives of the murderers themselves that are lost. Who would you rather live?

Many times, killers kill again and again, this proves to be the case in the prison system itself, as well as outside of prison. People have been killed for as little as a pack of cigarettes in prison because an inmate failed to pay his bills. Life is very cheap in prison, and life is just as cheap on the streets of our cities. If the recent movie theater massacre in Colorado has not brought home to us, as one many gunned down dozens of people, murdering 12 and injuring 70 others.

The system that is designed to deal with violent criminals is the flaw in the system here in the United States. You have **(1)** the mismanagement of evidence, **(2)** the intentional corrupting of evidence, **(3)** law enforcement and prosecutors blinded by anything outside of what they believe to be true, **(4)** the poor and minority receiving different levels of defense, **(5)** as well as the more strict punishments, **(6)** an over crowded system that lets dangerous offenders out in just a few years, and **(7)** most

---

[122] D. R. W. Wood and I. Howard Marshall, New Bible Dictionary, 3rd ed. (Leicester, England; Downers Grove, IL: InterVarsity Press, 1996), 57.

death row inmates do not get executed for 50-20 years because of all the appeals they receive.

Do these flaws within the system make a case for capital punishment unacceptable? Here again, we are back to the morality of whether we should carry out capital punishment. At what level are these corruptions within the system? There is little doubt that the poor receive far less in their defense against such charges. The defense attorney may only receive $6,000 for a murder trial that lasts a week, or $20,000.00 for a capital murder trial that lasts 2-3 weeks, while a wealthy defendant may spend tens of thousands to millions. The criminal justice system in the United States is so overwhelmed; it is literally impossible to meet out just to all. Of all cases that come before a judge, 98 percent of them are plead out to lesser included offenses, because not everyone can go to trial. However, almost all cases of murder go to trial. Even after having said all that, the United States criminal justice system is far fairer than any other country.

MORE EXECUTIONS, FEWER MURDERS

*per 66,000 people
Source: Bureau of Criminal Justice

Pro-death Penalty Webpage[123]

The Supreme Court case of Furman v. Georgia, 408 U.S. 238 (1972), brought an end to capital punishment 1972 through 1976. As you can see from the chart, when the death penalty was abolished for five years, the number of murders went up. However, stats are not always reflective of reality. The death penalty is only going to have a real effect on premeditative murder, not crimes of passion. There are other complications as well. With modern science, we are finding more and more people on death row, who are innocent. What the governments of

---

[123] http://www.wesleylowe.com/cp.html

the world do not realize, they are accountable for spilled blood, from the "the Judge of all the earth." (Gen. 18:25) While life for life is certainly fair justice, it is only fair under such conditions where one can be sure of the guilt.

Does Capital Punishment Devalue Life?

Some would argue that it is just the opposite; 'the lack of carrying out capital punishment devalues life.' If we looked at the individual states this way, we could say that Texas values life far more than any other state, because it has executed 483 people since 1976, with only a 109 being executed in Virginia, and Kansas with the least, zero!. We could think of it another way as well if we assess something as being of great value; then, we are willing to pay the ultimate price for it. Both are reasonable.

This is the way the United States sets up its criminal justice system. We attempt to make sure 'the punishment fits the crime.' If the person gets a parking ticket, it will be a small fine. If he assaults a person physically, he could receive a few months in the local county jail up to a few years in prison, depending if it is a misdemeanor assault or a felony assault. This so-called 'like for like' or punishment fitting the crime applies to capital murder as well. What would be the equal value of a human life? Would it not be "life for life"?—Deuteronomy 19:21, NEB.

The irony is that we humans can appreciate 'like for like' on everything, and would fight to no end, so as to not be short changed on our end if the 'like' process. However, the moment that human life for life comes into the picture, we pause. Whereas, when it was just a thing being considered, the emphasis (justice) was placed on the victim, who lost their end of the like, but once we move into the human life realm, the emphasis is not placed on the offender, and what is really just, like we do not know. Those who cannot stomach the execution of a human life will close their eyes to the victim, as well as any future victims and the value is then placed on the life of the murderer. They would scream from the courthouse steps, or in front of the prison on execution night, 'to execute this human, living, being is to cheapen life!' Now, is that really reasonable? They are not arguing innocence, as this person is guilty of say raping a mother and two daughters, then, beating them within an inch of their lives, before setting the house on fire, burning them to death. Many believe that if you just 'lock them up and throw away the key,' all is well. These once are still blinding themselves to the facts of how many inmates and correction officer are killed in a prison setting. In 2002, our of 2.1 million state prison inmates, 1,134 were murdered in prison.—BBC News 2005.

Many would argue that those who fail to exact equal punishment for the crime of taking a life are the ones who are cheapening life. We can get a picture of this imbalance in their thinking when we consider other aspects of when life is at risk. In the case of the death penalty, these ones are pro-life advocates of a few thousand inmates that have savagely taken the life (some murdering multiple people) of another, but these same ones will stand in front of abortion clinics, courthouses, or congress, arguing for the slaughter of an unborn child. Clearly, the preciousness of life only matters for a person who has wantonly taken the life or multiples lives of other(s).

Is Capital Punishment Legalized Murder?

Those part-time pro-life advocates of the murderers suggest that capital punishment is nothing more than "legalized murder." Let us analyze that thought for a minute. Killing is to cause something living to die, which can be done **lawfully** or **unlawfully**. Murder is deliberately taking another person's life unlawfully. Stealing is taking something unlawfully. If a police officer catches a criminal in an alley, mugging a person, and he takes that person's gun, is he stealing it? Hardly! It is a lawful taking of the gun. Therefore, when a governmental authority executes (kills) lawfully; it cannot be an unlawful taking of a life, murder. There is a clear distinction between murder and killing.

Again, as mentioned earlier, the law handed down by our Creator after the fall of humankind protected the man who may have accidently taken another person's life, voluntary or involuntary manslaughter. If the judges deemed that they were not intentionally trying to take the life of the other, they were not given the death penalty. However, those convicted of manslaughter in the Bible were punished, which once again shows that we should value life.—Numbers 35:6-32.

Are there Scriptural grounds for the governmental authorities to execute criminals guilty of intentional murder, with exaggerating circumstances? Yes, the Apostle Paul, informed the Christians in the capital of the Roman Empire "Let every person be subject to the governing authorities. For there is no authority except from God, and those that exist have been instituted by God. For he is God's servant for your good. But if you do wrong, be afraid, for he does not bear the sword in vain. For he is the servant of God, an avenger who carries out God's wrath on the wrongdoer." (Rom. 13:1, 4) The Apostle Peter makes the same case, "Be subject for the Lord's sake to every human institution, whether it be to the emperor as supreme, or to governors as sent by him to punish those who do evil and to praise those who do good."—1 Peter 2:13-14.

We can evaluate the seriousness of these men, as to just how serious they took the governmental power, by looking to the time when Paul was brought up on false charges, and his life hung in the balance. He stood before Governor Festus on charges that, if found guilty, would have brought the death penalty. Did he argue that the governmental did not have the authority? No, just the opposite, he said, "If then I am a wrongdoer and have committed anything for which I deserve to die, I do not seek to escape death."—Acts 25:11.

The Effect Capital Punishment on Society

When we lower 'punishment for the crime of aggravated murder,' so that it is equal to lesser crimes like robbery, burglary, and so on, the decision to risk getting caught starts to become worthwhile. If you will return to the chart again that deals with the level of murders committed in the United States from 1972 through 1976, you will see that there is a correlation to the value of life. Not the victim's life, but rather the offender valuing his own life. There is a constant level of murders for 30 years. However, when the abolished the death penalty for five years, the murder rate and other serious crimes almost tripled the 30-year average prior to 1972. Certainly, this alone is not the reason for such a jump, but the correlation is certainly there, between the skyrocket in the murder rate and the abolishment of the death penalty.

If the critics are correct, that capital punishment hardens and dehumanizes a society; it would certainly mean that if removed it should humanize a society. Of course, it could be argued, and rightly so that five years is hardly enough time without something, to see any correlation. However, we could add the statistic that when the United States made Kidnapping a death penalty case in the 1980's, it all but disappeared as a crime. However, once it was realized that no one was ever really sentenced to death over it, it began to rise yet again.

The only way that we could ever truly see a correlation between the capital punishment and the reduction of crime is if two factors came into play: **(1)** they sentenced all people who committed that crime to the death penalty, **(2)** which would be carried our within a month of being sentenced, no exceptions. The problems we face are trial and court errors, as well as corruption. Would a detective be less prone to alter evidence if he knew of such severe consequences, would lab technicians be more careful if they knew of such serious consequences? I have addressed many issues, but the actual purpose of this writing is to establish the moral significance of capital punishment.

Genesis 9:18-28 If it is Ham that saw Noah's nakedness, why is Canaan the one getting cursed?

Commenting on Genesis 9:24, which states that when Noah awoke from his wine he "got to know what his youngest son had done to him," a footnote in Rotherham's translation says, "Undoubtedly Canaan, and not Ham: Shem and Japheth, for their piety, are blessed; Canaan, for some unnamed baseness, is cursed; Ham, for his neglect, is neglected." Similarly, a Jewish publication, The Pentateuch, and Haftorahs, suggests that the brief narrative "refers to some abominable deed in which Canaan seems to have been implicated." (Edited by J. H. Hertz, London, 1972, p. 34) And, after noting that the Hebrew word translated "son" in verse 24 may mean "grandson," this source states: "The reference is evidently to Canaan." The Soncino Chumash also points out that some believe Canaan "indulged a perverted lust upon [Noah]," and that the expression "youngest son" refers to Canaan, who was the youngest son of Ham.— Edited by A. Cohen, London, 1956, p. 47.

As is generally the case, context can clear the muddied waters, to see more clearly. We should mention here that there is no explicit evidence for the inference that we are about to suggest, so we are not dogmatic about our understanding.

Genesis 9:18 Updated American Standard Version (UASV)

¹⁸ The sons of Noah who went forth from the ark were Shem, Ham, and Japheth. (Ham was the father of Canaan.)

One must ask why the account has an abrupt interruption here, with a parenthetical of introducing Canaan, before covering the drunkenness of Noah.

Genesis 9:22 Updated American Standard Version (UASV)

²² And Ham, the father of Canaan, saw the nakedness of his father and told his two brothers outside.

Here again, the account is pulling us back to Canaan. As the actions of Ham are being disclosed, the account goes out of its way to emphasize Canaan, saying "Ham, the father of Canaan." Both of these seem to imply that Canaan is an essential part of understanding the account.

We can accept that the expression "saw the nakedness of his father" as a means of expressing some kind of perversion or abuse on Noah by Canaan. If you turn to Leviticus, you will find that similar expressions are used in reference to sexual sins and incest. (Le 18:6-19; 20:17) Therefore, it is possible that Canaan committed some type of sexual abuse on the unconscious Noah, to which Ham had knowledge and did not take

159

measures to prevent or discipline if it was after the fact. Worse still, he made this known to the brothers, which brought more embarrassment and shame on Noah.

Then, there is the matter of the curse itself. "Cursed be Canaan; a servant of servants shall he be to his brothers." (Gen 9:25) There is no biblical evidence that Canaan was ever a servant to his uncles Shem or Japheth. However, we are dealing with Jehovah God, who possesses foreknowledge. Moreover, the curse is in the Word of God and thus shows that it was divinely inspired, and must therefore come true. We must keep in mind that God does not disfavor a person or people without a justifiable reason behind it. Is it possible that Canaan was already acting on some type of genetic leanings, such as lust for the same sex, and that Jehovah foresaw the outcome of that within the Canaanites, descendants of Canaan?

If you recall, Jehovah could read the heart-attitude of Cain, and had warned him of the results if he did not change his disposition. (Gen 4:3-7) In addition, God was able to discern the level of wickedness that was to be in the preflood population. (Gen 6:5) Moreover, God was able to detect the genetic bent of the unborn Jacob and Esau, while they were still in the womb. (Gen 25:23)

We see the justifiableness of God's curse on Canaan in the history of his descendants. They were so immoral that archaeologist that dug up their area was surprised that God had not destroyed them sooner. (Gen 15:15-16) They too had a lust for the same sex. The Bible is right alongside secular history in exposing the sordid past of the Canaanites. The curse was fulfilled about eight centuries after Noah uttered the words when the Israelites conquered the land of Canaan. Later too, they would be subjected even further by the descendants of Japheth, by way of Medo-Persia, Greece, and Rome.

Genesis 10:5 Chapter 10 (5, 20, 31) indicates that there were many languages, while 11:1 says one language." Why?

This is talking about two different time periods. In the earlier of the two, the tribes of Ham, Shem, and Japheth all spoke the same language. Later, the people rebelled against Jehovah's explicit command to spread out and fill the earth. (Gen 9:1) Therefore, God confused their languages, to facilitate his purpose that they fill the earth. Now that they could no longer understand each other, they had no alternative but to spread out and fill the earth. It should be noted that each person did not receive a new language, each family did, which kept the families (tribes) together.

160

Genesis 10:15-16 Were the "Amurru" the Amorites of the Bible?

Amorites.

"Semitic people found throughout the Fertile Crescent of the Near East at the beginning of the second millennium B.C. Amorites are first mentioned in the Bible as descendants of Canaan in a list of ancient peoples (Gen. 10:16; cf. 1 Chron. 1:13–16). Some of these nomadic people seem to have migrated from the Syrian desert into Mesopotamia, others into Palestine." (Baker Encyclopedia of the Bible Vol. 1, p. 76)[124] How can the Amorites be Semitic when the following texts say,

Genesis 10:6 (UASV)	Genesis 10:15-16 (UASV)	1 Chronicles 1:13-14 (UASV)
[6] The sons of Ham: Cush, Egypt, Put, and Canaan.	[15] Canaan fathered Sidon his firstborn and Heth, [16] and the Jebusites, the Amorites, the Girgashites,	[13] Canaan fathered Sidon his firstborn and Heth, [14] and the Jebusites, the Amorites, the Girgashites,

"The Amorites" In Genesis 10:15-16 above is listed as the sons of Canaan. However, elsewhere the Hebrew term is always in the singular but is used collectively for the major tribe in Canaan, which were the descendants of the original Amorite. Thus, they were not Semitic, but were of the Hamitic race, as is shown by Genesis 10:6. Most sources, like Holman Illustrated Bible Dictionary, say of the Amorites, "People who occupied part of the promised land and often fought Israel. Their history goes back before 2000 B.C.E. They took control of the administration of Babylonia for approximately 400 years (2000–1595), their most influential king being Hammurabi (1792–1750)." (p. 61.)[125]

Baker Encyclopedia of the Bible Vol. 1, p. 76[126] says, "Akkadian cuneiform inscriptions mention a relatively uncivilized people called *Amurruf* (translation of the Sumerian *Mar-tu*), perhaps named for a storm god. They overran the Sumerians and eventually most of Mesopotamia. The city of Mari, on the upper Euphrates River, fell to them about 2000 b.c.; Eshunna a short time later; Babylon by 1830 b.c.; and finally Assur around 1750 b.c. Mari had been an Akkadian city; archaeological investigations there from 1933 to 1960 uncovered more

---

[124] http://biblia.com/books/bkrencbib/VolumePage.V_1,_p_76
[125] http://biblia.com/books/hlmnillbbldict/Page.p_61
[126] http://biblia.com/books/bkrencbib/VolumePage.V_1,_p_76

than 20,000 clay tablets written in Akkadian but full of Amorite words and expressions." However, there is another possibility that the *Amurru* are not to be associated with the biblical Amorites, which descended from the original Amorite, which was fathered by Canaan, the son of Ham. The *Amurru* found in the Akkadian cuneiform inscriptions, means "west," in other words, geographically, the region "west" of Mesopotamia.

A. H. Sayce, in *The International Standard Bible Encyclopedia*, "*Varying Use of the Name* Amorites appears first in Mesopotamia in a divinatory text of the time of Sargon I (ca 2360–2305). There they are a nomadic people, possibly from the northwestern hill countries, but more likely (so Dossin) from the western deserts (kur-mar-tu=the desert countries). The name ("the Westerners") is therefore a purely geographical indication of their immediate origins, from the perspective of Mesopotamia, and conveys no information about their ethnic composition or their real name."[127] (Vol. 1, p. 113)

The International Standard Bible Encyclopedia goes on to say under part B, "*Early Amorite Kingdoms and Nomads in Syria and Mesopotamia* Between the 23rd and 21st [centuries] b.c. the Amorites penetrated into Babylonia, where, after the fall of the 3rd Dynasty of Ur (ca1950), they settled down. Thereafter Northwest Semitic dynasties ruled over Larsa (ca 1961–1699), Isin (ca 1958–1733), Mari (until 1693), and Babylon (ca 1830–1531, the 1st Dynasty of Babylon), further in Syria over Aleppo, Qatna, Alalakh, etc., showing a consistent ethnic and institutional pattern from Mesopotamia to Syria.[128] (Vol. 1, p. 113) However, we must keep in mind that the 20,000 clay tablets were written in the Semitic Akkadian, with "some names of West Semitic origin." As was mention at the outset, the biblical Amorites were Hamitic, not Semitic. Nevertheless, we would not dismiss the possibility that some branch of them may have assumed the Semitic tongue, we must admit that it is also just as possible that the *Amurru* were simply "westerners" of Semitic origin, who happen geographically to live west of Babylonia. Professor John Bright says,

> Of the greatest interest is the part played in these events by a people called the Amorites (a name known to the reader of the Bible, but with a narrower connotation). For some centuries [latter half of the 3rd millennium B.C.E. and early 2nd millennium B.C.E.], the people of northwestern Mesopotamia and northern Syria had been referred to in cuneiform texts as Amurru, i.e., 'Westerners.' This became, apparently, a general term applying to speakers of various Northwest-Semitic dialects

---

[127] Geoffrey W. Bromiley, ed., *The International Standard Bible Encyclopedia*, Revised (Wm. B. Eerdmans, 1979–1988), 113.
[128] IBID, 113.

found in the area including, in all probability, those strains from which later sprang both Hebrews and Arameans.[129]

Genesis 10:25 How was the earth "divided" in the days of Peleg?

It was "in his [Peleg's] days," that God confused the languages of the people, because of those involved in the building of Babel. Since they were no longer able to understand each other, there was a great confusion (Babel, "confusion"]. Therefore, the earth's population was divided in the days of Peleg, the earth being mankind. Peleg lived from 2269 to 2030 B.C.E.

Genesis 11:5 How could God have gone down to the city of Babylon?

Does not 2 Chronicles 6:18 (see, 1 Ki 8:27) tell us that "will God indeed dwell with man on the earth? Behold, heaven and the highest heaven cannot contain you, how much less this house that I have built!" Therefore, in what sense had Jehovah God come "down to see the city and the tower, which the children of man had built"?[130]

Should we think that it was necessary for Jehovah God truly to leave his heavenly throne to see the city and tower or take action? No! More reasonably, he took note; he turned his attention to the things on the earth. Therefore, when we read, "God first visited the Gentiles, to take from them a people for his name," it simply means that he turned his attention to the Gentiles. That is why we see a more dynamic translation rendering it, "God first showed an interest."—Acts 15:14, (AT).

At other times, and whether this is the case here as well, it does not explicitly say, God sent representatives to stand in his place, angelic messengers. There is no reason for the Creator of heaven and earth, to leave his heavenly place, to deliver a message to humans. There are only three instances in the Bible where God's voice was heard from heaven. (Matt. 3:17; 17:5; John 12:28) Otherwise, Jehovah God has either sent his Son in his prehuman existence or an angelic messenger. You will take note that not only was the Mosaic Law transmitted by angelic representatives, but they were viewed by Moses as though he were talking directly to God himself. "Why, then, the Law? It was added because of transgressions until the seed should arrive to whom the promise had been made; and it [the

---

[129] in *A History of Israel* (2000, p. 49)

[130] See Genesis 11:5-7; 18:21; Exodus 2:25; 3:8, 16; 4:3.

Law] was transmitted through angels by the hand of a mediator."—Galatians 3:19.

To help us appreciate that Moses was actually speaking with an angelic representative, we look to Acts 7:38, "This is the one who was in the congregation in the wilderness with the angel who spoke to him at Mount Sinai, and with our fathers. He received living oracles to give to us." That angelic representative was a personal spokesman for God and thus spoke to Moses, as if God himself were there, which the human being spoken to, viewed it this way as well.

You will also take note that the angel, who delivered the message to Moses at the burning bush. Exodus 3:2 identifies him as, "the angel of Jehovah appeared unto him in a flame of fire out of the midst of a bush." Please note what verse 4 adds to this, "When Jehovah saw that he turned aside to see, God called unto him out of the midst of the bush." In verse 6, this angelic representative said, "I am the God of thy father, the God of Abraham, the God of Isaac, and the God of Jacob. And Moses hid his face; for he was afraid to look upon God." We clearly see both the angelic representative and Moses, viewing the spokesperson as being none other than Jehovah God himself. We see this again at Exodus 4:10, "And Moses said unto Jehovah, Oh, Lord, I am not eloquent, neither heretofore, nor since thou hast spoken unto thy servant; for I am slow of speech, and of a slow tongue."

We have yet another example chapter 6 of Judges. Herein we find yet another man speaking to God through another angelic representative. Judges 6:11 says, "And the angel of Jehovah came, and sat under the oak which was in Ophrah, that pertained unto Joash the Abiezrite: and his son Gideon was beating out wheat in the winepress, to hide it from the Midianites." Here again, we find this angelic representative being viewed as Jehovah God himself. Take not over verses 14-5, "And Jehovah looked upon him, and said, Go in this thy might, and save Israel from the hand of Midian: have not I sent thee? And he said unto him, Oh, Lord, wherewith shall I save Israel? Behold, my family is the poorest in Manasseh, and I am the least in my father's house." Therefore, as is made clear here, the materialized angel that Gideon saw and spoke to, is viewed as Jehovah God himself in the biblical account.

Then too, we have Manoah and his wife, the parents of Samson. Here again, you have an account viewing the angel of Jehovah as Jehovah. The account says, "The angel of Jehovah appeared unto the woman." (vs 3) The wife reports to Manoah, "Then the woman came and told her husband, saying, A man of God came unto me, and his countenance was like the countenance of the angel of God." (vs 6) "Then Manoah entreated Jehovah, and said, Oh, Lord, I pray thee, let the man of God whom thou didst send come again unto us, and teach us what we shall do unto the child that shall be born." (vs 8) "And God [listened] to the voice of Manoah; and the angel of God came again unto the woman as she sat in the field: but Manoah her husband was not with her." The rest of the account up to verse 18 has a conversation between 'the angel of Jehovah and Manoah.' However, take a special note as to what Manoah says to his wife in verse 22, "We shall surely die because we have seen God." We know from Scripture that no one has seen Jehovah God, but Manoah and his wife felt that way because he has come into contact with an angelic spokesperson for God.

Genesis 11:26, 32; 12:1, 4 Was Abraham 135 or 75-years-old when he was called to leave Haran?

(**Genesis 12:1**) Now Jehovah said to Abram, "Go out from your land and from your relatives, and from the house of your father, to the land that I will show you. ("J")

After Terah, Abram's father, died, Abram is commanded to leave Haran.

(**Genesis 11:26**) When Terah had lived seventy years, he fathered Abram, Nahor, and Haran.

When Terah was 70, Abram was born.

(**Genesis 11:32**) And the days of Terah were two hundred and five years, and Terah died in Haran.

Terah died at the age of 205, which would make Abraham 135 when he left Ur.

(**Genesis 12:4, ASV**) So Abram went, as the Lord had told him, and Lot went with him. Abram was seventy-five years old when he departed from Haran.

Here we see that Abram was only 75 when he left Haran.

Discrepancy: According to 11:32, Terah died at the age of 205; hence, Abram must have been 135 when he was called to leave Haran. However, 12:4 says that he was only 75 when he left Haran. The Source Critic informs us that this seeming contradiction is resolved if Genesis chapter 12 is of a different source from the genealogy of Genesis chapter 11.

The above need not be a contradiction at all. True enough, it was at the age of 70 that Terah began having children (Gen. 11:26), but does Abraham have to be the firstborn child simply because he is listed first?

Ask yourself, what weight does the names Nahor and Haran play in the Bible account? Now ask yourself, what about the name Abraham? He is considered to be the father and founder of three of the greatest religions on this planet: Judaism, Christianity, and Islam. He is the third most prominent person named in God's Word. This practice, that of placing the most prominent son first in a list of sons even though they are not the firstborn is followed elsewhere in God's Word with other prominent men of great faith, for example, Shem and Isaac. (Gen. 5:32; 11:10; 1 Chron. 1:28) Therefore, let us keep it simple. Genesis 11:26 does not say that Abram was the firstborn; it simply says that Terah began fathering children, and then it goes on to list his three sons, listing the most prominent one first. Thus, it is obvious that Terah fathered Abram at the age of 130. (Gen. 11:26, 32; 12:4) In addition, it is true that Sarah was Abram's half-sister, not by the same mother, but by having Terah as the same father. (Gen. 20:12) Therefore, it is Haran, who is the firstborn of Terah, whose daughter was old enough to marry Nahor, another of Terah's three sons.—Genesis 11:29.

Genesis 11:28 Was Abraham's family from Ur of the Chaldeans or Haran?

At Genesis 11:28, we are told that "Haran died in the presence of his father Terah in the land of his kindred, in Ur of the Chaldeans." However, Genesis 29:4 says of Jacob, who is enquiring about his relatives, "My brothers [polite address to shepherds], where do you come from?" They said, "We are from Haran."

There is no conflict here, as Abraham's descendants originated from Ur, but later migrated up to Haran, when Abram was called by God. (Gen. 11:31-12:1) There is nothing strange about referencing Ur, one's birthplace as their homeland, nor doing the same with the place one lived up until they were 75-years-old. Moreover, he refers to his brother's children as being part of his family.

Genesis 11:28 The term "Chaldeans" was not recognized until several hundred years after Moses. So, did Moses pen the term Chaldeans?

Genesis 11:28 Updated American Standard Version (UASV)

²⁸ Haran died in the presence of his father Terah in the land of his birth, in Ur **of the Chaldeans.** (Bold mind)

As this book has clearly demonstrated, Moses is the inspired author of the Pentateuch. At best, we can accept that it is likely that Joshua may have updated the text in Deuteronomy chapter 34, which speaks of Moses' death, and it is possible that Joshua may have made the reference in Numbers 12:3 that refer to Moses as being 'the humblest man on the face of the earth.'[131] In addition, we can accept that a later copyist [or even possibly Ezra, another inspired author] updated Genesis 11:28, 31 to read "of the Chaldeans," a name of a land and its inhabitants in the southern portion of Babylonia that *possibly* was not recognized as Chaldea until several hundred years after Moses.

The origin of the Chaldeans is uncertain but may well be in the west, or else branches of the family may have moved there (cf. Job 1:17). The general name for the area in the earliest period is unknown, since it was part of Sumer (*see* Shinar); so it cannot be argued that the qualification of Abraham's home city Ur as "of the Chaldeans" (Gen. 11:28, 31; 15:7; as later Neh. 9:7; cf. Acts 7:4) is necessarily a later insertion in the text.[132]

The same would hold true of a copyist updating Genesis 36:31, which reads: "Now these are the kings who reigned in the land of Edom before *any king reigned over the sons of Israel.*" Moses and Joshua were long gone for hundreds of years before Israel ever had a king over them.[133] The same would hold true again for Genesis 14:14, which reads: "When Abram heard that his relative had been taken captive, he led out his trained men, born in his house, three hundred and eighteen, and went in pursuit *as far as Dan.*" Dan was an area settled long after Moses death after the Israelites had conquered the Promise Land. This too is, of course, an update as well, making it contemporary to its readers.[134]

---

[131] For the possibility of Moses penning these words, see my comments in the first paragraph of section four.

[132] Geoffrey W. Bromiley, vol. 1, *The International Standard Bible Encyclopedia, Revised* (Wm. B. Eerdmans, 1988; 2002), 630.

[133] Actually, this statement could belong to Moses, even though there were no kings in Israel at this time. How? He would be aware that Jehovah had promised Abraham that he would be so great that kings would come out of him (Gen 17:6) and the preparation for such is mentioned at Deuteronomy 17:14-20.

[134] It should be noted that this author does not accept higher criticisms unending desire to find source(s) for a book, because they have dissected it to no end. While there are a few details that may have been updated by a copyist, or even the inspired writer Ezra (writer of Chronicles and the book that bears his name), this does not mean that we accept the update, if it is such, as the inspired material that was originally written, unless it was done by another inspired writer like Joshua, Ezra, or Nehemiah, or even possibly Jeremiah. It is also possible that it could be an explanatory addition.

"Reference to "Ur of the Chaldeans" (11:28) identifies the native land of Haran but not necessarily of Terah and his sons Abram and Nahor. In fact, the inclusion of this

167

Genesis 12:10-20; 20:1-18 How could God let Abraham prosper by lying?

The standard of God is that there is no lying, which Exodus 20:16 makes all too clear, "You shall not bear false witness against your neighbor." However, When Abram was forced to go down to Egypt, because of a famine, he "said to Sarai his wife, 'I know that you are a woman beautiful in appearance, and when the Egyptians see you, they will say, 'This is his wife.' Then they will kill me, but they will let you live. Say you are my sister, that it may go well with me because of you, and that my life may be spared for your sake.'" (12:12-13) In Genesis chapter 20, we find Abraham repeating this behavior, even though it did not bode well for him the first time. Did Abraham lie these two times, and if so, why does the entire account of Abraham present him as righteously walking with God, the epitome of faith?

First, it should be mentioned that Sarah was the half-sister and wife of Abraham. Therefore, in essence, he did not lie about their relationship; he simply withheld information that would have been used by the enemy, resulting in Abraham being possibly killed. It is true malicious lying is prohibited in the Bible, which is to say something that is not true in a conscious effort to deceive or hurt somebody that is deserving of the truth. However, the Bible has examples or cases where a person has withheld information from an enemy, who would have used that information to hurt or cause harm to the person or another. The Bible seems to suggest that we are not under obligation to divulge information to the enemy, as that would cause oneself harm. The American legal system allows something like this as well. It is called The Fifth Amendment (Amendment V), which guarantees you do not have to testify against yourself.

Jesus Christ counseled, "Do not give dogs what is holy, and do not throw your pearls before pigs, lest they trample them underfoot and turn to attack you." (Matt 7:6) Even Jesus himself, who is incapable of malicious lying, on occasion, withheld information from those who were

---

information for Haran may suggest the ancestral home was elsewhere (for this discussion see comments on 12:1). "Ur of the Chaldeans" occurs three times in Genesis (11:28, 31; 15:7) and once elsewhere (Neh 9:7). Stephen identified the place of God's revelation to Abram as "Mesopotamia" from which he departed: "So he left the land of the Chaldeans and settled in Haran" (Acts 7:3-4). The "land [chōra] of the Chaldeans" rather than "Ur of the Chaldeans" is the Septuagint translation, as reflected in Stephen's sermon, which can be explained as either a textual slip due to the prior phrase "land of his birth" or the ancient translator's uncertainty about the identity of the site. J. W. Wevers proposes that due to the apposition of "land of his birth," the translator interpreted "Ur" as a region." K. A. Mathews, *Genesis 11:27–50:26*, vol. 1B, The New American Commentary (Nashville: Broadman & Holman Publishers, 2005), 99–100.

not worthy of it, and would have only used it to hurt him. (Matt. 15:1-6; 21:23-27; John 7:3-10) We see this same principle under way with Abraham, Isaac, Rehab, and Elish, as all pointed in the wrong direction or withheld all the facts from the enemies or non-worshipers.—Genesis 12:10-19; chap 20; 26:1-10; Joshua 2:1-6; James 2:25; 2Ki 6:11-23.

Genesis 13:5-11 Was Lot acting Selfish or Selfless in his choice of land?

Genesis 13:5-11 Updated American Standard Version (UASV)

⁵ And Lot, who went with Abram, also had flocks and herds and tents. ⁶ And the land could not support them while dwelling together, for their possessions were so great that they were not able to remain together. ⁷ And there was strife between the herdsmen of Abram's livestock and the herdsmen of Lot's livestock. At that time the Canaanites and the Perizzites were dwelling in the land.

⁸ Then Abram said to Lot, "Let there be no strife between you and me, and between your herdsmen and my herdsmen, for we are brothers. ⁹ Is not the whole land before you? Separate yourself from me. If you take the left hand, then I will go to the right, or if you take the right hand, then I will go to the left." ¹⁰ And Lot lifted up his eyes and saw that the Jordan Valley was well watered everywhere like the garden of Jehovah, like the land of Egypt, in the direction of Zoar. This was before Jehovah destroyed Sodom and Gomorrah. ¹¹ So Lot chose for himself all the plain of the Jordan, and Lot journeyed east. Thus they separated from each other.

We can see from this event and others in the life of Abraham that he certainly reflected the image of God. He would not allow a quarrel to continue between his herders and those of his nephew Lot. It was Abraham, who was the patriarch, who had the right to simply make a decision, who allowed Lot the first choice of the land he wanted. This was a selfless act on the part of Abraham.—Genesis 13:5-13.

Abraham and Lot stood up in the hill country of Bethel and Ai, which allowed them to see down into the Jordan Valley, as well as the area around Jericho. Even though the Dead Sea is nearby, the south end of the valley is described as "well watered everywhere like the garden of [Jehovah], like the land of Egypt." (13:10) This was the choice of Lot. Many commentators have said this was a selfish act of Lot. However, some factors need to be considered first, before we jump to that conclusion. **(1)** Why was Abraham or Lot never drawn to this area before now? If it is actually the preferred place, why were they not already occupying it? **(2)** This area was very hot and humid throughout the

169

summer, which would have been very uncomfortable for Abraham. **(3)** The hill country that they were in was more desirable all year-round. **(4)** Lot is the one that would have to pick up and move to the new area, adjusting to the new surroundings. **(5)** This allowed the elderly Abraham to stay where they had already chosen as being the best suited for human occupancy, avoiding the sweltering heat and humidity of the summer in the Jordan Valley. In other words, it is far more likely that Abraham was selfless in his gesture to let Lot go first, and Lot was just as selfless in taking the less desirable option. How did God view Lot? Well, he inspired Peter to pen,

2 Peter 2:7-8 Updated American Standard Version (UASV)

⁷ and if he rescued righteous Lot, greatly distressed by the sensual conduct of the irreverent[135] men ⁸ (for by what he saw and heard that righteous man, while living among them, felt his righteous soul tormented day after day by their lawless deeds),

Genesis 14:1-17 Can we trust the account of Abraham's defeat of the Mesopotamian kings, as being historically reliable?

Moses, in penning Genesis, presents the account as being historically true. However, the scholarship that has produced what is known as the Documentary Hypothesis, biblical criticism, says not only did Moses not even pen any of the first five books of the Bible, but that this account was written hundreds of years after him, and is completely fabricated.

It is true that we have very little archaeological evidence that can settle this as being a true historical account. What reason is offered to see it otherwise? Do we rightly dismiss an account because we have not found evidence of such? To do so, would be a serious indication of bias against the Bible, nothing more. We look at all the other writings of the Ancient Near East as evidence of historical events, but the manuscripts of the Old Testament are not viewed in the same light.

However, we do have indirect support from noted scholars H. Gunkel and W. F. Albright "In spite of our failure hitherto to fix the historical horizon of chapter 14, we may be certain that its contents are very ancient. There are several words and expressions found nowhere else in the Bible and are now known to belong to the second millennium [k.c.l. The names of the towns in Transjordania are also known to be very

---

[135] Gr *athesmos*; pertaining to refusing to be subjected to legal requirements—'lawless, unruly, not complying with law.' ... 'who was troubled by the licentious conduct of lawless people' 2 Pet 2:7.

ancient" (Alleman and Flack, Old Testament Commentary, Philadelphia: Fortress Press, 1954, 14). Therefore, we have no sound reasons for dismissing this for anything other than an authentic historical account of Abram defeating the Mesopotamian kings by way of the most high God.

Genesis 14:18-20 Who was Melchizedek?

Many have argued over just who Melchizedek was. Was he a real historical person, like Noah's son Shem? Was he an angel, or some superhuman being? Was he an appearance of Christ prior to his coming to earth as the Son of God? The Apostle Paul in the book of Hebrews, chapter 7, helps his readers to see that Melchizedek was a type of Christ, and Christ was a priest and kind in the manner of Melchizedek.

Melchizedek was a real historical person, who was born and died. However, the account can be used to highlight features of similarity by the greater Melchizedek, Jesus Christ. The Melchizedek account does not mention his mother and father, not his descendant, or the birth or death, it is simply left out. Accordingly, Melchizedek could aptly foreshadow Jesus Christ, who has an unending priesthood. Jesus had no predecessor or successor to his priesthood. Moreover, Jesus priesthood and Kingship are not the result of human ancestors, but by being appointed by Jehovah God.

Genesis 15:16 Did the Exodus take place in the fourth or in the sixth generation?

There seems to be a clear contradiction between what is said here in Genesis 15:16 about the Exodus coming in the "fourth generation," [(1) Levi, (2) Kohath, (3) Amram, and (4) Moses] while 1 Chronicles 2:1-9 and Matthew 1:3-4 have it has coming in the sixth generation [(1) Judah, (2)Perez, (3) Hezron, (4) Ram, (5) Amminadab, and (6) Nashon].

We have the term "generation" defined for us as being 100 years, since the "fourth generation" of verse 16 is equal to "four hundred years" as stated in verse 13. Therefore, the differences of the two are explained by the context. Genesis chapter 15 is referring to the amount of time that would pass, while 1 Chronicles is referring to the number of people involved in that same amount of time.

In addition, we remember that these 400 years is a part of the 430 years from the time the Abrahamic covenant started up unto the time of the Exodus. These 430 years is actually broken into two equal parts, 215 years before they entered Egypt and 215 years in Egypt before the Exodus. We can use just the tribe of Levi as our example, to calculate the 'four generations' after they had entered Egypt: (1) Levi [lived 137 years], (2) Kohath [lived 133 years], (3) Amram, and (4) Moses [lived 120 years].—Ex 6:16, 18, 20.

Genesis 15:17 Is not the phrase that the sun has gone down, or the sun has set contrary to science?

Conservative Christianity makes the claim that the Bible is accurate and fully inerrant in all that it says, including history, geography, and science. How can we make such claims when the statement at Genesis 15:17 and Genesis 19:23 are unscientific? The writers of the Bible are writing from a human perspective and were certainly not attempting to make a scientific claim. They were using observable language, just as we do today. On every newscast or newspaper across the United States, we still speak of the time the sun rises or sets. Even to use such an argument against the Bible shows the desperation on the part of the Bible critic.

Genesis 16:2 Was it appropriate for Sarai to offer her maidservant Hagar as a secondary wife (concubine) to Abram?

The custom in that time provided for the continuation of a family, by the husband taking a secondary wife or concubine, to compensate for his wife's barrenness. However, there were other families, who simply lived a polygamous life, and it had nothing to do with the need of an heir. The polygamous lifestyle goes back to the line of Cain. It became a custom, and even some worshipers of Jehovah took it up. (Gen. 4:17-19; 16:1-3; 29:21-28) However, the record is clear that Jehovah God intended one wife, monogamous marriage. There is nothing in Scripture to show that he ever abandoned that position. (Gen. 2:21, 22) Even the command is given to Noah and his family 'be fruitful and fill the earth,' was given to a family that all had one wife. (Gen. 7:7; 9:1; 2 Pet. 2:5) Moreover, Jesus very clearly clarified the one wife standard.—Matthew 19:4-8; 1 Timothy 3:2, 12.

Genesis 17:17-18; 18:9-15 How are we to Understand Abraham and Sarah's laughter at the angelic announcement of a son?

Both Abraham and Sarah laughed when the angel announced that, they were to have a son when Abraham was 100 years old, and Sarah was 90. (Gen. 18:16–21:7) We can note from the account that Abraham was **not** rebuked for his laughing, but Sarah was, which she even tried to deny. Therefore, there is no reason to see Abraham's laughter as nothing more than that of joy, for he was finally going to have a son with his beloved Sarah. However, Sarah's laughter was something more, as she saw this amazing prospect as humorous. In other words, the idea of having a child at the age of 90, when she had been barren all these years, struck her as funny. Maybe she was picturing her 90-year-old body being nine months pregnant and what she would have looked like. However, no one can rightfully look at the account, and come away with either Abraham or Sarah laughing because of contempt, disrespect or deliberate sarcasm as both are recorded as demonstrating faith in the promise God made.—Romans 4:18-22; Hebrews 11:1, 8-12.

Genesis 19:8 Why was Lot not condemned for offering his daughters to the Sodomites.

Genesis 19:8 Updated American Standard Version (UASV)

8 Now behold, I have two daughters who have not known[136] a man; please let me bring them out to you, and do to them as is good in your eyes;[137] only do nothing to these men, inasmuch as they have come under the shadow[138] of my roof."

In Chapter 19 of Genesis, we come to the event of where God sent two of His angels to visit Lot in Sodom. Showing the common hospitality of the Ancient Near Eastern family, Lot invited them to stay at his home. The evening certainly did not go as Lot had planned. The city surrounded the house, for the purpose of sexually assaulting the visitors. They stood outside demanding the visitors be brought out. Lot said, "I beg you, my brothers, do not act so wickedly. Behold, I have two daughters who have not known any man. Let me bring them out to you, and do to them as you please. Only do nothing to these men, for they have come under the shelter of my roof." But they said, ""Stand back!" And they said, "This fellow came to sojourn, and he has become the judge! Now we will deal worse with you than with them." Then they pressed hard against the man Lot and drew near to break the door down. But the men reached out their hands and brought Lot into the house with them and shut the door. And they struck with blindness the men who were at the entrance of the house, both small and great, so that they wore themselves out groping for the door.—Genesis 19:1-11.

---

[136] Hebrew idiom for *sexual intercourse* (See Gen 4:1) I.e. had intercourse

[137] I.e., *whatever you want*

[138] I.e., *under the shelter* (protection) *of my roof* (house)

This event has certainly caused quite a bit of confusion, as all of us ask ourselves, 'how on earth can we reconcile the fact that Lot offered his two daughters up, to circumstances in which they would surely be raped, in place of two total strangers?' Lot seems to be a coward, trying to save himself. Even more confusing, is how God would inspire the apostle Peter to pen these words: "and if he rescued righteous Lot, greatly distressed by the sensual conduct of the wicked (for as that righteous man lived among them day after day, he was tormenting his righteous soul over their lawless deeds that he saw and heard)." (2 Pet. 2:7-8) Did God approve of the behavior that appears so hideous to our modern-day minds?

We need to keep in mind that we are viewing the account through a modern-day mind, and this will cause us to misunderstand the account. In addition, we need to appreciate that, the Bible itself does not condone or condemn what actions Lot took that night. Moreover, it does not make us aware of what he may have been thinking and feeling, or what moved him to take the course he did.

We are not operating blindly though; we can infer some things from this account and other parts of the Bible. First, we know that Lot was no coward. There is no doubt that Lot found himself in what seemed like an impossible situation. We need to understand exactly what Lot meant by "for they have come under the shelter of my roof." We can understand that Lot would be moved to protect his visitors. However, just how far would he go? According to the Ancient Near East, it was a host's obligation to protect the guests in his home, defending them even to the point of death if necessary. Lot was certainly prepared to do that. In addition, Jewish historian Josephus reports that the Sodomites were "unjust towards men, and impious towards God ... They hated strangers, and abused themselves with Sodomitical practices." This is evidence that Lot was not a coward, as he went *out* to talk with this unreasonable mob, shutting the door behind him.—Genesis 19:6.

However, there is more to what is meant by 'one coming under the shelter of one's roof.' This will help us understand a small facet of why Lot would offer his daughters up, in place of two strangers. The Bible critics assume the worst, but let us try to reason out other possibilities. We know that Lot was a "righteous man," by the inspired words of Peter, which is, in essence, God's view of Lot. A righteous man would be a man of faith. Lot was the nephew of Abraham, and was traveling with him and Sarah up unto this point. He was able to see Jehovah act in behalf of Sarah firsthand. The powerful Pharaoh of Egypt took Sarah because of her great beauty. Jehovah God acted on behalf of her and Abraham before Pharaoh could violate Sarah. (Gen. 12:11-20) It is entirely reasonable that he had faith that Jehovah would do the same for his daughters. In fact, is that not what happened? The angels of Jehovah stepped in, and kept Lot and his daughters safe.

Another possibility was that Lot was trying to buy time. He knew the men were after the angels for homosexual purposes, and they would likely not find his daughters as an acceptable substitute. (Jude 7) In addition, these young women were engaged to two men in the city, and there is the possibility that this offer would cause a division among those men's households and the rest of the city. (Gen. 19:14) It is the old 'divide and conquer' approach.

Genesis 19:30-38 Did God condone the incest of Lot with his two daughters?

Genesis 19:30-38 Updated American Standard Version (UASV)

Lot and His Daughters

³⁰ Lot went up from Zoar, and stayed in the mountains, and his two daughters with him; for he was afraid to dwell in Zoar; and he dwelt in a cave, he and his two daughters. ³¹ And the firstborn said to the younger, "Our father is old, and there is not a man on earth to come in to us after the manner of all the earth. ³² Come, let us make our father drink wine, and we will lie with him, that we may preserve seed from our father."¹³⁹ ³³ So they made their father drink wine that night, and the firstborn went in and lay with her father; and he did not know when she lay down or when she arose. ³⁴ On the following day, the firstborn said to the younger, "Behold, I lay last night with my father; let us make him drink wine tonight also; then you go in and lie with him, that we may preserve seed from our father."¹⁴⁰ ³⁵ So they made their father drink wine that night also, and the younger arose and lay with him; and he did not know when she lay down or when she arose. ³⁶ Thus both the daughters of Lot were with child by their father. ³⁷ The firstborn bore a son, and called his name Moab; he is the father of the Moabites to this day. ³⁸ And the younger, she also bore a son, and called his name Ben-ammi; he is the father of the sons of Ammon to this day.

We must take a moment and look at the historical setting while looking at the rest of God's Word. Lot lost his wife in the destruction of Sodom and Gomorrah, his daughters surviving. They fled to Zoar, but they soon felt unsafe and moved on to a cave. (Gen. 19:30) It is at this time the older daughter said to the younger: "Our father is old, and there is not a man on earth to come in to us after the manner of all the earth.

---

¹³⁹ I.e., *preserve offspring from our father.*
¹⁴⁰ i.e., *preserve offspring from our father.*

Come, let us make our father drink wine, and we will lie with him, that we may preserve offspring from our father."—Gen. 19:31, 32.

One indicator that Lot would have not supported incest is the fact they plotted to get him intoxicated, knowing if he were sober, he would have rejected such an idea. We must realize the mindset of the daughters, knowing that there was no way to continue the family line. Being in the land of Canaan, with no family, it meant the end of their family name. Thus, living among the Sodomites and their debased way of thinking had influenced them to the point that they so easily came up with such a scheme. Considering all of this, we must ask, 'what the value of adding this account?'

It certainly was not added for its sexual content, or to justify incest. The sons that would be born to the daughters, and therefore, related to Abraham, would become the Moabites and Ammonites (Gen. 11:27), who would have historical dealings with the Israelites centuries later. As you know, the Israelites are the sons of Israel (Jacob), Abraham's grandson. This helps us to understand later accounts, like why the Israelites never trespassed on the land of Moab and Ammon, when they were taking over the land east of the Jordan.—Deuteronomy 2:9, 18, 19, 37.

What we have in Genesis, chapter 19 is the historical facts, for laying a foundation for events that would span about 3,000 years of Israelite history. Thus, there was no reason to include an approval or disapproval; it was simply an historical account. However, the Bible is not silent on drunkenness or incest. (Pro. 20:1; 23:20, 21, 29-35; 1 Cor. 6:9, 10; Lev. 18:6, 7, 29) The Bible critic will argue that the daughters lived hundreds of years before the Mosaic Law, so they were not under it. While this is true, Paul lets us know that God gave us an internal conscience that convicts us, or excuses us. This must have been the case with the daughters, why else get the father intoxicated? — Romans 2:14-15.

Why did God inspire Peter to call Lot a "righteous man"? This is certainly not because he condoned getting drunk, nor because he approved of the incest. However, we know that Lot is not perfect, and he was passed out during the incest. In addition, the Bible does not give us a historical picture of Lot as a drunkard. It is God, who is the reader of heart, who judged Lot as "righteous." Thus, we can surmise that most of his life was in walking with God. We could also see a very broken heart of a "righteous man" over the difficulty he found himself in, for the bad choices he made.

Instead of looking for contradictions, mistakes and evidence that the Bible is not inspired, the Lot account only reinforces our belief that the Bible is a book of truth. Jehovah God does not move his authors to cover up the mistakes of his prominent people, like that of secular history. Instead, he inspires the recounting of accurate and honest historical information, as background material, helping us, so we can better understand future events in His Word.

Genesis 21:8-10 How are we to understand Ishmael's mocking Isaac?

We should not view Ishmael, who was about nineteen years old, with Isaac being but a toddler, as simply playing with a child. It was far more, as the next verse implies, it could have been about the heirship. Paul, using allegory spoke of this event, showing that this was the beginning of persecution, not simple mistreatment. (Gal. 4:22-31)

The word in our passage (*mĕṣaḥēq, piel*), however, usually conveys a harmful nuance, and Sarah's stern and swift reaction agrees that some untoward behavior occurred. Exactly what Sarah witnessed is unstated. That Ishmael publicly ridiculed the name of the toddler or the celebratory events surrounding his birth fits well the negative nuance of the term and the obvious wordplay on the name "Isaac." The apostle Paul, in reviving this historical memory (Gal 4:29), assumed the passage portrayed harmful behavior ("persecuted the son [Isaac]").

Expulsion of the slave and her son for teasing the child raises the question of the appropriateness of Sarah's reaction, especially if the Hebrew should be interpreted as mere children's play. That Sarah or Abraham was not always above inexcusable behavior is transparent from earlier episodes, but here the verse nuances the action of Ishmael as hostile. We have already noted the negative meaning of the prevalent use of *mĕṣaḥēq*. (Matthews 2001, 269)

Genesis 21:32, 34 Who were the Philistines mentioned here in Genesis?

Here we have the Philistines in this area about 1900 B.C.E., while the earliest mention of the Philistines by the Palestinians and Egyptians is around 1200 B.C.E., some 700 years earlier. Did Moses get it wrong? At this point, we do not know when this ancient sea people journeyed from Crete to the part of Canaan that came to be called Philistia, the southwestern coastline between Joppa and Gaza. Therefore, if a Bible critic were to bring this up, it is a fallacy known as arguing from silence, which is a conclusion based on the silence of the opponent, failing to give evidence.

The Bible critics have a track record of doing such, drawing conclusions, because we lack historical evidence that such existed. They did this with the cities of Sodom and Gomorrah, saying that they were not historical. Then, there was the discovery of the Ebla tablet, by Italian archaeologist Paolo Matthiae and his team in 1974–75, removing the charge that Sodom and Gomorrah were myths. The Ebla tablets referred to both cities. Therefore, in time, we might have a similar discovery for the Philistines that dates back to the time of Abraham.

However, even if that does not prove to be the case, we have discovered more than enough to establish so much in the Bible, and have quieted the critics many times, so it is not always necessary to have a discovery. If the critic has raised issues dozens of times, and historical discoveries have debunked their criticisms repeatedly, why is there the need to continue listening them? Nor should we feel pressured to answer their argument from silence, as no evidence for something at a particular time, does not equate that the something did not exist at that time. Therefore, we have enough discoveries to support the trustworthiness of both the Old and New Testament many times over, so their argument from ignorance is just that, ignorant.

Genesis 22:2 Why did God tell Abraham to sacrifice his son when God condemned human sacrifice in Leviticus 18 and 20?

Leviticus 18:21 and 20:2 give us God's moral standards as to human sacrifice. It is specifically condemned.

Leviticus 18:21 Updated American Standard Version (UASV)

[21] You shall not give any of your offspring to offer them[141] to Molech, and so profane the name of your God: I am Jehovah.

Leviticus 20:2 Updated American Standard Version (UASV)

[2] "You shall also say to the sons of Israel, 'Any man from the sons of Israel or from the aliens sojourning in Israel who gives any of his offspring to Molech, shall surely be put to death; the people of the land shall stone him with stones.'

---

[141] Lit *cause to pass over*; *allow the passing through*; i.e. children devoted to or sacrifices in the fire to Molech

First, it should be kept in mind that Jehovah had no intention from the beginning of having Abraham offer up Isaac. (22:12) This was a great test as to Abraham's faith.

Genesis 22:12 Updated American Standard Version (UASV)

¹² He said, "Do not lay your hand on the boy or do anything to him, for now I know that you fear God,¹⁴² seeing you have not withheld your son, your only son, from me."

God was not after a sacrifice, but an evident demonstration of Abraham's faith, which was likely more for Abraham than for God. Abraham's actions confirmed God's confidence in him. By his actions, Abraham demonstrated beyond question that his original faith in God was beyond question, and is still genuine, as he was to become the father to a great nation. In addition, Jehovah is the God of the living, not the dead. Even though a person may lose their life, if they are in God's favor, to him they are not dead, but awaiting a resurrection.

Hebrews 11:17-19 Updated American Standard Version (UASV)

¹⁷ By faith Abraham, when he was tested, offered up¹⁴³ Isaac, and he who had received the promises was offering up¹⁴⁴ his only begotten son, ¹⁸ of whom it was said, "In Isaac your seed¹⁴⁵ shall be called," ¹⁹ having reasoned that God was able even to raise him from the dead, from which, figuratively speaking,¹⁴⁶ he did receive him back.

It is inferred in the account that Abraham must have believed that, even if he did offer Isaac, it was within Jehovah's power to bring him back. Take not of his comments before heading off to complete his task.

---

¹⁴² I.e. God-fearing (not dreadful fear), reverential fear of displeasing God out of ones love for God.

¹⁴³ An interpretive translation could read, "as good as offered up Isaac." The Greek verb here (*prosenenochen*) translated "offered up" is in the perfect tense, where the writer describes "a completed verbal action that occurred in the past but which produced a state of being or a result that exists in the present (in relation to the writer). The emphasis of the perfect is not the past action so much as it is as such but the present 'state of affairs' resulting from the past action." (GMSDT) Dods and Moffatt take the perfect tense to refer only to a past act with no emphasis being suggested by the author. (Dods, "Hebrews," 358; Moffatt, Hebrews, 176.)

¹⁴⁴ The Greek verb here (*prospheren*) translated "was offering up" is in the imperfect tense, "where the writer portrays an action in process or a state of being that is occurring in the past with no assessment of the action's completion." (GMSDT) Therefore, this rendering is in harmony with what actually happened.

¹⁴⁵ Or *descendants*; *offspring*

¹⁴⁶ Lit *in a parable*; Gr *enparabolei*

Genesis 22:5 Updated American Standard Version (UASV)

⁵ And Abraham said to his servants, "You stay here with the donkey, and I and the boy will go up there. We will worship, then **we will return to you.**"

Genesis 22:2 How could Isaac be Abraham's "only son" when he already had Ishmael?

Ishmael was born first, but to a concubine. He was not the heir to the inheritance, as Jehovah can choose who he wishes. We will see this with Solomon as well. Moreover, 'only son' can be an equivalent to a 'beloved son.'

Genesis 23 Who were the Hittites, since some archaeology does not have their kingdom until about 400 years later?

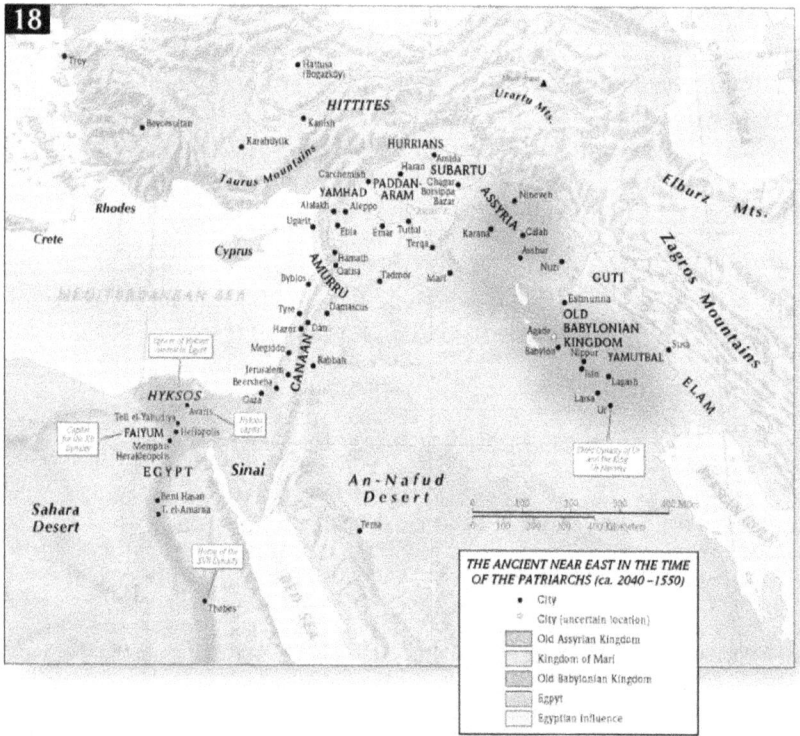

THE ANCIENT NEAR EAST IN THE TIME OF THE PATRIARCHS (ca. 2040 – 1550)

• City
◦ City (uncertain location)
▢ Old Assyrian Kingdom
▢ Kingdom of Mari
▢ Old Babylonian Kingdom
▢ Egypt
▢ Egyptian Influence

The Bible discloses that the Hittites were the offspring of Noah's great-grandson Heth. Heth was a son of Canaan and a grandson of Ham. Therefore, the Hittites were Canaanites.—Genesis 10:1, 6, 15.

Even prior to Abraham's sojourn into Canaan in 1943 C.C.E., the Hittites were well set up long enough before and sufficiently successful there. The Hittites were acknowledged to have lived in the mountainous areas of Palestine, more precisely in Hebron and its vicinity. (Gen. 15:18-20; 23:2-20) Hundreds of years later they were still to be found inhabiting mountainous areas. However, the range of their region is not exactly designated in the Bible.—Num. 13:29; Josh. 11:3.

Of the Canaanites, apparently, only the Hittites sustained a reputation and power as a nation for a significant time after the Israelite overthrow of the land. (1 Ki. 10:29) They are talked about in the Scriptures as having kings and military power as late as the reign of King Jehoram of Israel (c. 917-905 B.C.E.). (2 Ki. 7:6) Nevertheless, the Syrian, Assyrian and Babylonian invasions of the land seemingly crushed their power.

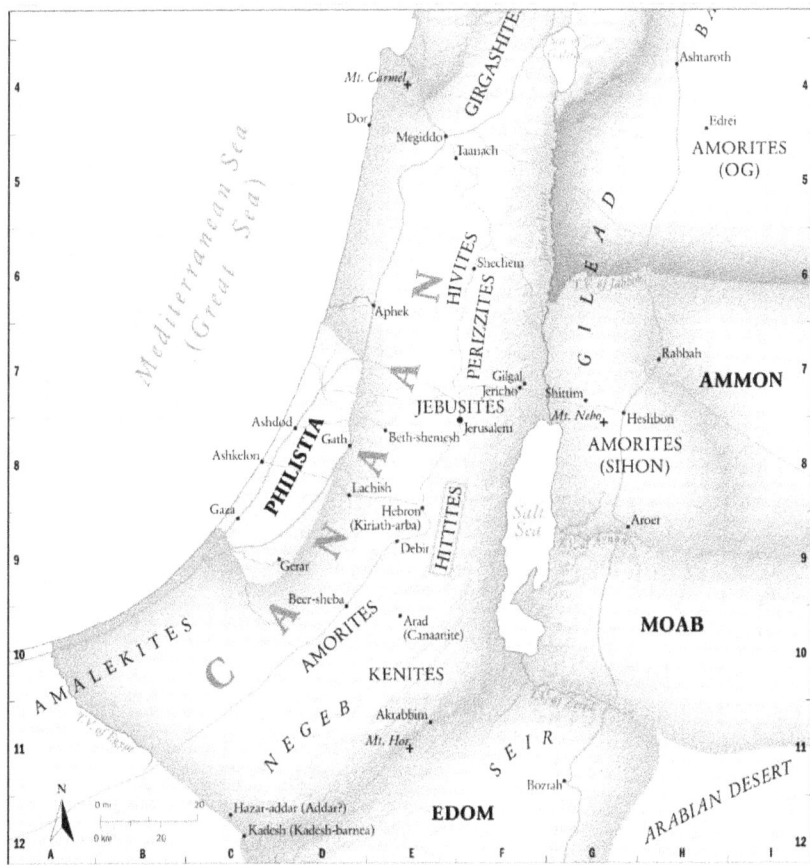

Genesis 23:3 Updated American Standard Version (UASV)

³ Then Abraham got up from before his dead and spoke to the sons of Heth, saying,

As you can see from Genesis 23, the Hittites, or the "sons of Heth" were in control of Hebron at the time of Sarah's death, about 1881 B.C.E. However, other scholars, have dated Sarah's death as earlier at about 2050 B.C.E.

Numbers 13:29 Updated American Standard Version (UASV)

²⁹ The Amalekites dwell in the land of the Negeb. The Hittites, the Jebusites, and the Amorites dwell in the hill country; and the Canaanites dwell by the sea, and along the Jordan."

In about 1473 B.C.E., the spies, who had secretly entered Canaan to investigate Centuries later, about 1473 B.C.E., the Hittites were still to be found inhabiting mountainous regions of Canaan, per the fearful report of the twelve spies when they returned from their expedition to Canaan.

Here is where the Bible difficulty comes in, as you have secular records that place the Hittite "old Kingdom" power in In Anatolia (Modern Turkey) in Asia Minor, at Boghazkoy, previously called "Hattusha,"[147] their capital. Moreover, the records have their rise in power and prominence in the Near East not coming until about 1650–1400 B.C.E, by way of the reign of king **Mursilis I**, who overthrew the first Babylonian dynasty in 1595 B.C.E. It is for this reason that many modern scholars doubt the historicity of the Hittites in Canaan as early as the 2050 B.C.E., at the time of Sarah's death and burial. While we feel the death of Sarah should be dated, according to Bible chronology, some 70 years later in about 1881 B.C.E., this still would not satisfy the Bible critics.

In Anatolia (Modern Turkey) in Asia Minor, archaeologists at Boghazkoy, previously called "Hattusha", have discovered much recent archaeological evidence from cuneiform tablets. These refer to battles in Anatolia, between several Hittite territories from about 1950 to 1850 B.C.E.

Even prior to these battles, there were a people of non-Indo-Europeans called Hattians. These early people were obviously attacked by an enemy force, defeated conclusively, and took over the territory around 2300 to 2000 B.C.E. These Indo- European invaders assumed the name, Hatti. In Semitic languages, Hatti and Hitti would have been written the same because they only wrote the consonants, not the vowels. The reader, guided by the context, much as an English-speaking

---

[147] King Hattushili I is credited with founding the capital.

person fills in the vowels for such abbreviations as "bldg", supplied the vowel sounds. (building), "blvd." (boulevard), and "hgt." (height). While it may very well be true that the Old Hittite Kingdom (1650-1400 B.C.E.) did not reach its high point until the 16th century B.C.E., there is more than enough evidence to corroborate a Hittite presence in Hebron at the time of the death of Sarah, being substantial enough to have control over the area.

Genesis 25:1 Keturah is called Abraham's wife here, but at 1 Chronicles 1:32, she is referred to as his concubine.

There is no real contradiction here, it just seems that way to the English reader of the Bible. The Hebrew word *ishshah* means "woman" (literally, a female man) or "wife." Genesis 25:1 should be understood as "Abraham took another **woman**, whose name was Keturah." Therefore, there is no conflict with Genesis 25:6 or 1 Chronicles 1:32.

In addition, among the Hebrews a concubine held a position in the nature of a secondary wife and was on occasion spoken of as a wife. Even still, the Hebrew word *pilegesh* for concubine used in 1 Chronicles 1:32, you have the same word being used at Genesis 25:6, in reference to the mothers of all his sons aside from Isaac. Furthermore, the Hebrew word *vayoseph* at Genesis 25:1, which means "and adding" or "in addition to," is not to say the addition of another wife, because Sarah was dead. (Gen 24:67) Therefore, we are to understand that Abraham was taking or adding to his concubines, at best a secondary wife.

Genesis 25:1-2 How is it that Abraham can have children so easily here when he was unable for almost 100 years?

It is not that Abraham was past the age of being fertile. While it is true that he was over a hundred years old, he lived to be 175 years old. Since he was still closer to the preflood people that had lived for centuries, he likely was fertile longer than our generation of people today that only live 70-80 years of age. Even today, men who live into their 80's are fertile into their 60's.

Obviously, Sarah must have either been unable to have children when she was fertile, or God withheld children, because he wanted the seed to be born at a given moment. One must admit, with 100 years of trying, to then have Isaac, it must have been a joy beyond all comprehension, appreciation beyond the norm. We do know that while

Abraham was unable to impregnate Sarah for decades, it did not take long when Sarah gave Abraham Hagar as a concubine.

Genesis 25:8 It says Abraham 'died and was gathered to his people.' Is this speaking of life after death?

Who were his people? Abraham's father was Terah of the city of Ur of the Chaldeans; and Genesis chapter eleven lists the forefathers of Abraham all the way back, to Shem, through nine generations, Noah's son. Most who do not delve into Bible genealogy are not aware that Noah lived up unto just two years before the birth of Abraham. Shem, on the other hand, lived 150 years into Abraham's life, dying a mere 25 years before Abraham. These forefathers, are the 'people to whom Abraham was gathered' in death. Abraham went in peace at death. What, then, does this mean? It means that Abraham joined his forefathers in death, and both Isaac and Jacob would follow him. Abraham slept with his forefathers in death, awaiting a future resurrection by Christ. (Compare 1 Ki 2:10, ESV)

Genesis 25:31-33 Did Jacob acquire the birthright through deception, and was God fine with this?

Genesis 25:31-33 Updated American Standard Version (UASV)

³¹ Jacob said, "Sell me your birthright today." ³² Esau said, "I am about to die; of what use is a birthright to me?" ³³ And Jacob said, "Swear to me today." So he swore to him and **sold his birthright to Jacob**.

When we go to chapter 37 of Genesis, we find that Jacob used a ruse of impersonating Esau to deceive his father Isaac in giving him the birthright. Was it proper for Jacob to impersonate Esau? There is no discrepancy here, as Jacob bought the birthright outright, but had to use deception to get it, as Esau was certainly not going to stick to his word.

If you read the full account, there is no doubt that Jacob had legal right to the blessing. Before the birth of Esau and Jacob, Jehovah had said to Rebekah, "the older shall serve the younger." (Gen 25:23) We know that Esau despised his birthright, and it is for this reason that Jehovah loved Jacob but hated Esau.[148] Therefore, when Jacob had the opportunity to acquire the birthright that he dearly valued, but Esau despised for a bowl of stew, he purchased it.—Genesis 25:29-34.

---

[148] "love but hated' is a Hebrew idiom that means the person loved the one more than the other, it does not mean that they literally hated the other.

Just why Rebekah and Jacob took care of the matter in the way they did, we do not know, but that both of them was aware that the blessing rightfully belonged to Jacob. Therefore, Jacob did not spitefully give an inaccurate or deliberately false account of himself in order to get something that did not rightfully belong to him. The Bible does not show and disapproval what Rebekah and Jacob did. The result was that Jacob received the rightful blessing.

Genesis 26:33 Was it Abraham or Isaac that gave the name to Beersheba?

Shibah is a well that the servants of Isaac dug, or dug again, at Beersheba. That same day the well-produced water and Isaac called its name Shibah, which means "Oath or Seven" and refers to an oath or statement confirmed by seven. (Gen 26:31-33) It seems that Isaac used the name "Shibah" (*Shebah*), to preserve the name Beersheba, which his father Abraham had given the place. The fact that this is Abraham's son makes it far more likely that this is the same well previously dug by Abraham, simply dug again by the servants of Isaac, which is verified at Genesis 26:18.

Genesis 26:34; 36:2-3 Who were Esau's wives?

Genesis 26:34 Updated American Standard Version (UASV)

³⁴ When Esau was forty years old, he took Judith **[wife 1]** the daughter of Beeri the Hittite to be his wife, and Basemath **[wife 2, also named Adah]** the daughter of Elon the Hittite;

Genesis 36:2 Updated American Standard Version (UASV)

² Esau took his wives from the daughters of Canaan: Adah **[either the same person as Basemath or her sister]** the daughter of Elon the Hittite, and Oholibamah **[wife 3]** the daughter of Anah and the granddaughter of Zibeon the Hivite;

Genesis 28:8-9 Updated American Standard Version (UASV)

⁸ So Esau saw that the daughters of Canaan were displeasing in the eyes of his father Isaac; ⁹ Esau went to Ishmael and took as his wife, besides the wives he had, Mahalath **[wife 4]** the daughter of Ishmael, Abraham's son, the sister of Nebaioth.

Judith was perhaps not cited in the ancestries in Genesis 36 because she gave birth to no children.

Genesis 29:21-30 When was Rachel given as Jacob's wife?

Genesis 29:27 Updated American Standard Version (UASV)

²⁷ Complete the week of this one, and we will give you the other also for the service which you shall serve with me for another seven years."

Notice that Laban is informing Jacob that he must complete the bridal week for Leah, and then he would be given Rachel. However, the contract also stated that Jacob must work another seven years to receive Rachel. Therefore, when was Jacob to receive Rachel, at the end of bridal week of Leah, or after another seven years of work?

Jacob received Rachel after Leah's bridal week of seven days. Then he was obligated to work the additional seven years for Rachel. This is made evident by the fact Rachel's maid presented Jacob with children before that time was up, and this would only be the case if Rachel were his wife, and having trouble bearing children.

Genesis 31:20 Did Jacob deceive Laban? If so, why would God bless him?

We can start with the fact that the Hebrew word for "deceived" really means, "stole the heart of." This Hebrew idiom can be rendered either "Jacob deceived" or "Jacob outwitted." Jacob was a grown man, who fulfilled his contract with Laban and far beyond. He was not obligated to inform him of anything. He outwitted Laban, because he knew Laban would cause trouble if he informed him, he was fearful of what Laban might do.

Genesis 31:32 Did God bless Rachel, a person, who had just stolen the teraphim?

God would not bless Rachael for stealing or lying about the action of stealing the teraphim. We need not assume that because Laban did not discover the teraphim, that it was because Jehovah God had worked on behalf of Rachel not to get discovered (i.e., he blessed her). No, it is just a simple fact that she did not get caught because she was crafty in her actions. Jehovah did not step in to expose her, or help her.

Genesis 32:30 Can the face of God be seen?

We find the following from Scripture . . .

Exodus 33:20 Updated American Standard Version (UASV)

²⁰ But he said, "You cannot see my face, for no man can see me and live!"

John 1:18 Updated American Standard Version (UASV)

¹⁸ No one has seen God at any time; the only begotten god[149] who is in the bosom of the Father,[150] that one has made him fully known.

1 John 4:12 Updated American Standard Version (UASV)

¹² No one has seen God at any time; if we love one another, God remains in us and his love is perfected in us.

Exodus 33:23 Updated American Standard Version (UASV)

²³ Then I will take away my hand, and you shall see my back, but my face shall not be seen."

However, Scripture than informs us that . . .

Genesis 32:20 Updated American Standard Version (UASV)

²⁰ and you shall say, 'Behold, your servant Jacob also is behind us.'" For he said, "I will appease him with the present that goes before me. Then afterward I will see his face; perhaps he will accept me."

Deuteronomy 5:4 Updated American Standard Version (UASV)

⁴ Jehovah spoke face to face with you in the mountain, out of the fire,

The expression "face to face" may denote intimate association or communication, to speak with someone personally, directly, or intimately. As Norman L. Geisler points out, even a blind man is able to speak with someone "face to face." This expression points to the way in which Moses communicated with God, not what he saw. Moses never saw God's face literally. On the contrary, as the setting shows, God was speaking through an angelic representative to Moses in open, verbal communication (as opposed to visions or dreams), which gave the basis for such an expression. (Num. 12:6-8; Ex. 33:20; Ac 7:35, 38; Gal. 3:19; compare Gen. 32:24-30; Hos. 12:3-4.) What God allowed Moses to see

---

[149] John 1:18: "only-begotten god", P⁶⁶ℵ*BC*Lsyrʰᵐᵍ·ᵖ; **[V1]** "the only-begotten god," P⁷⁵ℵ¹33copᵇᵒ; **[V2]** "the only-begotten Son." AC³(Wˢ)ΘΨf1.¹³ MajVgSyrᶜ

[150] Or *at the Father's side*

was His passing glory. (Ex. 33:21-23) Keep in mind that an angelic representative for God could convey His messages in the same sense as a cell phone can transmit our words to another person on the other side of the planet.

Genesis 37:25–28, 36; 38:1; 39:1 Was Joseph sold to Ishmaelites or to Midianites?

Genesis 37:25–28 Updated American Standard Version (UASV)

[25] Then they sat down to eat bread. And looking up they saw a caravan of Ishmaelites coming from Gilead, with their camels bearing labdanum gum, balsam, and and myrrh, on their way to carry it down to Egypt. [26] Then Judah said to his brothers, "What profit is it if we kill our brother and conceal his blood? [27] Come, let us sell him to the Ishmaelites, and let not our hand be upon him, for he is our brother, our own flesh." And his brothers listened to him. [28] Then Midianite traders passed by. And they drew Joseph up and lifted him out of the pit, and sold Joseph to the Ishmaelites for twenty shekels of silver. They took Joseph to Egypt.

Genesis 37:36 Updated American Standard Version (UASV)

[36] Meanwhile the Midianites had sold him in Egypt to Potiphar, an officer of Pharaoh, the captain of the guard.

Genesis 38:1 Updated American Standard Version (UASV)

[38] It happened at that time that Judah went down from his brothers and turned aside to a certain Adullamite, whose name was Hirah.

Genesis 39:1 Updated American Standard Version (UASV)

[39] Now Joseph had been brought down to Egypt, and Potiphar, an officer of Pharaoh, the captain of the guard, an Egyptian, had bought him from the hand of the Ishmaelites who had brought him down there.

Discrepancy: In Genesis 37:25 the Ishmaelites are passing by at the opportune time mentioned in verses 26 and 27, with Judah suggesting that instead of killing Joseph they sell him to the Ishmaelites. Yet, verse 28 switches in midstride to the Midianites, as they drew Joseph from the pit, selling him to the Ishmaelites. In verse 36, the Medanites (likely a scribal error; almost every translation has Midianites, so we will accept that as so) are selling Joseph to Potiphar in Egypt. Yet, the discrepancy pushes the envelope even further, for Genesis 39:1 says, it was the Ishmaelites who delivered and sold Joseph to Potiphar in Egypt. Was Joseph sold to Ishmaelites or to Midianites? In addition, who delivered and sold Joseph to Potiphar in Egypt? It seems that the higher critics are bent on using ambiguous passages (obscure at first glance to the casual reader) to facilitate their Documentary Hypothesis. You might say that these discrepancies are fuel for the engine that drives their Documentary Hypothesis locomotive. E. A. Speiser writes:

> The narrative is broken up into two originally independent versions. One of these (J) used the name Israel, featured Judah as Joseph's protector, and identified the Ishmaelites as the traders who bought Joseph from his brothers. The other (E) spoke of Jacob as the father and named Reuben as Joseph's friend; the slave traders in that version were Midianites who discovered Joseph by accident and sold him in Egypt to Potiphar.[151]

For Speiser, it is time to slice up the text and divide it up between our alleged "J"-Text and "E"-Text writers. It is also hypothesized that our "R"-Redactor edits the two and slips in some additional information as well, suggesting that the Midianites are the ones who were actually passing by, selling Joseph later to the Ishmaelites. Thus, it would be the Ishmaelites, who would deliver and sell Joseph to Potiphar in Egypt. Yes, at first glimpse, this would appear to make it all well, but we still have a problem: Genesis 37:36 states that it was the Midianites who sold Joseph to Potiphar in Egypt.

Actually, when one looks below the surface reading, there is no discrepancy here at all. Ishmael (son of Hagar and Abraham) and Midian (son of Keturah and Abraham) were half-brothers. It is highly likely that there was intermarriage between the descendants of these two, allowing for an interchangeable use of the expression "Ishmaelites" and "Midianites." (Genesis 25:1–4; 37:25–28; 39:1) We see this in the days of Judge Gideon when Israel was being attacked, with both terms "Ishmaelites" and "Midianites" being used to describe the attackers. (Judges 8:24; 7:25; 8:22, 26) Alternatively, even still you could have an Ishmaelite caravan encompassing Midianite merchants that were passing by, with the Midianites brokering the deal and delivering Joseph from the pit to the Ishmaelite caravan, where Joseph would be under the Ishmaelites' custody even if the Midianites were *detaining* him. Once they arrived at Potiphar's place in Egypt, it would be the Midianites to broker the deal with Potiphar. Thus, it can be stated, either way, the Ishmaelites or the Midianites delivered and sold Joseph to Potiphar in Egypt.

151. E. A. Speiser, *Genesis,* Anchor Bible (Garden City, N.Y.: Doubleday, 1964), 293–4.

Genesis 46:4 Did Jehovah bring Jacob out of Egypt or did he die there?

Here in verse 4 of chapter 46 that he would go down with him to Egypt and that he would bring him back to the Promise Land one day. However, Gen 49:33 says,

Genesis 49:33 Updated American Standard Version (UASV)

³³ When Jacob finished instructing his sons he drew his feet up to the bed and breathed his last, and was gathered to his people.

You will note that it was a promise not to Jacob personally that he would be brought up out of Egypt, but to his generations to come. We come to this by way of verse 3 of chapter 46, which says, "Do not be afraid to go down to Egypt, for there **I will make you into a great nation.**" Moreover, in all likelihood, Jacob was brought out of Egypt when Joseph was brought back, but it was his body that was brought back.

Genesis 50:25 Updated American Standard Version (UASV)

²⁵ Then Joseph made the sons of Israel swear, saying, "God will surely visit you, and you shall carry up my bones from here."

Exodus 13:19 Updated American Standard Version (UASV)

¹⁹ Moses took the bones of Joseph with him, for Joseph had made the sons of Israel solemnly swear, saying, "God will surely visit you, and you shall carry my bones from here with you."

Another aspect could come after Jacob is resurrected, in which he could and likely will return to the land.

Genesis 49:5-7 How can Jacob pronounce a curse upon Levi here and yet Moses blessed Levi in Deuteronomy 33:8-11?

This curse is coming up Levi and his brother Simeon, because of their executing vengeance on the Hivites of Shechem. (Gen 34:1-31) Levi's punishment was that his descendants would be scattered in Israel. (Gen 49:7; Jos 21:41) However, this curse would eventually be turned into a blessing for the tribes of Israel. It ended up that the scattered Levites would serve as teachers.

Deuteronomy 33:10 Updated American Standard Version (UASV)

¹⁰ They shall teach Jacob your ordinances
  and Israel your law;
they shall put incense before you
  and whole burnt offerings on your altar.

Therefore, there is no contradiction here. Levi was Scattered as the prophecy stated, and that position enabled them to serve as Moses had proclaimed (Deut. 33:10-11), as teachers and priests to Israel, proving to be a blessing.

Genesis 49:10 Who or what is "Shiloh" in this verse?

Shiloh means "he whose it is; he to whom it belongs." In uttering a blessing upon **Judah**, the dying patriarch Jacob said: "The **scepter** shall not depart from **Judah**, nor the ruler's **staff** from between his feet, until tribute, comes to him; and to him shall be the obedience of the peoples." (Gen. 49:10) Starting with the rule of the **Judean** David, power to rule (the ruler's staff) and the right to rule (the scepter) were the properties of the tribe of Judah. This was to remain as such until the coming of Shiloh, signifying that the royal line of Judah would come to an end in Shiloh as the everlasting heir. In addition, before the overthrow of the kingdom of Judah, God specified to the last Judean king, Zedekiah, that rulership would be "until he comes, the one to whom judgment belongs, and I will give it to him." (Eze. 21:26, 27) This would evidently be Shiloh, as the name "he whose it is; he to whom it belongs."

In the centuries that followed, Jesus Christ is the only successor of David to whom kingship was promised. In advance of the birth of Jesus, the angel Gabriel said to Mary: "the Lord God will give to him the throne of his father David, and he will reign over the house of Jacob forever, and of his kingdom, there will be no end." (Lu 1:32, 33) Therefore, Shiloh must be Jesus Christ, "the Lion that is of the tribe of Judah."—Revelation 5:5; compare Isa 11:10; Romans 15:12.

APPENDIX A Defending Moses as Author of the Pentateuch

It was in the latter half of the nineteenth century that higher criticism began to be taken seriously. These critics rejected Moses as the writer of the Pentateuch, arguing instead that the accounts in Genesis, Exodus, Leviticus, Numbers, and Deuteronomy were based on four other sources [writers] written between the 10th and the 6th centuries B.C.E. To differentiate these sources one from the other, they are simply known as the "J," "E," "D," and "P" sources. The letters are the initial to the name of these alleged sources, also known as the Documentary Hypothesis.

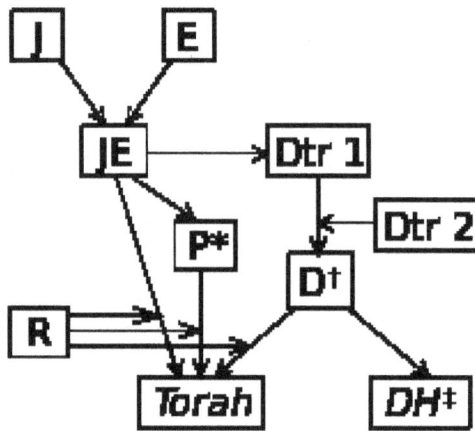

Image 1 Diagram of the Documentary Hypothesis.

*   includes most of Leviticus

†   includes most of Deuteronomy

‡   "Deuteronomic history": Joshua, Judges, 1 & 2 Samuel, 1 & 2 Kings – Wikipedia

Source Criticism, a sub-discipline of Higher Criticism, is an attempt by liberal Bible scholars to discover the original sources that the Bible writer(s) [not Moses] used to pen these five books. It should be noted that most scholars who engage in higher criticism start with liberal presuppositions. Dr. Gleason L. Archer, Jr., identifies many flaws in the reasoning of those who support the Documentary Hypothesis; however, this one flaw being quoted herein is indeed the most grievous and lays the foundation for other irrational reasoning in their thinking. Identifying their problem, Archer writes, "The Wellhausen school started with the pure assumption (which they have hardly bothered to demonstrate) that Israel's religion was of merely human origin like any other, and that it was to be explained as a mere product of evolution."[152] In other words, Wellhausen and those who followed him begin with the presupposition that God's Word is *not* that at all, the Word of God, but is the word of mere man, and then they reason **into** the Scripture not **out of** the Scriptures based on that premise. As to the effect, this has on God's Word and those who hold it as such; it is comparable to having a natural disaster wash the foundation right out from under our home.

Liberal Christianity says that Moses did not pen every word from Genesis through Deuteronomy. They conclude that this is nothing more than a tradition that originated in the times that the Jews returned from their exile in Babylon in 537 B.C.E. and the destruction of Jerusalem in 70 C.E. These source critics reason that there was and is a misunderstanding of Deuteronomy 31:9, which says that Moses "[wrote] this law, and delivered it unto the priests the sons of Levi, that bare the ark of the covenant of Jehovah, and unto all the elders of Israel." They argue that Deuteronomy only implies that Moses wrote the laws of Deuteronomy chapters 12–28; moreover, this was extended into a tradition that encompassed the belief that the entire Pentateuch was *not* written by Moses.

In addition, these source critics put forth that the language of Deuteronomy chapters 12–18, as well as the historical and theological context, places the writing and completion of these five books centuries after Moses died. According to these critics, this alleged tradition of Moses being the author of the first five books of our Bible was completely accepted as fact by the time Jesus Christ arrived on the scene in the first-century C.E. These critics further argue that Jesus, the Son of God, was also duped by this tradition and simply perpetuated it when he referred to "the book of Moses" (Mark 12:26), which to the Jews at that time counted Genesis, Exodus, Leviticus, Numbers, and Deuteronomy as a book by Moses. In addition, at John 17:23, Jesus spoke of "the law of Moses," which he and all others Jews had long held to be the Pentateuch. Thus, for the critic, Jesus simply handed this misunderstood tradition off to first-century Christianity.

We have read much in previous chapters thus far about these critical scholars, but it will not hurt to review, before delving into discrediting their hypothesis. How has such extreme thinking as this Documentary Hypothesis come down to us, going from being a hypothesis to being

---

[152] 152. Gleason L. Archer, A Survey of Old Testament Introduction (Moody Publishers, Chicago, 2007), 98.

accepted as *law* in secular universities and most seminaries? What is the relationship between a hypothesis, theory, and law? In the physical sciences, there are several steps before a description of a phenomenon becomes law.

(1) **Observation:** "I noticed that objects fall to the earth."

(2) **Hypothesis:** "I think something must be pulling these objects to the earth. Let me call it gravity."

(3) **Experimentation:** "Let me put this to the test by releasing different objects from that cliff. Umm, it seems that everything I let go falls. My hypothesis seems to be right."

(4) **Theory:** "I have noticed that every time I release an object, and wherever I do it, over the sidewalk, from the 32nd floor of that office building and even from the cruise ship—they fall to the earth as if pulled by something. It happens often enough to be called a theory."

(5) **Law:** "Well, this has consistently been occurring over the years. It must be absolutely true and therefore a Law."

Where does the "Documentary Hypothesis" fit into this scheme? Wellhausen *et al.* made certain **Observations** and then produced a **Hypothesis** to explain what they saw. I would argue that is as far as they made it in following the formula for the scientific method.

The Forefathers of Source Criticisms

Abraham Ibn Ezra (1089–1164) Ibn Ezra was, by far, the most famous Bible scholar of medieval times. True enough, he may have questioned the idea that Moses wrote the entire Torah; however, he chose not to do this in an outward way; he chose to be more subtle in presenting such an idea. For Ibn Ezra, several verses seemed not to have come from Moses, but one verse stood out above the others. Deuteronomy 1:1 reads: "These are the words that Moses spoke to all of Israel beyond the Jordan." The east side of the Jordan would be "this" side with the west side being the "other side." (Numbers 35:14; Joshua 22:4) The point of his contention here being the fact that Moses was never on the other side of the Jordan, the west side, with the Israelite nation. Therefore, the question begs to be asked, Why would Moses pen "beyond," a seeming reference to the west side? This will be answered soon enough.

Thomas Hobbes (1588–1679) writes, "It is therefore sufficiently evident that the five books of Moses were written after his time, though how long after it be not so manifest." Is Hobbes a friend or foe of Christianity? Like Francis Bacon before him, he deepened the crack in the acceptance of the Bible being a source of divine authority.[153]

Benedict Spinoza (1632–1677) writes, "It is thus clearer than the sun at noon the Pentateuch was not written by Moses but by someone who lived long after Moses." Spinoza lays the groundwork for higher criticism based on logical or reasonable deduction, believing that thought and actions should be governed by reason, deductive rationalism.[154] He writes that because "There are many passages in the Pentateuch which Moses could not have written, it follows that the belief that Moses was the author of the Pentateuch is ungrounded and irrational."[155] Moses was not the only Biblical author to lose his writership at the chopping block of Spinoza. "I pass on, then, to the prophetic books ... An examination of these assures me that the prophecies therein contained have been compiled from other books ... but are only such as were collected here and there, so that they are fragmentary." Daniel did not fare so well either, he is only credited with the last five chapters of his book. Spinoza presents the notion that the 39 books of the Hebrew Old Testament were set down by none other than the Pharisees. Moreover, the prophets spoke not by God, being inspired, but of their own accord. As to the apostles, Spinoza wrote, "The mode of expression and discourse adopted by [them] in the Epistles show very clearly that the latter are not written by revelation and divine command, but merely by the natural powers and judgment of the authors." Did Matthew, Mark, Luke, and John, fare any better? Hardly! Spinoza states: "It is scarcely credible that God can have designated to narrate the life of Christ four times over, and to communicate it thus to mankind."

Spinoza had no respect for those he deemed fools because of their belief in miracles. He writes, "Anyone who seeks for the true causes of miracles and strives to understand natural phenomena as an intelligent being, and not gaze upon them like a fool, is set down and denounced as an impious heretic by those, whom the masses adore as the interpreters of nature and the gods. Such a person knows that, with the removal of ignorance, the wonder which forms their only available means for proving and preserving their authority would vanish also. . . . A miracle, whether a contravention to, or beyond nature is a mere absurdity."[156]

---

[153] Garrett, Don, *The Cambridge companion to Spinoza* (Cambridge: Cambridge University Press, 1996), 389.
[154] Richard Elliot Friedman, *Who Wrote The Bible* (San Francisco: Harper Collins, 1997), 21.
[155] R. H. M. Elwes, *A Theologico-political Treatise, and a Political Treatise* (New York, NY: Cosimo Classics , 2005), 126.
[156] Norman L. Geisler, *Inerrancy* (Grand Rapids, MI: Zondervan, 1980), 318.

Such a dogmatic disbelief in miracles is a contributing factor to Spinoza being the father of modern-day higher criticism.

Richard Simon (1638–1712). This French Catholic priest accepted Moses as the author for most of the Pentateuch, but he is the first to notice repetition with certain portions that would come to be known as doublets.

- two different creation stories

- two stories of the Abrahamic covenant

- two stories where Abraham names his son, Isaac

- two stories where Abraham claims Sarah as his sister

- two stories of Jacob's journey to Haran

- two stories where God revealed himself to Jacob at Bethel

- two stories where God changes Jacob's name to Israel

- two stories of when Moses got water from a rock at Meribah

Jean Astruc (1684–1766) This French physician and professor of medicine would, by a rather naïve observation, get the Documentary Hypothesis underway. While Astruc never denied Mosaic writership, he had observed that there seemed to be two sources for Moses' penning the early chapters of Genesis: one that favored the title God (Elohim), and another that favored the personal name of God (Jehovah). This theory seemed to carry even more support by duplicate material, as Astruc viewed Genesis chapter one as one creation account and Genesis chapter two as another. It should be kept in mind that Astruc credited Moses as the writer, but was simply looking for what Moses may have drawn on in penning the Pentateuch.[157]

David Hume (1711–1776) was an eighteenth-century Scottish philosopher whose influence on the denial of divine authority, miracles, and prophecy has had a major impact that has reached down to the twenty-first century! Hume has three major pillars that hold up his refutation of divine authority. First, he writes, "A miracle is a violation of the laws of nature."[158] The laws of nature have been with man since his start. If a person falls from a high place, he will hit the ground. If a rock is dropped into the sea, it will sink. Each morning our sun comes over the horizon and each night it goes down, and so on. Without a doubt, there

---

[157] Norman L. Geisler and William E. Nix, *A General Introduction to the Bible*. Rev. and Expanded (Chicago, IL: Moody Press, c.1986, 1996), 156.
[158] David Hume, *An Enquiry Concerning Human Understanding* (Boston, MA: Digireads.com, 2006), 65.

are laws of nature that never fail to follow their purpose. Therefore, for Hume, there is nothing that would ever violate the laws of nature. This 'conclusive evidence,' Hume felt, "is as entire as any argument from experience" that there could never be miracles.

Hume's second pillar is based on his belief that humankind is gullible. Moreover, he reasons that the masses of 'religious persons' want to believe in miracles. In addition, there have been many who have lied about so-called miracles, which have been nothing but a sham. For his third pillar, Hume argues that miracles have occurred only in the time periods of ignorance; as the enlightenment of man grew the miraculous diminished. Hume reported, "Such prodigious events never happen in our days." Hume rejected the inspiration of Scripture on two grounds: (1) he denied the possibility of miracles and prophecy, and (2) he rejected the Bible's divine authority as a whole because, to him, it was based upon perception or feeling, rather than upon fact, nor could it be proved by observation and experiment. Thus, for Hume, the result is that the Bible "contains nothing but sophistry and illusion."[159] As we can see, Hume's conclusion is obvious: Because the Bible is, in fact, not inspired, it could never be a true source of knowledge that it claims, and it is certainly not God's Word for humankind.

Johann Gottfried Eichhorn (1752–1827) took Jean Astruc's conjectures beyond Genesis to other books of the Pentateuch, arguing that the Pentateuch contained three primary sources that were distinct by vocabulary, style, and theological features. He also borrowed the phrase "higher criticism" from Presbyterian minister and scientist Joseph Priestly, and he was the first to name these alleged sources "E" (for Elohim) and "J" for Jehovah.[160]

Karl Heinrich Graf (1815–1869), aside from Julius Wellhausen, was the person we look to most for the modern documentary hypothesis. For Graf the "J" source was the earliest, composed in the ninth century B.C.E.;[161] the "E" source was written shortly thereafter. The author of Deuteronomy wrote shortly before Josiah's clearing away false worship in the seventh century B.C.E., and finally, the "P" source was written in the sixth century after the exile.

In 1878, the German Bible critic **Julius Wellhausen (1844–1918),** writing in *Prolegomena zur Geschichte Israels (Prolegomena to the History*

---

[159] Ibid., 90.

[160] Norman L. Geisler and William E. Nix, *A General Introduction to the Bible. Rev. and Expanded* (Chicago, IL: Moody Press, c.1986, 1996), 157.

[161] B.C.E. means "before the Common Era," which is more accurate than B.C. ("before Christ"). C.E. denotes "Common Era," often called A.D., for anno Domini, meaning "in the year of our Lord."

of Israel), popularized the ideas of the above scholars that the first five books of the Bible, as well as Joshua, were written from the 9th century into the 5th century B.C.E., over a millennium [1,000 years] after the events described.[162]

The capital letter "J" is used to represent an alleged writer. In this case it stands for any place God's personal name, Jehovah, is used. It is argued that this author is perhaps a woman as it is the only one of their presented authors who is not a priest. (Harold Bloom, *The Book of "J"*) They date the portion set out to "J" to c.850 B.C.E. Some scholars place this author in the southern portion of the Promised Land, Judah.[163]

Another writer is put forth as "E," for it stands for the portion that has Jehovah's title Elohim, God. Most higher critics place this author c.750–700 B.C.E. Unlike "J," this author "E" is said to reside in the northern kingdom of Israel. As stated earlier, this author is reckoned a priest, with his lineage going back to Moses. It is also proffered that he bought this office. In addition, it is argued that an editor combined "J" and "E" after the destruction of Israel by the Assyrians but before the destruction of Jerusalem by the Babylonians, which they date to about 722 BC.E.[164]

These same critics hold out that the language and theological content of "D," Deuteronomy, is different from Genesis, Exodus, Leviticus, and Numbers. Thus they have another author. They argue that the priests living in the northern kingdom of Israel gathered "D" over several hundred years; however, it was not until much later that "D" was combined with the earlier works. It is also said that the "D" writer (source) was also behind Joshua, Judges, 1 and 2 Samuel and 1 and 2 Kings (Dtr). It is suggested strongly that, in fact, this is the book found in the temple by Hilkiah the high priest and given to King Josiah. (2 Kings 22:8) It is further put forth that J/E/D were fused together as one document in about 586 B.C.E.[165]

The source critics use the capital letter "P" for Priestly. This is because this portion of the Pentateuch usually relates to the priesthood. For instance, things like the sacrifices would be tagged as belonging to this author. Many scholars suggest that "P" was written before the destruction of Jerusalem, which they date at 586 B.C.E. Others put forth that it was written during the exile of seventy years, the Priest(s) composing this holy

---

[162] Ernest Nicholson, *The Pentateuch in the Twentieth Century: The Legacy of Julius Wellhausen* (New York: Oxford University Press, 1998), 36–47.

[163] Mark F. Rooker, *Leviticus: The New American Commentary* (Nashville: Broadman & Holman, 2001), 23.

[164] Ibid., 23.

[165] Ibid., 23.

portion for the people who would return from exile, while others say it was written after the exile, about 450 B.C.E. These liberal scholars find no consensus on when this supposed author "P" wrote this portion of the first five books. The critics tell us that the final form of J/E/D/P was composed into one document about 400 B.C.E.[166]

The capital "R" represents the editor(s) who put it together and may have altered some portions to facilitate their social-circumstances of their day. The "R" comes from the German word *Redakteur* (Redactor), which is an editor or reviser of a work.

With all the focus on Wellhausen and the impetus he has given to the Documentary Hypothesis, one would conclude that he had made an enormous, critical investigation of the text, which, in essence, moved him to cosign with his predecessors. If that is your conclusion, you will have to regroup, for it was simply a feeling that something was not quite right that moved Wellhausen to accept a system of understanding without any evidence whatsoever. In his book *Prolegomena to the History of Israel*, first published in 1878, Wellhausen helps his readers to appreciate just how he came about his expressed interest in the Documentary Hypothesis:

> In my early student days I was attracted by the stories of Saul and David, Ahab and Elijah; the discourses of Amos and Isaiah laid strong hold on me, and I read myself well into the prophetic and historical books of the Old Testament. Thanks to such aids as were accessible to me, I even considered that I understood them tolerably, but at the same time was troubled with a bad conscience, as if I were beginning with the roof instead of the foundation; for I had no thorough acquaintance with the Law, of which I was accustomed to be told that it was the basis and postulate of the whole literature. At last I took courage and made my way through Exodus, Leviticus, Numbers, and even through Knobel's Commentary to these books. But it was in vain that I looked for the light which was to be shed from this source on the historical and prophetical books. On the contrary, my enjoyment of the latter was marred by the Law; it did not bring them any nearer me, but intruded itself uneasily, like a ghost that makes a noise indeed, but is not visible and really effects nothing. Even where there were points of contact between it and them, differences also made themselves felt, and I found it impossible to give a candid decision in favour of the priority of the Law. Dimly I began to perceive that throughout there was between them all the difference that separates two

---

[166] Ibid., 23–24.

wholly distinct worlds. Yet, so far from attaining clear conceptions, I only fell into deeper confusion, which was worse confounded by the explanations of Ewald in the second volume of history of Israel. At last, in the course of a casual visit in Göttingen in the summer of 1867, I learned through Ritschl that Karl Heinrich Graf placed the law later than the Prophets, and, almost without knowing his reasons for the hypothesis, I was prepared to accept it; I readily acknowledged to myself the possibility of understanding Hebrew antiquity without the book of the Torah.[167]

Martin Noth (1902–1968) A liberal twentieth-century German scholar who specialized in the pre-Exilic history of the Jewish people. Noth presented what he called the "Deuteronomic Historian." He argued that the language and theological outlook of Joshua, Judges, 1 and 2 Samuel and 1 and 2 Kings was the same as the book of Deuteronomy. Noth believed this writer lived during the exile because of a reference from 2 Kings to the exile. Modern critics, however, believed this writer lived before the exile, with 2 Kings 25:27 being a later addition.

Frank M. Cross, Jr., Hebrew and Biblical scholar' muddies the water even more with his proposition that there was not one Deuteronomistic history, but two. The first he proposed to be written during the reign of the Judean King Josiah to aid him in cleaning up the false worship going on within Judah. After the destruction of Jerusalem, Cross said the same writer or possibly another goes back to edit this work, to add in the destruction of Jerusalem and the exile to Babylon.

Redaction Criticism

I briefly address the Redaction Theory here because of its relationship to the Documentary Hypothesis. As stated above in our alphabet soup of alleged authors ("J," "E," "D," "P," and "R"), a redactor is an editor or reviser of a work. Redaction Criticism is another form of Biblical criticism that intends to investigate the Scriptures and draw conclusions concerning their authorship, historicity, and time of writing. This form of criticism as well as the others has really done nothing more than tear down God's Word. R. E. Friedman, the Documentary Hypothesis' biggest advocate, asserts that the "J" document was composed between 922–722 B.C.E. in the southern kingdom of Judah, while the northern kingdom of Israel was composing the "E" document during these same years. Friedman contends that sometime thereafter a compiler of history put these two sources together, resulting in "J/E," with the compiler being known as "RJE."

---

[167] Julius Wellhausen, *Prolegomena to the History of Israel* (1878), 3–4

Friedman states that shortly thereafter, the priesthood in Jerusalem put out yet another document, known today as "P," this being another story to be added to the above "J/E." Going back to their authors for the first five books of the Bible, Friedman and these critics claim a redactor, or editor put the whole Pentateuch together using "D," "P," and the combination of "J/E." For them this editor (Deuteronomist) used the written sources he had available to make his additions for dealing with the social conditions of his day. They claim this editor's express purpose was to alter Scripture to bring comfort and hope to those who were in exile in Babylon. Wellhausen's theories, with some adjustments, have spread like a contagious disease, until they have consumed the body of Christendom. However, the real question is, Do these higher critics have any serious evidence to overturn thousands of years of belief by three major religious groups (Jews, Christians, and Muslims) that the Pentateuch was written by Moses?

What these critics have are pebbles, each representing minute inferences and implications [circumstantial evidence at best] that they place on one side of a scale. These are weighed out against the conservative evidence of Moses' authorship of the Pentateuch. As unsuspecting readers work their way through the books and articles written by these critics, the scales seem to be tilted all to one side, as if there were no evidence for the other side. Thus, like a jury, many uninformed readers; conclude that there is no alternative but to accept the idea that there are multiple authors for the Pentateuch instead of Moses, who is traditionally held to be the sole author.

Just what impact has the Documentary Hypothesis had on academia? Let us allow R. Rendtorf, professor Emeritus of the University of Heidelberg, to answer:

> Current international study of the Pentateuch presents at first glance a picture of complete unanimity. The overwhelming majority of scholars in almost all countries where scholarly study of Old Testament is pursued, take the documentary hypothesis as the virtually uncontested point of departure for their work; and their interest in the most precise understanding of the nature and theological purposes of the individual written sources seems undisturbed.[168]

Let us take a moment to look at many of these pebbles and see which side of the scale they are to be placed on. As stated at the outset,

---

[168] R. Rendtorff, "The Problem of the Process of Transmission in the Pentateuch," *JSOT* (1990): 101.

we will address the major arguments as a case against the whole. Some of these pebbles are major obstacles for honest-hearted Christians.

Arguments of Higher Critics for the Documentary Hypothesis

We will address four areas of argumentation from the higher critics: (1) the divine names, (2) discrepancies, (3) repetition, known as "doublets," and (4) differences in language and style. We will give at least one example of each and address at least one example under the evidence for Moses' writership.

Divine Names

The higher critics argue that every Bible verse that contains the Hebrew word for God, ('Elohim'), set off by itself has its own writer, designated by the capital "E" ("Elohist"). On the other hand, any verse that contains the Tetragrammaton, (Jehovah, Yahweh), God's personal name, is attributed to yet another writer, "J" ("Jawist"). (Cassuto, 18-21) Let us see how they explain this. The critics argue that "God" ('Elohim') is restricted in use exclusively in the first chapter of Genesis (1:1–31) in relation to God's creation activity, and that starting in Genesis 2:4 through the end of the second chapter we find God's personal name.

R. E. Friedman speaks of a discovery by three men: "One was a minister, one was a physician, and one was a professor. The discovery that they made ultimately came down to the combination of two pieces of evidence: doublets and the names of God. They saw that there were apparently two versions each of a large number of Biblical stories: two accounts of the creation, two accounts each of several stories about the patriarchs Abraham and Jacob, and so on. Then, they noticed that, quite often, one of the two versions of a story would refer to God by one name and the other version would refer to God by a different name." (R. E. Friedman, 50)

Different settings, however, require different uses. This principle holds true throughout the whole of the entire Old Testament. Moses may choose to use ('Elohim') in a setting in which he wants to show a particular quality clearly, like power, creative activity, and so on. On the other hand, Moses may choose to use God's personal name (Jehovah, Yahweh) when the setting begs for that personal relationship between the Father and his children, the Israelites, or even more personable, a one-on-one conversation between Jehovah God and a faithful servant.

The Divine Names: The weakness of claiming multiple authors because of the different names used for God is quite evident when we look at just one small portion of the book of Genesis in the *American Standard Version* (1901). God is called "God Most High," "possessor (or maker) of heaven and earth," "O Lord Jehovah," "a God that seeth," "God Almighty," "God," "[the] God,"[169] and "the Judge of all the earth." (Genesis 14:18, 19; 15:2; 16:13; 17:1, 3; 18:25) It is difficult to believe that different authors wrote these verses. Moreover, let us look at Genesis 28:13, which says, "And, behold, Jehovah stood above it, and said, I am Jehovah, the God ["Elohim"] of Abraham thy father, and the God of Isaac: the land whereon thou liest, to thee will I give it, and to thy seed." Another scripture, Psalm 47:5, says, "God is gone up with a shout, Jehovah with the sound of a trumpet."[170] In applying their documentary analysis, we would have to accept the idea that two authors worked together on each of these two verses.

Many conservative scholars have come to realize that in a narrative format one will often find a ruler being referred to not only by name but also by a title, such as "king." M. H. Segal observes: "Just as those interchanges of human proper names and their respective appellative common nouns cannot by any stretch of the imagination be ascribed to a change of author or source of document, so also the corresponding interchanges of the divine names in the Pentateuch must not be attributed to such a literary cause."[171] If one were to look up "Adolf Hitler" using *Academic American Encyclopedia*, within three paragraphs he will find the terms "Führer," "Adolf Hitler," and simply "Hitler." Who is so bold as to suggest that there are three different authors for these three paragraphs?

Dr. John J. Davis[172] helps us to appreciate that there is "no other religious document from the ancient Near East [that] was compiled in such a manner; a documentary analysis of the Gilgameš Epic or Enūma Eliš would be complete folly. The author of Genesis may have selected divine names on the basis of theological emphasis rather than dogmatic preference. Many divine names were probably interchangeable; Baal and

---

[169] The title *'Elo·him'* preceded by the definite article *ha*, giving the expression *ha·'Elo·him'*.

[170] See also Psalm 46:11; 48:1, 8.

[171] See also Psalm 46:11; 48:1, 8.

[172] John J. Davis, *Paradise to Prison: Studies in Genesis* (Salem: Sheffield, 1975), 22–23.

Hadad were used interchangeably in the Hadad Tablet from Ugarit,[173] and similar examples could be cited from Egyptian texts."[174]

In fact, we now know that there were many deities in the ancient Near East that had multiple names. As stated above with the Babylonian Creation account, the Enuma Elish, the god Marduk (Merodach), chief deity of Babylon, also had some 50 different names.[175] It would not even be thinkable to apply any of the Documentary Hypothesis analysis to any of these works. Why? Not only because we can see that ancient writers are no different than modern writers and are able to use different names and titles interchangeably within their work, but they were written on stone, so to speak. If one has one clay tablet that has both a personal name and two different titles for the same king, it would be difficult to argue that there were two or three different authors for the one tablet. Bible scholar Mark F. Rooker has the following to say about the use of Elohim and Yahweh in the Old Testament:

> Moreover, it is clear that throughout the Old Testament that the occurrence of the names of God as Elohim or Yahweh is to be attributed to contextual and semantic issues, not the existence of sources. This conclusion is borne out by the fact that the names consistently occur in predictable genre. In the legal and prophetic texts the name Yahweh always appears, while in wisdom literature the name for God is invariably Elohim. In narrative literature, which includes much of the Pentateuch, both Yahweh and Elohim are used.[176] Yet consistently the names do not indicate different sources but were chosen by design. The name Elohim was used in passages to express the abstract idea of Deity as evident in God's role as Creator of the universe and the Ruler of nature. Yahweh, on the other hand, is the special covenant name of God who has entered into a relationship with the Israelites since the name reflects God's ethical character. (Cassuto, 31) Given the understanding of the meaning of these names for God, it is no wonder that the source which contains the name Yahweh

---

[173] G. R. Driver, *Canaanite Myths and Legends* (New York: T. & T. Clark, 1971), 70-72.

[174] For example, see the "Stele of Ikhernofret" in James B. Pritchard, ed., *Ancient Near Eastern Texts*, 2nd ed. Princeton: Princeton University Press, 1955, pp. 329–30.

[175] K. A. Kitchen, *On the Reliability of the Old Testament* (Grand Rapids: Eerdmans, 2003), 424–5.

[176] Similarly, Livingston has pointed out that the cognate West Semitic divine names il and ya(w) appear to be interchangeable in the Eblaite tablets. (*The Pentateuch in Its Cultural Environment*, 224.)

would appear to reflect a different theology from a selected group of texts which contained the name Elohim."[177]

Let us, on a small scale, do our own analysis of the divine names in the first two chapters of Genesis. The Hebrew word (*'elohim'*) is most often agreed upon to be from a root meaning "be strong," "mighty," or "power."[178] It should be said too that by far, most Hebrew scholars recognize the plural form (*im*) of this title *'elo·him'* to be used as a plural of "majesty," "greatness," or "excellence." The Hebrew word (*'elo·him'*) is used for the Creator 35 times from Genesis 1:1 to 2:4a. Exactly what is the context of this use? It is used in a setting that deals with God's power, his greatness, his excellence, his creation activity, all of which seems appropriate, does it not?

Moving on to Genesis 2:4b–25, we find God now being referred to by his personal name, the Tetragrammaton (YHWH, JHVH), which is translated "Jehovah" (KJV, ASV, NW, NEB, etc.) or "Yahweh" (AT, NAB, JB, HCSB, etc.). It is found in verses 4b–25 eleven times; however, it comes before his title (*'elohim'*).[179] Why the switch, and what is the context of this use? This personal name of God is used in a setting that deals with his personal relationship with man and woman. This is not a second creation account; it is a more detailed account of the creation of man, which was only briefly mentioned in chapter one in passing, as each feature of creation was ticked off. In chapter two, the Creator becomes a person as he speaks to his intelligent creation, giving them the prospect of an perfect eternal life in a paradise garden, which is to be cultivated earth wide, to be filled with perfect offspring. Therefore, we see a personal interchange between God and man as He lays out His plans to Adam, which seems very appropriate, does it not when switching from using a title in chapter one to using a personal name in chapter two? In chapter two, we have the coupling of the personal name "Jehovah" with the title "God," to show that we are still talking about this 'great,' 'majestic,' 'all powerful' Creator, but personalized as he introduces himself to his new earthly creation.

Thus, there is no reason to assume that we are talking about two different writers. No, it is two different settings in which a skilled writer would make the transition just as Moses did. It would be no different than if a modern-day news commentator was giving as a report about the United States President visiting Russia to meet with Dmitry Anatolyevich Medvedev, in which he used the title President predominately. The

---

[177] Mark F. Rooker, *Leviticus: The New American Commentary* (Nashville: Broadman & Holman, 2001), 26–27.

[178] Ibid., 27.

[179] "Jehovah God." Heb., *Yehwah' 'Elohim'*.

following week the same news commentator may be covering the President visiting a hospital with injured children who had survived a tornado, and refer to the President as President Obama. It isn't difficult to see that one is an official setting where the President needs to be portrayed as powerful, while in the other setting; he needs to be portrayed as personable. The same principles used herein apply to the rest of the Pentateuch and the Old Testament as a whole.

Discrepancies

Discrepancies, or should I say "perceived" discrepancies, are the critic's favorite pebble. These perceived discrepancies set off an alarm for the critic, and then he rushes off with his pebble like a child to add it to the multiple-authors side of the scale. To differentiate between the supposed different sources texts, I will lay them out as follows:

("J") will be used to represent an alleged writer. In this case, it stands for any place God's name Jehovah is used.

("E") will be for the portion that has Jehovah's title, *Elohim*, God.

("P") will be for the portion of priestly activities.

("D") Deuteronomy is different from Genesis, Exodus, Leviticus, and Numbers. Thus, it has another author.

("RJE") will represent the compiler who put "J" and "E" together.

("R") will represent the editor(s), who put it all together and may have altered some portions to express their social circumstances of their day.

("U") will represent the alleged "unknown independent texts."

"Narrative Discrepancy" (Genesis 12:1, ASV) Now Jehovah said unto Abram, Get thee out of thy country, and from thy kindred, and from thy father's house, unto the land that I will show thee: ("J") (after Terah, Abram's father, died, Abram is commanded to leave Haran)

> **(Genesis 11:26, ESV)** When Terah had lived 70 years, he fathered Abram, Nahor, and Haran ("U"). (When Terah was 70, Abram was born.)

(Genesis 11:32, ESV) The days of Terah were 205 years ("U"): and Terah died in Haran ("R"). (Terah died at the age of 205, which would make Abraham 135 when he left Ur.)

(Genesis 12:4, ASV) So Abram went, as Jehovah had spoken unto him; and Lot went with him ("J"): and Abram was seventy and five years old when he departed out ("P") of Haran ("R"). (12:4 has Abram being only 75 when he leaves Haran.)

Discrepancy: According to 11:32, Terah died at the age of 205; hence, Abram must have been 135 when he was called to leave Haran. However, 12:4 says that he was only 75 when he left Haran. The Source Critic informs us that this seeming contradiction is resolved if Genesis chapter 12 is of a different source from the genealogy of Genesis chapter 11.

The above need not be a contradiction at all. True enough, it was at the age of 70 that Terah began having children (Genesis 11:26), but does Abraham have to be the firstborn child simply because he is listed first? Consider, what weight does the names Nahor and Haran play in the Bible account? Now consider, what about the name Abraham? He is considered the father and founder of three of the greatest religions on this planet: Judaism, Christianity, and Islam. He is the third most prominent person named in God's Word. This practice, that of placing the most prominent son first in a list of sons even though they are not the firstborn is followed elsewhere in God's Word with other prominent men of great faith, for example, Shem and Isaac. (Genesis 5:32; 11:10; 1 Chronicles 1:28) Therefore, let us keep it simple. Genesis 11:26 does not say that Abram was the firstborn; it simply says that Terah began fathering children, and then it goes on to list his three sons, listing the most prominent one first. Thus, it is obvious that Terah fathered Abram at the age of 130. (Genesis 11:26, 32; 12:4) In addition, it is true that Sarah was Abram's half-sister, not by the same mother, but by having Terah as the same father. (Genesis 20:12) Therefore, in all likelihood, it is Haran who is the firstborn of Terah, whose daughter was old enough to marry Nahor, another of Terah's three sons. – Genesis 11:29.

"Narrative Discrepancy" (Genesis 37:25–28, 36; 38:1; 39:1, YLT)

(Genesis 37:25–28, YLT) And they sit down to eat bread ("E"), and they lift up their eyes, and look, and lo, a company of Ishmaelites coming from Gilead, and their camels bearing spices, and balm, and myrrh, going to take [them] down to Egypt. 26 And Judah saith unto his brethren, 'What gain when we slay our brother, and have concealed his blood? 27 Come, and we sell him to the Ishmaelites, and our hands are not on him, for he [is] our brother—our flesh;' and his brethren hearken ("J"). 28 And Midianite merchantmen pass by and they draw out and bring up Joseph out of the pit ("E"), and sold him to the Ishmaelites for twenty shekels of silver. They took Joseph to Egypt ("J"). (Genesis 37:36) And the Medanites have sold him unto Egypt, to Potiphar, a eunuch of Pharaoh, head of the executioners ("E"). (Genesis 38:1) And it cometh to pass, at that time, that Judah goeth down from his brethren, and turneth aside unto a man, an Adullamite, whose name [is] Hirah ("J"). (Genesis 39:1) And Joseph hath been brought down to Egypt, and Potiphar, a eunuch of Pharaoh, head of the executioners, an Egyptian man, buyeth him out of the hands of the Ishmaelites who have brought him thither ("J").

Discrepancy: In Genesis 37:25 the Ishmaelites are passing by at the opportune time mentioned in verses 26 and 27, with Judah suggesting that instead of killing Joseph they sell him to the Ishmaelites. Yet, verse 28 switches in midstride to the Midianites, as they drew Joseph from the pit, selling him to the Ishmaelites. In verse 36, the Medanites (likely a scribal error; almost every translation has Midianites, so we will accept that as so) are selling Joseph to Potiphar in Egypt. Yet, the discrepancy pushes the envelope even further, for Genesis 39:1 says, it was the Ishmaelites who delivered and sold Joseph to Potiphar in Egypt. Was Joseph sold to Ishmaelites or to Midianites? In addition, who delivered and sold Joseph to Potiphar in Egypt? It seems that the higher critics are bent on using ambiguous passages (ambiguous at first glance to the casual reader) to facilitate their Documentary Hypothesis. You might say that these discrepancies are fuel for the engine that drives their Documentary Hypothesis locomotive. E. A. Speiser writes:

> The narrative is broken up into two originally independent versions. One of these (J) used the name Israel, featured Judah as Joseph's protector, and identified the Ishmaelites as the traders who bought Joseph from his brothers. The other (E) spoke of Jacob as the father and named Reuben as Joseph's friend; the slave traders in that version were Midianites who discovered Joseph by accident and sold him in Egypt to Potiphar.[180]

For Speiser, it is time to slice up the text and divide it up between our alleged "J"-Text and "E"-Text writers. It is also hypothesized that our "R"-Redactor edits the two and slips in some additional information as

---

[180] E. A. Speiser, *Genesis*, Anchor Bible (Garden City, N.Y.: Doubleday, 1964), 293–4.

well, suggesting that the Midianites are the ones who were actually passing by, selling Joseph later to the Ishmaelites. Thus, it would be the Ishmaelites, who would deliver and sell Joseph to Potiphar in Egypt. Yes, at first glimpse, this would appear to make it all well, but we still have a problem: Genesis 37:36 states that it was the Midianites, who sold Joseph to Potiphar in Egypt.

Actually, when one looks below the surface reading, there is no discrepancy here at all. Ishmael (son of Hagar and Abraham) and Midian (son of Keturah and Abraham) were half-brothers. It is highly likely that there was intermarriage between the descendants of these two, allowing for an interchangeable use of the expression "Ishmaelites" and "Midianites." (Genesis 25:1–4; 37:25–28; 39:1) We see this in the days of Judge Gideon when Israel was being attacked, with both terms "Ishmaelites" and "Midianites" being used to describe the attackers. (Judges 8:24; 7:25; 8:22, 26) Alternatively, even still we could have an Ishmaelite caravan encompassing Midianite merchants that were passing by, with the Midianites brokering the deal and delivering Joseph from the pit to the Ishmaelite caravan, where Joseph would be under the Ishmaelites' custody even if he was being *detained* by the Midianites. Once they arrived at Potiphar's place in Egypt, it would be the Midianites to broker the deal with Potiphar. Thus, it can be stated either way, the Ishmaelites or the Midianites delivered and sold Joseph to Potiphar in Egypt.

Repetitions (Doublets)

What are doublets? It is the telling of the same story twice, making the same events appear to happen more than once. For example,

(1) there are two stories of the creation account,

(2) two stories of God's covenant with Abraham,

(3) two stories where Abraham names his son Isaac,

(4) two stories where Abraham claims Sarah is his sister, two stories of Jacob's journey to Haran,

(5) two stories where God revealed himself to Jacob at Bethel,

(6) two stories where God changes Jacob's name to Israel,

(7) two stories of when Moses got water from the rock at Meribah, and a detailed description in Exodus 24–29 of how to build the tabernacle, then within five chapters a retelling of how they did it, repeating the details again in chapters 34–40.

The critic goes on to point out that, there is more to this "doublet" story than meets the eye; they argue that one of the doublets will contain the title for the Creator, God (*Elohim*); while the other doublet of the same story will contain the personal name for the Creator, Jehovah. Moreover, they argue that there are other defining features that are only within one side or the other.

(Genesis 1:27, ESV) So God created man in his own image, in the image of God he created him; male and female he created them.

(Genesis 2:7, ASV) And Jehovah God formed man of the dust of the ground, and breathed into his nostrils the breath of life; and man became a living soul.

Within two chapters, we have two verses where the writer, if one person, informs us of the creation of man twice, the second as though the first was never mentioned at all. Again, the source critic will argue that there were two sources of the same information on the creation of man and the compiler allowed both to remain. What the source critic fails to tell his reader is that there are sense breaks within the various accounts in these first three chapters. Genesis 1:1–2:3 is the basic creation account. Genesis 2:4–25 is the restating of day three (verses 5, 6) and the subsequent preparation of the earth for the settling of man and woman in the Garden of Eden. Genesis 3:1–24 is specifically about the temptation, the entry of sin and death into the world, the promise of a seed to save humankind, a description of the conditions of imperfection and of man's loss of the Garden of Eden.

Bible scholar Leon Kass, who supports the Documentary Hypothesis, had this to say about the creation account of Genesis chapters 1 and 2:

Once we recognize the independence of the two creation stories, we are compelled to adopt a critical principle of reading if we mean to understand each story on its own terms. We must scrupulously avoid reading into the second story any facts or notions taken from the first, and vice versa. Thus, in reading about the origin of man in the story of the Garden of Eden, we must not say or even think that man is here created in God's image or that man is to be the ruler over the animals. Neither, when we try to understand the relation of man and woman in the Garden, are we to think about or make use of the first story's account of the coequal coeval creation of man and woman. Only after we have read and interpreted each story entirely on its own should we try to integrate the two disparate teachings. By proceeding in this way, we will discover why these two separate and divergent accounts have been juxtaposed and how they function to convey a coherent, noncontradictory teaching about human life. [181]

Let us look at another example in which the critic has argued that one source says forty days while the other speaks of 150 days:

(Gen 7:12, NET) And the rain fell on the earth forty days and forty nights.

(Gen 7:24, NET) The waters prevailed over the earth for 150 days.

Genesis 7:24 and 8:3 say the floodwaters lasted for 150 days, yet; Genesis 7:4, 12 and 17 say it was only forty days. Once again, the difference is solved with a simple explanation. Each is referring to two different time periods. Let us look at these verses again (italics mine):

(Gen 7:12, NET) And the rain fell on the earth forty days and forty nights. [Notice that the 40-days refer to how long the rain fell—"the rain fell."]

(Gen 7:24, NET) The waters prevailed over the earth for 150 days. [Notice that the 150-days refer to how long the flood lasted—"waters prevailed."]

(Gen 8:3, NET) The waters kept receding steadily from the earth, so that they had gone down by the end of the 150 days.

(Gen 8:4, NET) On the seventeenth day of the seventh month, the ark came to rest on one of the mountains of Ararat.

(Gen 7:11; 8:13, 14, NET) In the *six hundredth year of Noah's life*, in *the second month*, on the seventeenth day of the month, on that day all the fountains of the great deep burst open and the floodgates of the heavens were opened. *In Noah's six hundred and first year*, in the first day of the first month, *the waters had dried up* from the earth, and Noah removed the covering from the ark and saw that *the surface of the ground was dry*. And *by the twenty-seventh day of the second month the earth was dry.*

By the end of the 150 days, the water had gone down [Gen 8:3]. Five months from the beginning of the rain, the ark comes to rest on

---

[181] Leon R. Kass, *The Beginning of Wisdom: Reading Genesis* (New York: Free Press, 2003), 56.

Mount Ararat [8:4]. Eleven months later the waters dried up [7:11; 8:13]. Exactly 370 days from the start (lunar months), Noah and his family left the ark and were on dry ground.

Yet another example is found in 2 Kings 24:10-16. Verses 10-14 say, "At that time the servants of Nebuchadnezzar king of Babylon came up to Jerusalem, and the city was besieged. And Nebuchadnezzar king of Babylon came to the city while his servants were besieging it, and Jehoiachin the king of Judah gave himself up to the king of Babylon, himself and his mother and his servants and his officials and his palace officials. The king of Babylon took him prisoner in the eighth year of his reign and carried off all the treasures of the house of the LORD and the treasures of the king's house, and cut in pieces all the vessels of gold in the temple of the LORD, which Solomon king of Israel had made, as the LORD had foretold. He carried away all Jerusalem and all the officials and all the mighty men of valor, 10,000 captives, and all the craftsmen and the smiths. None remained, except the poorest people of the land."

Verses 15-16 say, "And he carried away Jehoiachin to Babylon. The king's mother, the king's wives, his officials, and the chief men of the land he took into captivity from Jerusalem to Babylon. And the king of Babylon brought captive to Babylon all the men of valor, 7,000, and the craftsmen and the metal workers, 1,000, all of them strong and fit for war."

Here we have a repetition of the same events back-to-back. Why? Is it multiple sources and the redactor simply keeping both? In an attempt to stave off the conservative view of Moses' writership, scholar, and critic Richard Elliot Friedman writes:

> Those who defended the traditional belief in Mosaic authorship argued that the doublets were always complementary, not repetitive, and that they did not contradict each other, but came to teach us a lesson by their 'apparent' contradiction. But another clue was discovered that undermined this traditional response. Investigators found that in most cases one of the two versions of a doublet story would refer to the deity by the divine name, Yahweh . . . , and the other version of the story would refer to the deity simply as 'God.' That is, the doublets lined up into two groups of parallel versions of stories. Each group was almost always consistent with the name it used. Moreover, the investigators found that it was not only the names of the deity that lined up. They found various other terms and characteristics that regularly appeared in one of the other group. This tended to support the hypothesis that someone had taken two different old source documents, cut

them up, and woven them together to form the continuous story in the Five Books of Moses.[182]

Ancient Semitic literature has other similar examples of repetition. Moreover, the use of Elohim in one instance and Jehovah in another is due to context and semantic issues. Notice Friedman's use of the phrases "in most cases" and "almost always." Which is it? And as we will see, he is overstating his case to the point of exaggeration. Let us look at the most popular example in the "Matriarch in Danger." It has three occurrences in Genesis: Sarah in Egypt with Pharaoh (Genesis 12:10–20), Sarah in Gerar with Abimelech (Genesis 20:1–18), and Rebekah in Gerar with Abimelech (Genesis 26:7–11). Friedman would argue that we simply have one story with three different sources that had been maintained over time. The personal name of God, Jehovah, is used in the account of Sarah in Egypt with Pharaoh (vs. 17). The title Elohim is used in the account about Sarah in Gerar with Abimelech (vs. 3), but so is Jehovah (vs. 18). In the account of Rebekah in Gerar with Abimelech, neither Elohim nor Jehovah is used. Therefore, Friedman's case is really no case at all, because both Jehovah and Elohim appear in one account with Sarah in Gerar with Abimelech and neither Jehovah nor Elohim appear in the account with Rebekah in Gerar with Abimelech. It should be noted that all three occurrences are in reference to Abimelech and Pharaoh, but both times that the name Jehovah is used, it is in reference to Jehovah executing a punishment of these rulers. If their best example does not even come close to their claims, then what are we to think of the others? Before moving on to the differences in language and style, we should close with one last point about the literature of the Ancient Near East (ANE). One of the features of ANE literature, which includes Hebrew, is its parallelism, repetition, the telling of stories that are similar to stress patterns that are important. Even in the book of Acts, you have three different accounts of Paul's conversion (Ac 9:3-8; 22:6-11; 26:12-18). It is repetition for emphasis. At the outset of this section, we mentioned that chapters 24-29 of Exodus give a detailed description of how the tabernacle was built, and chapters 34-40 repeat the very same information. Chapters 24-29 contain the directions, and chapters 34-40 show how they did it; thus, the repetition is emphasizing that they did exactly what Jehovah had asked them to do.

Differences in Language and Style

Supporters of the Documentary Hypothesis would argue that within the Pentateuch we see such things as preferences for certain words, differences in vocabulary, reoccurring expressions in Deuteronomy that

---

[182] Richard Elliot Friedman, *Who Wrote The Bible* (San Francisco: Harper Collins, 1997), 22.

are not found in Genesis, Exodus, Leviticus, and Numbers, all evidence for the higher critics and their multiple source theory. Also, there are individual characteristics in grammar and syntax. Further, the critic describes "P" as being very boring, completely lacking in interest or excitement, dry; while the writers of "J" and "E" are very vivid and lively, holding the reader's interest in their storytelling. Additionally, "D" uses expressions like 'with all your heart and all your soul,' which the rest of the Pentateuch lacks in those types of expressions. Their conclusion is that there is no alternative but to have multiple writers as the differences in language and style dictate.

If the alleged writers of the Pentateuch were so narrow in their vocabulary and writing abilities that they would use only one given word for a given idea and never use another when dealing with that idea, it would be easy to suggest a division of actual sources. Yet this is not the case at all. The writers of the Hebrew Scriptures throughout ancient Israel actually expressed a great variety of words in their work. Douglas K. Stuart (Ph.D., Harvard University), Professor of Old Testament at Gordon–Conwell Theological Seminary, is of the same opinion:

> In fact, the contrary situation appears to be true. In ancient Israel there were four demonstrable indications of a preference for variety in written expression rather than for desire for stylistic consistency. (1) If there were two different ways of spelling a word the Israelites chose to preserve both spellings as valid and to include both of them frequently in any document. Thus with regard to spelling (orthography), ancient Israelites had no commitment to consistency to style, but the free use of alternative spellings was regarded as not only proper, but desirable. (2) In the case of common expressions, a similar phenomenon can be observed. Where variation was possible, it apparently was not avoided, but preferred. Alternative ways of forming a given multiword expression were employed commonly so that both alternatives were preserved. Thus, in the case of repeated phraseology in prose contexts, there was no commitment to consistency of style, but rather the alternative formulation was regarded not only proper, but desirable. (3) With regard to variation in grammatical forms, a similar phenomenon is observed. If there existed two different ways of saying something, even in the case of a common verb form, both ways were used so as to preserve both in the common discourse. Again, the preference appears to have been for inclusion of variety rather than for consistency of one form if two existed. (4) The Masoretic system of *Kethib-Qere* represents a fourth indicator of the tendency in past times to

preserve variance rather than to select one option and to employ it consistently, a tendency that extended into the medieval period when the Masoretes worked. This system arose from a desire to include, not merely side-by-side, but actually within the same word, two variant readings rather than two select ones. The Masoretes provide the consonants of one text option in the vowels of another. They indicated their preferred reading, but did not omit the reading they regarded as inferior, they simply did not localize it.[183]

Differences in Style and Vocabulary: An investigator would not be honest if he were simply to reject these differences out of hand, as though they did not exist. Therefore, rightly, we need to investigate these differences, giving an answer that has substance. I will cite one of their pillar examples, to demonstrate the principle that if they are so far off base here, then we can conclude their foundation in this area is really no foundation at all. Before we get started, let us do a little review of Biblical Hebrew, to be better able to address our example.

(**Qal**): Qal is the simple form of the verb, meaning "light" or "easy." This is the simple active stem of the verb.

(**Hiphil**): This is generally called the "*causative*" form because it reveals the *causative* action of the qal verb. The "*h*" is prefixed to the stem, which modifies the root.

QAL   yalad (to give birth)

HIPHIL   holid (he caused to give birth)

Examples:

Gen. 14:18: Irad begat (*yalad*) Mehujael

Gen. 5:4: Adam after he begat (*holid*) Seth

The advocates of the Documentary Hypothesis argue that to find *yalad* in the genealogy of Cain in Genesis chapter 4, the Table of Nations in Genesis chapter 10, and Nahor's family line in Genesis chapter 22 (all being of the "J" author), while finding *holid* in Adam's history down to Noah in Genesis chapter 5 as well as the genealogy of Shem found in

---

[183] Douglas K. Stuart, *The New American Commentary: An Exegetical Theological Exposition of Holy Scripture: EXODUS* (Nashville: Broadman & Holman, 2006). See pp. 30–31 for examples of the above four points.

Genesis chapter 11 (being of the "P" author) is nothing more than proof positive that there are two authors: "J" and "P."

In short, we are not dealing with a word or phrase that is peculiar to an individual writer like "J" or "P." No, this is nothing more than an example of following the basic rules of Hebrew grammar and syntax. In many cases, it could not have been written in any other way, because it is the socially accepted usage of the Hebrew language. When those who support the Documentary Hypothesis pull Hebrew words or even phrases out of their setting (as I have done above), looking at them in isolation, their reasoning becomes based solely on personal wishes, feelings, or perceptions, rather than on linguistic rules, reasons, or principles of the language itself. Hebrew, like any other language, conforms to the socially accepted style, with the regular and specific order, or arrangement. The Hebrew language has its own rules and allowable combinations of how words are joined together to make sense to the Hebrew mind. Umberto Cassuto, also known as Moshe David Cassuto, (1883–1951), who held the chair of Biblical studies at the Hebrew University of Jerusalem had this to say concerning the usage of *yalad* and *holid*:

> It will suffice to note the fact that the verb *yaladh* occurs in the signification of *holidh* only in the *past tense* [perfect] and the *present* [participle]. We say, "so-and-so *yaladh* [mas. sing. perfect] so-and-so," and we say *yoledh* [participle mas. Sing.: "is begetting"]; but we do not say in the *future tense* [imperfect] so-and-so *yeledh* [to signify: "he will beget"] (or *wayyeledh* [imperfect with *waw* conversive, to connote: "and he begot"]) so-and-so." In the imperfect, the *Qal* is employed only with reference to the mother, for example, so-and-so *teledh* ["will give birth to"] (*watteledh* ["and gave birth to"]) so and so." In connection with the father one can only say, *yolidh* [hiphil imperfect; "he will beget"] or *wayyoledh* [hiphil imperfect with *waw* conversive; "and he begot"] (although we find in Prov. xxvii 1: what a day may bring forth ["*yeledh*"; *Qal* imperfect] the verb is used there not in connotation of "begetting" but actually in the sense of "giving birth"). Similarly, we do not say, using the infinitive, Aajare *lidhto* [to signify: "after his begetting"] but only Aajare *lidhtah* ["after her giving birth"]; with regard to the father we can only say Aajare *holidho* ["after his begetting"]. This is clear to anyone who is sensitive to the Hebrew idiom. In the genealogies from Adam to Noah and from Noah to Abraham, it would have been impossible to write anything else but *wayyoledh* and Aajare *hoilidho*; every Hebrew author would have had no option but to write thus and not

otherwise. It is not a question of sources but of the general usage of the Hebrew tongue.[184]

Professor K. A. Kitchen, one of the leading experts on Biblical history, notes in his book *Ancient Orient and Old Testament:* "Stylistic differences are meaningless, and reflect the differences in detailed subject-matter." He says that similar style variations can also be found "in ancient texts whose literary unity is beyond all doubt."[185]

A 1981 news report relates to this debate and provides some interesting facts.[186]

TEL AVIV, Israel (UPI)—A five-year long computer study of the Bible strongly indicates that one author—and not three as widely held in modern criticism—wrote the book of Genesis.

"The probability of Genesis' having been written by one author is enormously high—82 percent statistically," a member of the research team said in an article published in Wednesday's *Jerusalem Post.*

Professor Yehuda Radday, a Bible scholar from the Technion, a Haifa university, said more than 20,000 words of Genesis were fed into a computer which conducted a painstaking analysis of its linguistic makeup.

Bible critics widely hold that Genesis had three authors—the Jawhist or "J" author, the Elohist or "E" author and a priestly writer, dubbed "P."

"We found the J and E narratives to be linguistically indistinguishable," Radday told a news conference today. But the P sections differ widely from them.

"This is only to be expected, since dramatic tales and legal documents must necessarily display different 'behavior,'" he said. "If you compared love letters and a telephone directory written by the same person, linguistic analysis would point to different authors."

The team combined statistical and linguistic methods with computer science and Bible scholarship to reach their conclusions. They used 54 analysis criteria, including word

---

[184] Umberto Cassuto, *The Documentary Hypothesis* (New York, NY: Shalem Press, 2006), 55-56.
[185] K. A Kitchen, *Ancient Orient and Old Testament* (Downers Grove, IL: InterVarsity Press, 1975), 125.
[186] As published in the *St. Petersburg Times:* http://tinyurl.com/noke4m

length, the use of the definite article and the conjunction "and," richness of vocabulary and transition frequencies between word categories.

"These criteria are a reliable gauge of authorship because these traits are beyond an author's conscious control and furthermore are countable," Radday said.

A mathematics expert on the team ran a computer check against classical German works by Goethe, Herder and Kant and found that the statistical probability of their being the sole authors of their own work were only 22 percent, 7 percent and 9 percent respectively.

As mentioned above, Jewish and Christian conservatives accept one writer for the first five books of the Bible, namely, Moses. The critics, however, argue that although Moses is definitely the main character of the Pentateuch because they are unable to find any *direct mention* within it of Moses having written these five books, it is for them simply a tradition that Moses is the writer. This author is certain that is not the impression you will have after reading the next chapter.

Internal and External Evidence for Moses Authorship

First, it is obvious that Moses did *not* write *every word* of the Pentateuch. Why? The section that relates his death would be something that Joshua could have added after Moses' death. (Deuteronomy 34:1–8) In addition, the critic would argue, it would hardly seem very meek to pen these words about oneself: "Now the man Moses was very meek, more than all people who were on the face of the earth." (Numbers 12:3, ESV) Nevertheless, consider that Jesus said of himself: "I am gentle and lowly in heart" (Matthew 11:29, *ESV*), which no one would fault Jesus with as though he were boasting. Both Moses and Jesus were simply stating a fact. The amount of possible material that may have been added by Joshua, another inspired writer is next to nothing and does not negate Moses' authorship.

What Does the Biblical Evidence from the Old Testament Report?

Exodus 17:14 (ASV)	Exodus 24:4 (ASV)	Exodus 34:27 (ASV)
[14] And Jehovah said unto Moses, Write this	[4] And Moses wrote all the words of Jehovah,	[27] And Jehovah said unto Moses, Write

for a memorial in a book, and rehearse it in the ears of Joshua: that I will utterly blot out the remembrance of Amalek from under heaven.

and rose up early in the morning, and builded an altar under the mount, and twelve pillars, according to the twelve tribes of Israel.

thou these words: for after the tenor of these words I have made a covenant with thee and with Israel.

Leviticus 26:46 (ASV)

46 These are the statutes and ordinances and laws, which Jehovah made between him and the children of Israel in mount Sinai by Moses.

Leviticus 27:34 (ASV)

34 These are the commandments, which Jehovah commanded Moses for the children of Israel in mount Sinai.

Numbers 33:2 (ASV)

2 And Moses wrote their goings out according to their journeys by the commandment of Jehovah: and these are their journeys according to their goings out.

Numbers 36:13 (ASV)

13 These are the commandments and the ordinances which Jehovah commanded by Moses unto the children of Israel in the plains of Moab by the Jordan at Jericho.

Deuteronomy 1:1 (ASV)

1 These are the words which Moses spake unto all Israel beyond the Jordan in the wilderness, in the Arabah over against Suph, between Paran, and Tophel, and Laban, and Hazeroth, and Di-zahab.

Deuteronomy 31:9 (ASV)

9 And Moses wrote this law, and delivered it unto the priests the sons of Levi, that bare the ark of the covenant of Jehovah, and unto all the elders of Israel.

Deuteronomy 31:22 (ASV)

22 So Moses wrote this song the same day, and taught it the children of Israel.

Deuteronomy 31:24 (ASV)

24 And it came to pass, when Moses had made an end of writing the words of this law in a book, until they were

Joshua 1:7 (ASV)

7 Only be strong and very courageous, to observe to do according to all the law, which Moses my servant commanded thee:

finished,

Joshua 8:31 (ASV)	1 Kings 2:3 (ASV)	2 Kings 14:6 (ASV)
31 as Moses the servant of Jehovah commanded the children of Israel, as it is written in the book of the law of Moses, an altar of unhewn stones, upon which no man had lifted up any iron: and they offered thereon burnt-offerings unto Jehovah, and sacrificed peace-offerings.	3 and keep the charge of Jehovah thy God, to walk in his ways, to keep his statutes, and his commandments, and his ordinances, and his testimonies, according to that which is written in the law of Moses, that thou may prosper in all that thou does, and whithersoever thou turn thyself.	6 but the children of the murderers he put not to death; according to that which is written in the book of the law of Moses, as Jehovah commanded, saying, The fathers shall not be put to death for the children, nor the children be put to death for the fathers; but every man shall die for his own sin.
2 Kings 21:8 (ASV)	**Ezra 6:18 (ASV)**	**Nehemiah 13:1 (ASV)**
8 neither will I cause the feet of Israel to wander any more out of the land which I gave their fathers, if only they will observe to do according to all that I have commanded them, and according to all the law that my servant Moses commanded them.	18 And they set the priests in their divisions, and the Levites in their courses, for the service of God, which is at Jerusalem; as it is written in the book of Moses.	1 On that day they read in the book of Moses in the audience of the people; and therein was found written, that an Ammonite and a Moabite should not enter into the assembly of God for ever,
Daniel 9:13 (ASV)	**Malachi 4:4 (ASV)**	
13 As it is written in the law of Moses, all this evil is come upon us: yet have we not entreated the favor of Jehovah our God, that ...	4 Remember ye the law of Moses my servant, which I commanded unto him in Horeb for all Israel, even statutes and ordinances.	

To reject Moses as the writer of the Pentateuch is to reject these inspired writers and suggest they are not reliable; moreover, this would mean they were not inspired, because those under inspiration would not make such errors. If these critics are correct, then all the above is merely a great conspiracy. This author hardly thinks so!

What Does the Biblical Evidence from Jesus Christ Report?

Matthew 8:4 (ESV)	Matthew 11:23-24 (ESV)
4And Jesus said to him, "See that you say nothing to anyone, but go, show yourself to the priest and offer the gift that Moses commanded, for a proof to them."	23And you, Capernaum, will you be exalted to heaven? You will be brought down to Hades. For if the mighty works done in you had been done in Sodom, it would have remained until this day. 24 But I tell you that it will be more tolerable on the day of judgment for the land of Sodom than for you."
Matthew 19:4-5 (ESV)	**Matthew 19:8 (ESV)**
4He answered, "Have you not read that he who created them from the beginning made them male and female, 5and said, 'Therefore a man shall leave his father and his mother and hold fast to his wife, and the two shall become one flesh'?	8He said to them, "Because of your hardness of heart Moses allowed you to divorce your wives, but from the beginning it was not so.
Matthew 24:37 (ESV)	**Mark 10:5 (ESV)**
37 For as were the days of Noah, so will be the coming of the Son of Man.	5And Jesus said to them, "Because of your hardness of heart he wrote you this commandment.
Mark 12:26 (ESV)	**Mark 1:44 (ESV)**
26And as for the dead being raised, have you not read in the book of Moses, in the passage about the bush, how God spoke to him, saying, 'I am the God of Abraham,	44and said to him, "See that you say nothing to anyone, but go, show yourself to the priest and offer for your cleansing what Moses

and the God of Isaac, and the God of Jacob'?	commanded, for a proof to them."

Mark 7:10 (ESV) ¹⁰For Moses said, 'Honor your father and your mother'; and, 'Whoever reviles father or mother must surely die.'	**Luke 5:14 (ESV)** ¹⁴And he charged him to tell no one, but "go and show yourself to the priest, and make an offering for your cleansing, as Moses commanded, for a proof to them."

Luke 11:51 (ESV) ⁵¹from the blood of Abel to the blood of Zechariah, who perished between the altar and the sanctuary. Yes, I tell you, it will be required of this generation.	**Luke 17:32 (ESV)** ³² Remember Lot's wife.

Luke 24:27, 44 English Standard Version (ESV) ²⁷And beginning with Moses and all the Prophets, he interpreted to them in all the Scriptures the things concerning himself. ⁴⁴Then he said to them, "These are my words that I spoke to you while I was still with you, that everything written about me in the Law of Moses and the Prophets and the Psalms must be fulfilled."	**John 5:46 English Standard Version (ESV)** ⁴⁶For if you believed Moses, you would believe me; for he wrote of me.

John 7:19 English Standard Version (ESV) ¹⁹ Has not Moses given you the law? Yet none of you keeps the law. Why do you seek to kill me?"	**John 8:58 (UASV)** Jesus said to them, "Truly, truly, I say to you, before Abraham came to be I have been in existence."[187]

How does one ignore the strongest evidence of Moses' writership of these five books, which is specifically referred to by Jesus Christ and numerous other inspired writers? Being on trial by the modern day critic, I

---

[187] K. L. McKay, A New Syntax of the Verb in New Testament Greek (New York: Peter Lang, 1994), p. 42.

am certain Moses would appreciate the numerous witnesses that can be called to the stand on his behalf.[188]

What Does the Biblical Evidence from the Apostles Report?

Acts 2:32 (ESV)	Acts 6:14 (ESV)	Acts 15:5 (ESV)
[32]This Jesus God raised up, and of that we all are witnesses.	[14]for we have heard him say that this Jesus of Nazareth will destroy this place and will change the customs that Moses delivered to us."	[5]But some believers who belonged to the party of the Pharisees rose up and said, "It is necessary to circumcise them and to order them to keep the law of Moses."
Acts 26:22 (ESV)	**Acts 28:23 (ESV)**	**Romans 10:5 (ESV)**
[22] To this day I have had the help that comes from God, and so I stand here testifying both to small and great, saying nothing but what the prophets and Moses said would come to pass:	[23]When they had appointed a day for him, they came to him at his lodging in greater numbers. From morning till evening he expounded to them, testifying to the kingdom of God and trying to convince them about Jesus both from the Law of Moses and from the Prophets.	[5]For Moses writes about the righteousness that is based on the law, that the person who does the commandments shall live by them.
1 Corinthians 9:9 (ESV) [9]For it is written in the	**Hebrews 9:19 (ESV)** [19]For when every commandment of the	**Hebrews 10:28 (ESV)** [28] Anyone who has set

---

[188] Old Testament witnesses to Moses' writership of the Pentateuch: Joshua 1:7; 8:32–35; 14:10; 1 Kings 2:3; 1 Chronicles 6:49; 2 Chronicles 33:8; 34:14; 35:12; Ezra 3:2; 6:18; 7:6; Nehemiah 1:7, 8; 8:1, 14, 15; Daniel 9:11, 13; Malachi 4:4. New Testament witnesses to Moses' writership of the Pentateuch: Matthew 8:2–4; 19:7; Mark 1:44; 12:26; Luke 2:22; 16:29, 31; 24:27, 44; John 1:45; 7:22; 8:5; 9:29; 19:7 [Leviticus 24:16]; Acts 3:22; 6:14; 15:5; 26:22; 28:23; Romans 10:5; 1 Corinthians 9:9; Hebrews 9:19; 10:28.

| Law of Moses, "You shall not muzzle an ox when it treads out the grain." Is it for oxen that God is concerned? | law had been declared by Moses to all the people, he took the blood of calves and ... | aside the law of Moses dies without mercy on the evidence of two or three witnesses. |

What Does the Internal Evidence Report?

If the writer(s) of the Pentateuch were, in fact, living from the ninth century into the fifth century B.C.E., more than a millennium [1,000 years] after the events described, they would have had to be thoroughly familiar with, even an expert in geology, geography,[189] horticulture, archaeology, toponymy, onomatology (Archer, 1974), botany, zoology,[190] climatology,[191] and history. **Alternatively**, he would have to have been an eyewitness who walked through the events and situations detailed in the Pentateuch; thus, the writer. Here is how I defend these affirmations:

- He would need to have a thorough knowledge of Egyptian names and titles that match inscriptions.

- He would need to have been an expert in toponymy, the study of place-names.

- He would need to have been an expert in onomatology, the study of proper names of all kinds and the origin of names.

- He would need to be aware of the customs and cultures and religious practices of Egypt, desert dwellers, and life in Canaan 1,000 years into the past.

- He would need to have a thorough knowledge of the environment, climate, and the physical features of three regions.

- He would need to have a thorough knowledge of botany, being aware of naturally occurring plant life in three regions 1,000-years before his time.

- He would need to have a thorough knowledge of the environment, climate, and the physical features of three regions.

---

[189] Genesis 13:10; 33:18; Numbers 13:22.

[190] Leviticus 11 and Deuteronomy 14.

[191] Exodus 9:31, 32; Exodus 16–Deuteronomy.

This internal evidence deals with the proof within the Pentateuch about Moses: the customs and culture of some 3,500 years ago, literary forms used as well as the language itself, and the unity of these five books. As to dating the Pentateuch based on literary forms, one needs look no further than the titles by which God is referred to within the Hebrew Scriptures. From the years of 850–450 B.C.E., we find the Hebrew expression *Yehowah´ tseva'ohth´*, "Jehovah of armies," being used in a significant way. It is found 243 times, with variations, in the Scriptures: 62 times in Isaiah, 77 in Jeremiah, 2 in Micah, 4 in Nahum, 2 in Habakkuk, 2 in Zephaniah, 15 in Haggai, 54 in Zechariah, and 25 in Malachi. This is the same time period, in which higher criticism places the writing of the books of the Pentateuch. If they were penned or constructed during this time period, one would expect to find a high number of occurrences of the expression "Jehovah of armies." Yet, we find just the opposite: there is not one occurrence of this expression to be found in the five books of the Pentateuch. This evidence demonstrates that these books were written prior to the book of Isaiah, before 800 B.C.E., which invalidates the Documentary Hypothesis. Moreover, many aspects of the priesthood that had been adjusted over the centuries, under inspiration, would have been evident if the Pentateuch were written after David[192] and others had made such adjustments.

The building of the tabernacle at the foot of Mount Sinai fits in with the environment of that area. F. C. Cook stated, "In form, structure, and materials, the tabernacle belongs altogether to the wilderness. The wood used in the structure is found there in abundance."[193] The external evidence validates names, customs, and culture, religious practices, geography, places and materials of the book of Exodus, which would have been privy only to an eyewitness. The geographical references by this writer are so vast, detailed, and tremendously precise that it is almost impossible to have him be anyone other than an eyewitness.

Deuteronomy reads, "Then we . . . went through all that great and terrifying wilderness." This region in which the annual rainfall is less than 25 cm./10 in. is not different even today, which puts the nomadic traveler on a constant search for water and pasture. In addition, we have meticulous directions as to the encampment of the Israelites (Numbers 1:52, 53), the marching orders (Numbers 2:9, 16, 17, 24, 31), and the signals of the trumpet (Numbers 10:2–6) that directed their every move as evidence that these accounts were written in the "great and terrifying

---

[192] David organized the tens of thousands of Levites into their many divisions of service, including a great chorus of singers and musicians.—1 Chronicles 23:1–29:19; 2 Chronicles 8:14; 23:18; 29:25; Ezra 3:10.

[193] F. C. Cook, *Exodus* (1874), 247.

wilderness." Numbers 13:22 makes reference to the time Hebron was built, using the city of Zoan as a reference point: "They went up into the Negeb and came to Hebron. Ahiman, Sheshai, and Talmai, the descendants of Anak, were there. (Hebron was built seven years before Zoan in Egypt.)" Moses "was instructed in all the wisdom of the Egyptians" (Acts 7:22); thus, he would have knowledge of the building of Zoan, an Egyptian city, and of Hebron, a city on one of the trade routes between Memphis in Egypt and Damascus in Syria.

From the internal evidence, it is clearly obvious that the writer must have had an intimate knowledge of the desert, being an eyewitness to that environment. (See Leviticus 18:3; Deuteronomy 12:9; 15:4, 7; Numbers 2:1; Leviticus 14:8; 16:21; 17:3, 9.) The evidence is such because it is something that cannot be retained for a thousand years, but must come from an eyewitness. The details are extremely exact, and some would not have existed hundreds of years later: "Then they came to Elim, where there were twelve wells of water and seventy palm trees, and they camped there by the water," and "ram skins dyed red, fine leather, acacia wood." – Exodus 15:27; 25:5

Again, it should be noted that Moses "was instructed in all the wisdom of the Egyptians." (Acts 7:22) It is also obvious that the writer was quite familiar with Egyptian names: Pithom, meaning "House of Atum;" On, meaning "City of the Pillar" (the Greeks called the city Heliopolis); Potiphera·[194] meaning "He Whom Ra Has Given;" and Asenath, her name deriving from Egyptian, meaning: "Holy to Anath."

In addition, the writer used Egyptian words generously. "He had Joseph ride in his second chariot, and [servants] called out before him, 'Abrek!' So he placed him over all the land of Egypt." (Genesis 41:43) The exact meaning of this expression transliterated from Egyptian into Hebrew has not yet been determined. Some feel that it is an Egyptian word meaning (*Attention!*) while others see it as a Hebrew word meaning *Kneel* or *Bow down!* One misstep and the writer will lose credibility. However, this is never the case with the writer of the Pentateuch. He mentions the acacia tree, which is found in Egypt and Sinai but not in the land of Canaan. Moreover, this writer refers to numerous animals that are to be found primarily in Egypt or Sinai. – See Deuteronomy. 14:5; Leviticus 16:11.

The old form of words in the Pentateuch are of the time frame of the fifteenth century B.C.E. as well, and had no longer been in use for centuries by the time of the supposed writer(s) and redactor(s) of the

---

[194] A funeral pillar (stele) discovered in 1935 and now in the Cairo Museum refers to a personage named Potiphare.

ninth to the sixth centuries B.C.E. Dr. John J. Davis gives us the most widely recognized example, "The pronoun *she*, which appears as *hiw*' instead of *hî*'. Another example is the word *young girl*, spelled *na'ar* instead of *na'ărâ*, the feminine form."[195]

All who engaged in idolatry or prophesying falsely were to be stoned to death, no exceptions. (Deuteronomy 13:2–11) This included not only individuals but also entire communities, every person within a city (verses 12–17). One has to ask, why would a writer include this if it were penned during the time period of 850–450 B.C.E. when most of the time Israel was shoulder deep in idolatry and false prophets abounded? This would mean certain destruction for every city in the kingdom. It would have been mere foolishness to incorporate these laws, which could never be enforced and would cause nothing but resistance to the law. However, it makes perfectly good sense for laws such as these to be given to people living in the time of Moses who had just exited an idolatrous nation and who was preparing to go in and conquer a number of other nations who lived and breathed idolatry.

What Does the External Evidence Report?

"The book of the law of Moses," as Joshua called the Pentateuch, was accepted by Jews, Christians, and Muslims as containing evidence of inspiration. The fact that Moses is the writer of these five books is **not** something that grew up out of tradition; it is something Moses himself claims, saying he wrote under the divine command of Jehovah God. Moreover, the Jewish communities throughout the Roman empire were in total harmony with the fact that Moses was the writer of the Pentateuch, this being supported by the Samaritan Pentateuch, the Palestinian Talmud, the Babylonian Talmud, the Apocrypha, Philo Judaeus (a contemporary of Jesus and Paul and the first century), and by Jewish historian Flavius Josephus (37–100 C.E.).[196] What about the early Christian writers, who wrote about Christianity between 150 C.E. and 400 C.E.?

Moses, the servant of God, recorded, through the Holy Spirit, the very beginning of the creation of the world. First he spoke of the things concerning the creation and genesis of the world, including the first man and everything that happened afterwards in the order of events. He also indicated the number

---

[195] John J. Davis, *Paradise to Prison: Studies in Genesis* (Salem: Sheffield, 1975), 26.

[196] See Ecclesiasticus 45:5; 2 Maccabees 7:30; Philo (*On the Life of Moses* II; III, 12–14; IV, 20; VIII, 45–48, pp. 93–95); Josephus (*The Antiquities of the Jews*, 3.8.10); Exodus 17:14; 24:4.

of years that elapsed before the Deluge.—*Theophilus* (c. 180, E), 2.118.[197]

The origin of that know ledge should not, on that account, be considered as originating with the Pentateuch. For knowledge of the Creator did not begin with the volume of Moses. Rather from the very first it is traced from Adam and paradise.—*Tertullian* (c. 207, W), 3.278.[198]

What portion of scripture can give us more information concerning the creation of the world than the account that Moses has transmitted?--*Origen* (c. 225, E), 4.341.[199]

The destruction of Sodom and Gomorrah by fire on account of their sins is related by Moses in Genesis.--*Origen* (c. 248, E), 4.505.[200]

Moses said, "And the Lord God saw that the wickedness of men was overflowing upon the Earth" [Gen. 6:5–7].--*Novatian* (c. 235, W), 5.658.[201]

It is contained in the book of Moses, which he wrote about creation, in which is called Genesis.--*Victorinus* (c. 280, W), 7.341.[202]

If you will look at the books of Moses, David, Solomon, Isaiah, or the Prophets who follow . . . . You will see what offspring they have left.--*Methodious* (c. 290, E), 6.333.[203]

Let the following books be considered venerable and holy by you, both of the clergy and the laity. Of the Old Testament: The five books of Moses—Genesis, Exodus, Leviticus, Numbers, and Deuteronomy. . . .--*Apostolic Constitutions* (compiled c. 390, E), 7.505.[204]

---

[197] David W. Bercot, *A Dictionary of Early Christian Beliefs* (Peabody: Hendrickson, 1998), 599.
198. Ibid., 600.
199. Ibid., 600.
200. Ibid., 600.
201. Ibid., 601.
202. Ibid., 601.
203. Ibid., 601.
204. Ibid., 602.

Archaeology and the Bible

Unlike higher criticism, archaeology is a field of study that has a solid foundation in physical evidence, instead of presenting only hypotheses, inferences, and implications. Within archaeology, one has both explicit and direct evidence as well as implicit evidence. There are many great publications that will undoubtedly go into this area in much greater detail, but suffice it to say that the Biblical events, the characters, geography, agriculture, plants and trees and settings are all in harmony with and accessible through archaeology.

While archaeology is not a total vindicator, it has defended God's Word. No one can argue against the fact that our understanding of ancient times has increased tremendously over the past 150 years and is being continuously refined. At present, one could list thousands of events within the Scriptures that are in complete harmony with the archaeological record. In fact, Wellhausen had nothing like what is available to the modern scholar. If he had, one would have to wonder if he would have come to the same conclusions. Conveying this exact point, Dr. Mark F. Rooker, Professor of Old Testament and Hebrew, stated:

> Regarding the issue of differing divine names, it is now clear from archaeological data not available to Wellhausen and early critical scholars that deities in the ancient Near East often had multiple names. This fact is especially clear in the conclusion to the Babylonian Creation account, the *Enuma Elish*, where the god Marduk is declared to be preeminent and his fifty different names are mentioned in celebration of his conquest.[22] No one has suggested that each name represents a different source, as was done in biblical studies. On the contrary, it would have been impossible to attribute these different names to different sources that have been pasted or joined together in the literary account because the Mesopotamian writing system involved inscription in stone! Moreover, it is clear that throughout the Old Testament the occurrence of the names of God as Elohim or Yahweh are to be attributed to contextual and semantic issues, not the existence of sources. This conclusion is borne out by the fact that the names consistently occur in predictable genre. . . . Thus through scientific discovery and analysis the criterion of the differing divine names, which gave rise to the Documentary Hypothesis, has been found wanting. If this information would have been known in the last years of the

nineteenth century, it is safe to assume that the critical approach to the Pentateuch would never have seen the light of day.[205]

Much archaeological evidence as well as other forms of evidence has been uncovered to reveal the accuracy of the record. The ziggurat located at Uruk (Erech) was found to be built with clay, baked bricks for stone, and asphalt (bitumen) for mortar.[206] The Egyptian names and titles that Moses penned in the book of Exodus match Egyptian inscriptions. The book of Exodus shows that the Hebrew people were allowed to live in the land of Egypt as foreigners, as long as they kept separate from the Egyptians. Archaeology supports this custom. Likely, you will recall that Pharaoh's daughter bathed in the Nile (Exodus 2:5), which "was a common practice in ancient Egypt," according to Cook's *Commentary*. "The Nile was worshipped as an emanation . . . of Osiris, and a peculiar power of imparting life and fertility was attributed to its waters."

> The fact that a king's daughter should bathe in the open river is certainly opposed to the customs of the modern, Mohammedan East, where this is only done by women of the lower orders, and that in remote places (Lane, *Manners and Customs*); but it is in harmony with the customs of ancient Egypt,[207]* and in perfect agreement with the notions of the early Egyptians respecting the sanctity of the Nile, to which divine honours even were paid (vid., Hengstenberg's *Egypt*, etc. pp. 109, 110), and with the belief, which was common to both ancient and modern Egyptians, in the power of its waters to impart fruitfulness and prolong life (vid., *Strabo*, xv. p. 695, etc., and Seetzen, *Travels* iii. p. 204).[208]

In addition, history also testifies to the fact that magicians were a well-known feature of Egyptian life during the period of Moses.--Genesis 11:1-9; Exodus 8:22; 2:5; 5:6, 7, 18; 7:11.

Bricks have been found made with and without straw. The painting below was found in the private tomb of Vizier Rekhmire (the highest official under Pharaoh) on the west bank of ancient Thebes. Archaeology also supports "taskmasters--Egyptian overseers, appointed to exact labor

---

205. Mark F. Rooker, *Leviticus: The New American Commentary* (Nashville: Broadman & Holman, 2001), 26–27.

206 (Genesis 11:3, *ESV*) "And they said to one another, 'Come, let us make bricks, and burn them thoroughly.' And they had brick for stone, and bitumen for mortar."

207 Wilkinson gave a picture of a bathing scene in which an Egyptian woman of rank is introduced, attended by four female servants.

208. Carl Friedric Keil and Franz Delitzsch, *Commentary on the Old Testament* (Peabody, MA: Hendrickson, 2002), S. 1:278.

of the Israelites,"[209] as well as strictly controlled or enforced quotas that had to be met. (Exodus 5:6) Moreover, Egyptian papyri express serious concern for the needed straw (which was lacking at times) to be mixed with the mud to make these bricks. (Exodus 1:13, 14) The Papyri Anastasi, from ancient Egypt, reads, "There was no one to mould bricks, and there was no straw in the neighbourhood."[210]

Furthermore, the historical conditions and surroundings are in accord precisely with the occasions and assertions in the book of Numbers. We have references to Edom, Egypt, Moab, Canaan, Ammon, and Amalek, which are true to the times, and the names of places are free from error.[211] Archaeology is never absolute proof of anything, but it continues to add evidence, weighty at times to the fact that Moses had to be the writer of the Pentateuch. *Halley's Bible Handbook* writes, "Archaeology has been speaking so loudly of late that it is causing a decided reaction toward the conservative view. The theory that writing was unknown in Moses' day is absolutely exploded. And every year there are being dug up in Egypt, Palestine and Mesopotamia, evidences, both in inscriptions and earth layers, that the narratives of the Old Testament are true historical records. And 'scholarship' is coming to have decidedly more respect for the tradition of Mosaic authorship."[212]

The Silver Amulet is one of many archaeological nails in the coffin of the Documentary Hypothesis. Why? This portion of Numbers is argued by the critics to be part of the "P" document that was supposedly penned between 550 and 400 B.C.E. However, initially, it was dated to the late seventh / early sixth centuries B.C.E.

Of course, this dating was subsequently challenged by Johannes Renz and Wolfgang Rollig (*Handbuch der Althebraischen Epigraphik*, 1995) because the silver was cracked and blemished to the point of making many words and a few lines unreadable. This allowed these critics to argue for a date in the third to second centuries B.C.E. period, which would remove this stain on the lifeless body of their Documentary Hypothesis.

Then it was shipped to the University of Southern California to be examined under photographic and computer imaging. The results? The

209. Robert Jamieson, A. R. Fausset, and David Brown. *A Commentary, Critical and Explanatory, On the Old and New Testaments* (Oak Harbor: Scranton & Company, 1997), 51.

210. Adolf Erman and H. M. Tirard. *Life in Ancient Egypt* (Whitefish: Kessinger, 2003), 117.

211. "Sirion . . . Senir." These names appear in the Ugaritic texts found at Ras Shamra, Syria, and in the documents from Bogazköy, Turkey.

212. Henry Halley, *Halley's Bible Handbook* (Grand Rapids: Zondervan, 1988), 56.

researchers stated that they could "read fully and [had] analyzed with far greater precision," which resulted in the final analysis of being yet another vindication for Moses—the original dating stands: late seventh century B.C.E.

Exodus 14:6, 7 (*ESV*) reads, "So he [the Pharaoh] made ready his chariot and took his army with him, and took six hundred chosen chariots and all the other chariots of Egypt with officers over all of them." Pharaoh, being the god of the world and the supreme chief of his army, personally led the army into battle. Archaeology supports this custom.

Why are there no Egyptian records of the Exodus of the Israelites from Egypt? The critics may also ask why is there no archaeological evidence to support the Israelite's 215-year stay in Egypt (some of which was in slavery) and the devastation that was executed on the gods of Egypt. There is, in fact, one simple answer that archaeology has provided us: Any new Egyptian dynasty would erase any unflattering history prior to their dynasty, if such even existed, as it was their custom never to record any defeats that might be viewed as embarrassing or critical, which could damage the dignity of their people, for they were an extremely prideful empire.[213]

For example, Thutmose III ordered others to chisel Queen Hatshepsut out of the history books when he removed the name and representation of Queen Hatshepsut on a monumental stone record later uncovered at Deir al-Bahri in Egypt as well as from any other monuments she had built. Hatshepsut, daughter of Thutmose I, would eventually gain the throne upon her father's death even though Thutmose II (husband and half-brother to Hatshepsut) technically ascended the throne in name only. At best, Thutmose II lasted only three or four years before dying of a skin disease. Thutmose III was too young to rule, thus, Queen Hatshepsut simply held her own as the first female Pharaoh. Embarrassing for Thutmose III, indeed! Thus, as he grew, his hatred mounted for Hatshepsut and Senmut (her lover). After her death, Thutmose III worked vigorously to remove her name and the name of her lover from Egyptian history. If this was embarrassing, how much more so would be the ten plagues that had humiliated numerous gods of Egypt, including the Pharaoh himself? The exodus of 600,000 male slaves and their families, plus Egyptians who had chosen Jehovah as God instead of the Pharaoh of Egypt would have been quite embarrassing, indeed!

In 1925, discoveries of clay tablets were made at the ancient town of Nuzi in northeastern Mesopotamia; it was here that archaeologists found

---

213. Joseph P. Free, *Archaeology and Bible History* (Grand Rapids, MI: Zondervan Publishing, 1964).

a tremendous number of legal contracts dating to the fifteenth-century B.C.E. These actually shed much light on the life of people of that time. Due to the slow-moving life condition of the ancient Near East, they reflect life conditions for many years on both sides of the fifteenth century. Thus, what we now possess and know from studies of these Nuzi Tablets is that there are numerous customs in the Patriarchal period that were very much in common practice among the ancient Hurrians who lived in northern Mesopotamia, encompassing Haran, which was the home of Abraham after he left Ur and where Isaac later found his wife Rebekah.

Abraham's Contract. Eliezer was to be the legal inheritor of childless Abraham's property and position after Abraham's death. In fact, Abraham referred to Eliezer when he said, "a slave born in my house will be my heir." (Genesis 15:2, 3) Tablets from Nuzi discovered by archaeologists help the modern-day reader understand how a servant could become heir to his master's household. Mesopotamian records from the time of Abraham (2018–1843 B.C.E.); makes mention of the tradition of a childless couple adopting a son in their old age to have him take care of them up unto their death, and thereafter inheriting the household property. But if for some reason the couple would end up having a child, the child would become the primary heir instead, with the adopted servant or son getting a minor portion of the property as well. (Wood, 1996) In a culture that passed history down orally through its generations, we find Moses being only three generations removed from Abraham's great-grandson Levi (Levi, Kohath, Amram, and Moses) while our alleged "J" was a thousand years removed from Abraham, and the redactor even further. It is only by means of modern-day archaeology that we are aware of just how accurate the Genesis account is with minor details such as the legal system of adoption rights in Mesopotamia from 2000 B.C.E. (time of Abraham) to 1500 B.C.E. (time of Moses), knowledge that would not be available to our alleged composers. Thus, archaeology puts the Genesis account right back into the hands of its true writer, Moses.

The Price of a Slave. Joseph was the son of Jacob by Rachel, the grandson of Isaac, and the great-grandson of Abraham, and was sold as a slave to some Midianite merchants for a mere 20 pieces of silver by his jealous brothers in about 1750 B.C.E. (Genesis 37:28; 42:21) Throughout the stream of time, we find inflation in the slave trade, and the Biblical account of the price for Joseph falls exactly where it should to be in harmony with secular archaeology, as you can see in chart 1. Again, our alleged "J," "E," "D," and "P" composers would be a thousand years removed from Abraham, and "R" (the redactor) even further; thus they would have no access to this information so as to have gotten it correct.

Only the actual writer, Moses, would be aware of this information by family records or oral tradition.

The Inflation of the Slave Trade in Biblical Times (Wood, 1996)

SOURCE	DATE	PRICE OF A SLAVE IN SILVER
Akkad and 3rd Ur Dynasties	2000 B.C.E.	8–10 pieces of silver
Joseph (Genesis 37:2, 28)	1750 B.C.E.	20 pieces of silver
Hammurabi Code	1799–1700 B.C.E.	20 pieces of silver
Old Babylonian Tablets	B.C.E.	15–30 pieces of silver
Mari tablets	1799–1600 B.C.E.	20 pieces of silver
Exodus 21:32	1520–1470 B.C.E.	30 pieces of silver
Nuzi tablets	1499–1400 B.C.E.	30 pieces of silver
Ugarit tablets	1399–1200 B.C.E.	30–40 pieces of silver
Assyria	First millennium B.C.E.	50–60 pieces of silver
2 Kings 15:20	790 B.C.E.	50 pieces of silver
Persia	750–500 B.C.E.	90–120 pieces of silver

Seti I began much like his father Ramses, as a military commander. His military prowess led to many triumphs that are recorded on the walls of the temple of Amon-Ra at Karnak. Here Seti I recorded his military triumphs; captives are shown being seized by their hair. As was expressed earlier, victories were proudly recorded on Egyptian monuments, but embarrassing or critical events were ignored, that is, never chiseled into their annals of history.

Concluding Thoughts

I had given much thought to a conclusion that contained quotations from many reputable scholars who use thought-provoking points to support the writership of Moses for the Pentateuch, but what would that prove? Certainly, if you quote a reputable scholar you would add weight to an argument, but it does not make the case. It only validates that you are not alone in your reasoning. Therefore, I have added quotations of only two scholars to make just that point. One does not count the number of people who believe one thing as opposed to another and those with the most votes win. No, the results should be based on evidence. In fact, the higher critics will infer that they are in the right by saying, 'Today, you will hardly find one scholar in the world who will argue for the writership of Moses for the Pentateuch.' If that makes them in the right, it also makes them in the wrong. Why? Because for centuries, for millenniums, the majority of Bible scholars—in the Jewish world, the Christian world, and the Islamic world—accepted Moses' writership; that is, until the Age of Reason within the eighteenth and nineteenth centuries when people started to question not only the writership of Moses but the very existence of God.

Would any Christian living in 1700 C.E. have ever doubted the writership of Moses? Hardly! So how did the Documentary Hypothesis become Documentary Fact? All it took was for some leading professors at major universities to plant seeds of doubt within their students. Being at the entrance of the era of higher criticism and skepticism of the nineteenth century, this Documentary Hypothesis had a well-cultivated field in which to grow. It created a domino effect as a few scholars produced a generation of students, who would then be the next generation of scholars, and so on.

As we moved into the twentieth century, these questions had become "facts" in the eyes of many; in fact, it became in vogue to challenge the Bible. Leading schools and leading scholars of higher criticism were the norm, and soon the conservative Christian was isolated. The twentieth-century student received a lean diet from those few scholars who still accepted God's Word as just that, the Word of God, fully inerrant, with 40 writers of 66 books over a period of about 1,600 years. No, these students would now be fed mostly liberal theology, and any who disagreed were portrayed as ignorant and naïve. This planting of uncertainty or mistrust, with question after question bringing Moses' writership into doubt, with most literature focusing on this type of propaganda, would create the latest generation of scholars, and today they dominate the world of scholarship.

How did this progressive takeover come off without a hitch? The conservative scholarship of the early twentieth century saw these liberal naysayers as nothing more than a fly at a picnic. Most did not even deem it necessary to address their questions, so by 1950–1970, the Documentary Hypothesis machine was in full throttle. It was about this same time that the sleeping giant finally awoke to find that conservative scholarship had taken a backseat to this new creature, liberal scholarship. It is only within the last 30–40 years that some very influential conservative scholars have started to publish books in a move to dislodge this liberal movement.* Is it too little, too late?

*This is not to say that the 19th and early 20th century did not have any apologist defending against biblical criticism. There were some giants in this field, like R. A. Torrey.

It is possible to displace higher criticism, but many factors stand in the way. For one, any opposition is painted as uninformed and inexperienced regarding the subject matter. Moreover, the books that tear down the Bible with all their alleged critical analysis sell far better than those do that encourage putting faith in God's Word. In addition, many conservative scholars tend to sit on the sideline and watch as a few leading scholars attempt to do the work of the many. In addition, there are liberal scholars continually putting out numerous articles and books, dominating the market. Unlike the conservative scholars in the first part of the twentieth century, these liberal scholars in the first part of the twenty-first century are not slowing down. Moreover, they have become more aggressive.

The book *Introduction to the Bible*, by John Laux, explains just what the Documentary Hypothesis would have meant for the Israelites if it were true:

> The Documentary Theory is built up on assertions which are either arbitrary or absolutely false. . . . If the extreme Documentary Theory were true, the Israelites would have been the victims of a clumsy deception when they permitted the heavy burden of the Law to be imposed upon them. It would have been the greatest hoax ever perpetrated in the history of the world.[214]

It goes much further than that; it would mean that the Son of God was either fooled by what these higher critics argue, that there was a tradition of Moses being the writer of the Pentateuch, which developed through time and was accepted as reality during Jesus' day, or that Jesus was a liar, because he had lived in heaven prior to his coming down to earth and was aware of the deception but had continued a tradition that he knew to be false. The truth is that the Son of God was well aware that Moses was, in fact, the writer of the Pentateuch and he presented Moses as such because he was there at the time!

So again, because Jesus taught that Moses was, in fact, the writer of the Pentateuch, we have three options:

- Jesus knew Moses was the writer because Jesus was there, in heaven, prior to his Virgin birth and observed Moses as the writer; or

---

214. John Laux, *Introduction to the Bible* (Chicago: Tan Books & Pub., 1992), 186.

- Jesus knew that Moses was not the writer and simply perpetuated a Jewish tradition that Moses was the writer; or

- Jesus possessed a limited knowledge and simply believed something that was a tradition because he was unaware of it being such.

So if Jesus knew Moses was *not* the writer and purposely conveyed misinformation for the sake of Jewish tradition, this makes Jesus a liar and therefore a sinner, which would contradict what Hebrews 4:15 says of him, that "he was without sin." If he was simply in ignorance and was mistakenly conveying misinformation, this certainly does away with Jesus having a prehuman existence. (John 1:1–2; 3:13; 6:38, 62; 8:23, 42, 58; Colossians 1:15–18; Revelation 3:14; Proverbs 8:22–30) Based on the scriptures and other evidence presented, we can conclude that Jesus was well aware that Moses was the writer, and that is what he truthfully taught.

Duane Garrett makes the following observation concerning the Documentary Hypothesis:

> The time has long passed for scholars of every theological persuasion to recognize that the Graf-Wellhausen theory, as a starting point for continued research, is dead. The Documentary Hypothesis and the arguments that support it have been effectively demolished by scholars from many different theological perspectives and areas of expertise. Even so, the ghost of Wellhausen hovers over Old Testament studies and symposiums like a thick fog. . . . One wonders if we will ever return to the day when discussions of Genesis will not be stilted by interminable references to P and J. There are indications that such a day is coming. Many scholars are exploring the inadequacies of the Documentary Hypothesis and looking toward new models for explaining the Pentateuch.[215]

These world-renowned scholars who have gone left of center are witty and able to express thoughts, ideas, and feelings coherently, having conviction that leads unsuspecting ones who are not aware of the facts to accept ideas that are made to appear as smooth-fitting pieces in a large puzzle, thinking that they are nothing more than long-awaited answers. Sadly, many unsuspecting readers have taken their words as absolute truth.

Jesus quotes or alludes to 23 of the 39 books of the Hebrew Scriptures. Specifically, he quotes all five of the books attributed to

---

[215] Garrett, Duane. *Rethinking Genesis: The Sources and Authorship of the First Book of the Pentateuch* (Grand Rapids: Baker Books, 1991), 13.

Moses—the book of Deuteronomy 16 times alone, this obviously being one of his favorites. As we close this chapter, we are going to let our greatest witness take the stand. As you read Jesus' references to Moses and the Law you will undoubtedly notice that he viewed Moses' writership as historically true, completely authoritative, and inspired of God. If one does not accept, Moses, as the writer of the Pentateuch as Jesus did, is that not calling Jesus a liar.

As Christians, we accept what the Bible teaches as true. By way of common sense and sound reasoning, the vast majority of the issues of higher criticism's Social Progressive Christian and Christian Modernists have been answered quite easily by the conservative scholar in absolute terms: for example, F. David Farnell, Gleason L. Archer Jr., C. John Collins, K. A. Kitchen, Norman L. Geisler, and others. For the handful of issues left, we still have reasonable answers, which are not beyond a reasonable doubt at this time; we are quite content to wait until we are provided with the concrete answers that will make these few issues beyond all reasonable doubt. The last 150 years of evidence that has come in by way of archaeological discoveries, a better understanding of the original language, historical-cultural and contextual understanding, as well as manuscripts has answered almost all those doubtful areas that have been called into question by the higher critics. Therefore, because we lack the complete answers for a few remaining issues means nothing.

Consider this: A critic raises an issue, but it is answered by a new archaeological discovery a few years later. The critic runs to another issue, and it is later answered by an improved understanding of the original languages. Then he runs to look for yet another issue, and it is answered by thousands of manuscripts that are uncovered over a period of two decades. This has been the case with thousands of issues. What are we to think the agenda is of those who continue scouring God's Word looking for errors, discrepancies, and contradictions? How many times must they raise objections and be proven wrong before we stop listening to their cries? If that is the case, why do their books still outsell those that expose their erroneous thinking? Does that say something about the Christian community and their desire for tabloid scholarship (sensationalized stories)? Would the average Christian rather read an article or book by Dan Brown on how Jesus allegedly married and had sexual relations with Mary Magdalene and fathered children (false, of course), or read an article or book on the actual, even more fascinating account of Jesus' earthly life, based on the four Gospels?

For today's Christian, there is no more important study than the life and ministry of the real, historical Jesus Christ. The writer of the book of Hebrews exhorts us to **"fix our eyes on** Jesus," to **"consider him** who endured such opposition from sinful men." Moreover, Jehovah God himself commanded: "This is my Son, whom I love; with him I am well pleased. **Listen to him!**" (*NIV*, bolding added) While an apologetic of the study of the "*Historical Jesus*," or "*The Case for the Resurrection of Jesus*"[216] is certainly fine, the primary source of the four Gospels accounts of Matthew, Mark, Luke, and John should be first place, the starting point of any real investigation of Jesus' life and ministry. A life and ministry that viewed the Old Testament as historically true and of the greatest importance to his followers that he would leave behind after his ascension back to heaven.

We return to Wellhausen, who investigated his documentary hypothesis under the worldview of Israelite religion from an evolutionary model: (1) at the beginning it was animistic and spiritistic, (2) gradually developing into polytheism, (3) moving eventually into henotheism (choosing one god out of many), and finally (4) gravitating to monotheism. Wellhausen could not accept that this development took place in a short period, but was an evolution that took more than a millennium. This evolutionary process is no longer held among today's critical scholarship.

Another obstacle was that Wellhausen did not believe in the miraculous and could not accept prophetic statements (for example, Genesis 49) happening before the actual events. This mindset was the catalyst behind his research.[217] Consequently, Wellhausen investigated the text with this way of thinking and that state of mind contributed to his discovering the Documentary Hypothesis issues of different uses of the divine name, discrepancies, repetitions (doublets), and differences in style and language, reading his views into the text (eisegesis).

The above facts of this book have easily demonstrated that the evidence of the documentary hypothesis is really no evidence at all. The modern-day critic has to deal with the lack of consensus on the part of his colleagues, who lack in agreement for the explanation of the sources.

This failure to achieve consensus is represented by the occasional division of source strata into multiple layers (see Smend's J1 and J2) that often occasions the appearance of new

---

216. **Recommended**: Gary R. Habermas, *The Historical Jesus: Ancient Evidence for the Life of Christ* (Joplin, MO: College Press, 1996); Gary R. Habermas, *The Case for the Resurrection of Jesus* (Grand Rapids, MI: Kregel, 2004); Craig A. Evans, *Fabricating Jesus: How Modern Scholars Distort the Gospels* (Downers Grove, IL: IVP Books, 2006); Timothy Paul Jones, *Misquoting Truth: A Guide to the Fallacies of Bart Ehrman's Misquoting Jesus* (Downers Grove, IL: IVP Books, 2007).

217 Tremper Longman III, and Raymond B. Dillard, *An Introduction to the Old Testament* (Grand Rapids: Zondervan, 2006), 43–44.

sigla (for instance, Eissfeldt's L [aienquelle], Noth's G[rundschrift], Fohrer's N [for Nomadic], and Pfeiffer's S [for Seir]. A further indication of the collapse of the traditional documentary hypothesis is the widely expressed doubt that E was ever an independent source (Voz, Rudolph, Mowinckel; cf. Kaiser, IOT, 42 n. 18). Similar disagreements are also found in the dating of the sources. J has been dated to the period of Solomon by Von Rad, though Schmidt would argue for the seventh century, and Van Seters (1992, 34) has advocated an exile date. While most scholars believe P is postexilic, Haran has argued that it is to be associated with Hezekiah's reforms in the eighth century BC.[218]

While the lack of consensus is not in and of itself capable of disproving the proposition of sources other than Moses for the writing of the Pentateuch, it does cast even more doubt on the critical scholar's proposal that the new school of the Documentary Hypothesis has any more to offer than the old school of Wellhausen.

As this book has clearly demonstrated, Moses is the inspired author of the Pentateuch. At best, we can accept that it is likely that Joshua may have updated the text in Deuteronomy chapter 34, which speaks of Moses' death, and it is possible that Joshua may have made the reference in Numbers 12:3 that refer to Moses as being 'the humblest man on the face of the earth.'[219] In addition, we can accept that a later copyist [or even possibly Ezra, another inspired author] updated Genesis 11:28, 31 to read "of the Chaldeans," a name of a land and its inhabitants in the southern portion of Babylonia that *possibly* was not recognized as Chaldea until several hundred years after Moses.

> The origin of the Chaldeans is uncertain but may well be in the west, or else branches of the family may have moved there (cf. Job 1:17). The general name for the area in the earliest period is unknown, since it was part of Sumer (*see* SHINAR); so it cannot be argued that the qualification of Abraham's home city UR as "of the Chaldeans" (Gen. 11:28, 31; 15:7; as later Neh. 9:7; cf. Acts 7:4) is necessarily a later insertion in the text.[220]

The same would hold true of a copyist updating Genesis 36:31, which reads: "Now these are the kings who reigned in the land of Edom before *any king reigned over the sons of Israel*." Moses and Joshua were

---

218. Ibid., 49–50.

219 For the possibility of Moses penning these words, see my comments in the first paragraph of section four.

220 Geoffrey W. Bromiley, vol. 1, *The International Standard Bible Encyclopedia, Revised* (Wm. B. Eerdmans, 1988; 2002), 630.

long gone for hundreds of years before Israel ever had a king over them.[221] The same would hold true again for Genesis 14:14, which reads: When Abram heard that his relative had been taken captive, he led out his trained men, born in his house, three hundred and eighteen, and went in pursuit *as far as Dan.* Dan was an area settled long after Moses death, after the Israelites had conquered the Promise Land. This too is obviously an update as well, making it contemporary to its readers.[222]

Reference to "Ur of the Chaldeans"[223] (11:28) identifies the native land of Haran but not necessarily of Terah and his sons Abram and Nahor. In fact, the inclusion of this information for Haran may suggest the ancestral home was elsewhere (for this discussion see comments on 12:1). "Ur of the Chaldeans" occurs three times in Genesis (11:28, 31; 15:7) and once elsewhere (Neh 9:7). Stephen identified the place of God's revelation to Abram as "Mesopotamia" from which he departed: "So he left the land of the Chaldeans and settled in Haran" (Acts 7:3–4). The "land [*chōra*] of the Chaldeans" rather than "Ur of the Chaldeans" is the Septuagint translation, as reflected in Stephen's sermon, which can be explained as either a textual slip due to the prior phrase "land of his birth" or the ancient translator's uncertainty about the identity of the site. J. W. Wevers proposes that due to the apposition of "land of his birth," the translator interpreted "Ur" as a region.[224, 225]

As we have already stated, the critic is fond of finding portions of the text that lack secular support, and then summarily dismissing it as not being a real historical account. Once evidence surfaces to support their dismissal as being wrong and premature, they simply never mention this section again, but move on to another. The question that begs to be

---

[221] It should be noted that even this statement could belong to Moses, even though there were no kings in Israel at this time. How? He would be aware that Jehovah had promised Abraham that he would be so great that kings would come out of him (Gen 17:6) and the preparation for such is mentioned at Deuteronomy 17:14-20.

[222] It should be noted that this author does not accept higher criticisms unending desire to find source(s) for a book, because they have dissected it to no end. While there are a few details that may have been updated by a copyist, or even the inspired writer Ezra (writer of Chronicles and the book that bears his name), this does not mean that we accept the update, if it is such, as the inspired material that was originally written, unless it was done by another inspired writer like Joshua, Ezra, or Nehemiah, or even possibly Jeremiah. It is also possible that it could be an explanatory addition.

[223] Hb. "Chaldeans" כַּשְׂדִּים is *kaldu* (Akk.) in Assyrian texts, and the Gk. has καλδαιοι; the original *sd* has undergone a change to *ld* (see R. S. Hess, "Chaldea," *ABD* 1.886–87).

[224] J. W. Wevers, *Notes on the Greek Text of Genesis*, Septuagint and Cognate Studies 35 (Atlanta: Scholars Press, 1993), 158.

[225] K. A. Mathews, vol. 1B, *Genesis 11:27-50:26*, electronic ed., Logos Library System; The New American Commentary (Nashville: Broadman & Holman Publishers, 2007), 99–100.

asked by the logical and reasonable mind is, how many times must this take place before they stop and accept the Bible as sound and reliable history? Let us look at the historicity of the above account of Abraham's men defeating the Mesopotamian kings, for it is historically sound. Information had become known in the 20th century that vindicates this account as being historically true, and removes yet another arguing point from those supporters of the documentary hypothesis:

> The name of Chedorlaomer, King of Elam, contains familiar Elamite components: *kudur* meant "servant," and *Lagamar* was a high goddess in the Elamite pantheon. Kitchen (Ancient Orient, p. 44) generally prefers the vocalization Kutir instead of Kudur and gives the references for at least three Elamite royal names of this type. He equates tidal with a Hittite name, Tudkhaliya, attested from the nineteenth century B.C. As for Arioch, one King of Larsa ("El-Larsa") from this era was Eri-aku ("Servant of the Moon-god"), whose name in Akkadian was *Arad-Sin* (with the same meaning). The Mari tablets refer to persons by the name of Ariyuk. The cuneiform of the original of Amraphel, formerly equated with Hammurabi of Babylon, is not demonstrable for the twentieth century (Hammurabi himself dates from the eighteenth century, but there may possibly be a connection with Amorite names like *Amud-pa-ila*, according to H. B. Huffman. . . . It should be added that according to G. Pettinato, the leading epigraphist of the Ebla documents dating from 2400–2250 B.C., mention is made in the Ebla tablets of Sodom (spelled *Si-da-mu*), Gomorrah (spelled in Sumerian cuneiform *I-ma-ar*), and Zoar (*Za-e-ar*). He feels that quite possibly these may be the same cities mentioned in the Abrahamic narrative.[226]

> W. F. Albright comments: In spite of our failure hitherto to fix the historical horizon of this chapter, we may be certain that its contents are very ancient. There are several words and expressions found nowhere else in the Bible and now known to belong to the second millenium. The names of the towns in Transjordania are also known to be very ancient.[227]

In the final analysis, based on both the internal and external evidence, we can absolute confidence that Moses was the author of the Pentateuch. The minor additions of Joshua, who was himself an inspired

---

226. Gleason L. Archer, *Encyclopedia of Bible Difficulties* (Grand Rapids: Zondervan, 1982), 90–91.

227. H. C. Alleman and E. E. Flack, *Old Testament Commentary* (Philadelphia: Fortress, 1954), 14.

writer, as well as the handful of updates in the text to make it clearer to the then-current reader does no harm to the inspired message that God wished to convey.

Bibliography

Akin, Daniel L. *The New American Commentary: 1, 2, 3 John.* Nashville, TN: Broadman & Holman , 2001.

Aland, Kurt and Barbara. *The Text of the New Testament.* Grand Rapids: Eerdmans, 1987.

Alden, Robert L. *Job, The New American Commentary, vol. 11 .* Nashville: Broadman & Holman Publishers, 2001.

Aldrich, C Joseph. *Lifestyle Evangelism.* Portland, OR: Multnoma Press, 1981.

Alleman, H. C., and E. E. Flack. *Old Testament Commentary.* Philadelphia: Fortress Press, 1954.

Anders, Max. *Holman New Testament Commentary: vol. 8, Galatians-Colossians .* Nashville, TN: Broadman & Holman Publishers, 1999.

—. *Holman New Testament Commentary: vol. 8, Galatians, Ephesians, Philippians, Colossians.* Nashville, TN: Broadman & Holman Publishers, 1999.

—. *Holman Old Testament Commentary - Proverbs .* Nashville: B&H Publishing, 2005.

Anders, Max, and Trent Butler. *Holman Old Testament Commentary: Isaiah.* Nashiville, TN: B&H Publishing, 2002.

Andrews, Edward D. *THE COMPLETE GUIDE TO BIBLE TRANSLATION: Bible Translation Choices and Principles.* Cambridge: Christian Publishing House, 2012.

—. *THE EVANGELISM HANDBOOK: How All Christians Can Effectively Share God's Word in Their Community.* Cambridge: Christian Publishing House, 2013.

Andrews, Edward D. *AN INTRODUCTION TO BIBLE DIFFICULTIES So-Called Errors and Contradictions.* Cambridge: Christian Publishing House, 2011.

—. *An Introduction to Bible Difficulties: So-called Errors and Contradictions.* Cambridge, OH: Christian Publlishing House, 2012.

—. *BIBLE DIFFICULTIES: Debunking the Documentary Hypothesis.* Cambridge: Christian Publishing House, 2011.

—. *BOOKS OF 2 JOHN 3 JOHN and JUDE CPH New Testament Commentary.* Cambridge: Christian Publishing House, 2013.

—. *CHRISTIAN THEOLOGY: The Evangelism Study Tool.* Cambridge, OH: Christian Publishing House, 2016.

—. *CONVERSATIONAL EVANGELISM: Defending the Faith, Reasoning from the Scriptures, Explaining and Proving, Instructing in Sound Doctrine, and Overturning False Reasoning.* Cambridge, OH: Christian Publishing House, 2015.

—. *THE CHRISTIAN APOLOGIST: Always Being Prepared to Make a Defense .* Cambridge: Christian Publishing House, 2014.

—. *The Text of the New Testament: A Beginner's Guide to New Testament Textual Criticism.* Cambridge, OH: Bible-Translation.Net Books, 2012.

Archer, Gleason L. *A Survey of Old Testament Introduction (Revised and Expanded).* Chicago: Moody, 1994.

—. *A Survey of Old Testament Introduction.* Chicago: Moody, 1994.

—. *Encyclopedia of Bible Difficulties.* Grand Rapids: Zondervan, 1982.

Arndt, William, Frederick W. Danker, and Walter Bauer. *A Greek-English Lexicon of the New Testament and Other Early Christian Literature. 3rd ed.* . Chicago: University of Chicago Press, 2000.

Arnold, Clinton E. *Zondervan Illustrated Bible Backgrounds Commentary Volume 2: John, Acts.* . Grand Rapids, MI: Zondervan, 2002.

—. *Zondervan Illustrated Bible Backgrounds Commentary Volume 3: Romans to Philemon.* Grand Rapids: Zondervan, 2002.

—. *Zondervan Illustrated Bible Backgrounds Commentary Volume 4: Hebrews to Revelation.* Grand Rapids, MI: Zondervan, 2002.

—. *Zondervan Illustrated Bible Backgrounds Commentary: Matthew, Mark, Luke, vol. 1.* Grand Rapids, MI: Zondervan, 2002.

Baer, Daniel. *The Unquenchable Fire.* Maitland, FL: Xulon Press, 2007.

Bahnsen, Greg, and Van Til. *Apologetic .* (Phillipsburg, NJ: Presbyterian and Reformed, 1998.

Barbour, R. S. *Traditio-Historical Criticism of the Gospels.* London: SPCK, 1972.

Barclay, William. *The Letter to the Hebrews (New Daily Study Bible).* Louisville, KY: Westminster John Knox Press, 2002.

Barnett, Paul. *The Birth of Christianity: The First Twenty Years (After Jesus, Vol. 1)* . Grand Rapids, MI: Wm. B. Eerdmans , 2005.

Barton, John. *The Nature of Biblical Criticism.* Louisville: Westminster John Knox Press, 2007.

Barton, S.C. "'The Communal Dimension of Earliest Christianity'." *JTS 43*, 1992: 399–427.

—. *Discipleship and Family Ties in Mark and Matthew.* Cambridge: Cambridge University Press, 1994.

Bercot, David W. *A Dictionary of Early Christian Beliefs.* Peabody: Hendrickson, 1998.

Berkhof, Louis. *New Testament Introduction.* Grand Rapids: Eerdman-Sevensma, 1915.

—. *Principles of Biblical Interpretation.* . Grand Rapids, MI: Baker House, 1992.

Black, Allen, and Mark C Black. *THE COLLEGE PRESS NIV COMMENTARY 1 & 2 PETER.* Joplin: College Press Publishing Company, 1998.

Blenkinsopp, Joseph. *Isaiah 56-66: A New Translation with Introduction and Commentary.* New York: Anchor Bible, 2003.

Blomberg, Craig L. *Historical Reliability of the Gospels.* Downer Groves, IL: IVP Academic, 2007.

Blomberg, Craig L. "New Testament miracles and Higher Criticism: Climbing Up the Slippery Slope." *JETS 27/4*, December 1984: 436.

Blomberg, Craig L, and Stanley E., Stovell, Beth M Porter Jr. *Biblical Hermeneutics Five Views.* Downers Grove: InterVarsity Press, 2012.

Blomberg, Craig. *The New American Commentary: Matthew* . Nashville, TN : Broadman & Holman Publishers, 2001.

Boa, Kenneth, and Kruidenier. *Holman New Testament Commentary: Romans.* Nashville: Broadman & Holman, 2000.

Bock, Darrell L. *"Form Criticism," in New Testament Criticism and Interpretation. Edited by David A. Black and David S. Dockery.* Grand Rapids: Zondervan, 1991.

—. *Studying the Historical Jesus: A Guide to Sources and Methods.* Grand Rapids, MI: Baker, 2002.

—. *The Missing Gospels: Unerthing the Truth Behind Alternative Christianities.* Nashville, TN: Thomas Nelson, 2006.

Borchert, Gerald L. *The New American Commentary: John 1-11* . Nashville, TN: Broadman & Holman Publishers, 2001.

Borchert, Gerald L. *The New American Commentary vol. 25B, John 12– 21*. Nashville: Broadman & Holman Publishers, 2002.

Bradley, Anthony B. *Liberating Black Theology: The Bible and the Black Experience in America*. Wheaton: Crossway, 2010.

Brand, Chad, Charles Draper, and England Archie. *Holman Illustrated Bible Dictionary: Revised, Updated and Expanded*. Nashville, TN: Holman, 2003.

Bratcher, Robert. "Inerrancy: Clearing Away Confusion." *Christianity Today*, May 29, 1981: 12.

Bray, Gerald. *Biblical Interpretation: Past and Present*. Downers Grove, IL: InterVarsity Press, 1996.

Bridges, Jerry. *The Practice of Godliness* . Colorado Springs, CO: : NavPress, 1983.

Briley, Terry R. *The College Press NIV Commentary: Isaiah*. Joplin, MO: ollege Press Pub, 2000.

Bromiley, Geoffrey W. *The International Standard Bible Encyclopedia (Vol. 1-4)*. Grand Rapids, MI: William B. Eerdmans Publishing Co., 1986.

Bromiley, Geoffrey W., and Gerhard Friedrich. *Theological Dictionary of the New Testament, ed. Gerhard Kittel, vol. 4*. Grand Rapids, MI: Eerdmans, 1964-.

Brotzman, Ellis R. *Old Testament Textual Criticism*. Grand Rapids: Baker Academic, 1994.

Bruce, F. F. *The New International Commentary on the New Testament: The Epistle to the Hebrews (Revised)*. Grand Rapids, MI: William B. Eermans Publishing Company, 1990.

Bucher, Christina. "New Directions in Biblical Interpretation Revisited." *Bretheren Life and Thought 60, no. 1*, Spring 2015: 36.

Bultmann, Rudolf. *The History of the Synoptic Tradition*. Peabody: Hendrickson, 1990.

—. *The History of the Synoptic Tradition. Translated by John Marsh. Revised Edition*. Peabody, MA: Hendrickson, 1963.

Bultmann, Rudolf. "The New Approach to the Synoptic Problem." *Journal of Religion*, July, 1926: 345.

Bultmann, Rudolf, and Frederick C. Translated by Grant. *"The Study of the Synoptic Gospels,"* in *Form Criticism, Two Essays on New Testament Research.* . New York: Harper & Brothers, 1932.

Burge, Gary M. *Interpreting the Fourth Gospel, Guides to New Testament Exegesis, vol. 3.* Grand Rapids, MI: Baker Book House, 1992.

Buter, Trent C. *Holman New Testament Commentary: Luke.* Nashville, TN: Broadman & Holman Publishers, 2000.

Byrne, James M. *Religion and the Enlightenment from Descartes to Kant.* Louisville: Westminster John Knox Press, 1996.

Caba, Tedl et al.,. *The Apologetics Study Bible: Real Questions, Straight Answers, Stronger Faith.* Nashville: Holman Bible Publishers, 2007.

Caird, George B. "The Study of the Gospels: II. Form Criticism." *Expository Times LXXXVII*, February 1976: 139.

Carson, D. A, and Douglas J Moo. *An Introduction to the New Testament.* Grand Rapids, MI: Zondervan, 2005.

Carson, D. A. *New Bible Commentary: 21st Century Edition. 4th ed.* Downers Grove: Inter-Varisity Press, 1994.

Cassuto, Umberto. *The Documentary Hypothesis: And The Composition of the Pentateuch.* Jerusalem: Shalem Press, 2006.

Coleman, E. Robert. *The Master Plan of Evangelism.* Westwood, NJ: Fleming H. Revell Company, 1964.

Collins, John. *Genesis 1-4: A Linguistic, Literary, and Theological Commentary.* Philipsburg: P&R, 2006.

Comfort, Philip. *Encountering the Manuscripts: An Introduction to New Testament Paleography and Textual Criticism.* Nashville: Broadman & Holman, 2005.

—. *Encounterring the Manuscripts: An Introduction to New Testament Paleography and Textual Criticism.* Nashville: Broadman & Holman, 2005.

Comfort, Philip W. *New Testament Text and Translation Commentary.* Carol Stream: Tyndale House Publishers, 2008.

Comfort, Philip, and David Barret. *The Text of the Earliest New Testament Greek Manuscripts.* Wheaton: Tyndale House Publishers, 2001.

Cook, Stephen L. "Introduction: Case Studies from the Second Wave of Research in the Social World of the Hebrew Bible," ed. Ronald Simkins and Athalya Brenner." *Semeia 87*, 1999: 1-2.

Cooper, Lamar Eugene. *The New American Commentary, Ezekiel, vol. 17.* Nashville, TN: Broadman & Holman Publishers, 1994.

Cottrell, Peter, and Maxwell Turner. *Linguistics and Biblical Interpretation.* Downers Grove: InterVarsity Press, 1989.

Cruse, C. F. *Eusebius' Eccliatical History.* Peabody, MA: Hendrickson, 1998.

Daly, Mary. *Beyond God the Father: Toward a Philosophy of Liberation.* Boston: Beacon Press, 1973.

Davies, William D. *Invitation to the New Testament, A Guide to Its Main Witnesses.* Garden City, N.Y.: Doubleday, 1966.

Davis, John J. *Paradise to Prison: Studies in Genesis.* Salem: Sheffield, 1975.

Dayton, Donald W. "The Battle for the Bible: Renewing the Inerrancy Debate." *The Christian Century* , Nov 10, 1976: 976-80.

Delahaunty, R. J. *Spinoza: Arguments of the Philosophers.* London: Routledge & Kegan Paul Books, 1985.

Dockery, David S., Kenneth A. Matthews, and Robert B. Sloan. *Foundations for Biblical Interpretation.* Nashville: Broadman & Holman Publishers, 1994.

Dodd, C. H. *History and the Gospel.* London: Nisbet, 1938.

Donald A. Hanger, The Jewish Reclamation of Jesus. Eugene: Wipf and Stock, 1997.

Driver, G R. *Canaanite Myths and Legends.* New York: T. & T. Clark, 1971.

Dunn, James D. G. *"The Messianic Secret in Mark,"* in The Messianic Secret Edited by Christopher Tuckett. Philadelphia: Fortress, 1983.

Easley, Kendell H. *Holman New Testament Commentary, vol. 12, Revelation.* (Nashville, TN: Broadman & Holman Publishers, 1998.

Eims, LeRoy. *One to One Evangelism.* Wheaton, IL: Victor Books, 1974, 1990.

Ellingworth, Paul. *The Epistle to the Hebrews: A Commentary on the Greek Text.* Grand Rapids, MI: W.B. Eerdmans, 1993.

Elliott, J.H. *A Home for the Homeless: A Sociological Exegesis of I Peter: Its Situation and Strategy* . London: SCM Press, 1982.

Elliott, John H. "Social-Scientific Criticism of the New Testament: More on Methods and Models." *Semeia 35*, 1986: 6-7.

—. *What is Social Scientific Criticism?* . Minneapolis: Fortress Press, 1993.

Elwell, Walter A. *Evangelical Dictionary of Theology (Second Edition)*. Grand Rapids: Baker Academic, 2001.

Elwes, R H M. *A Theologico-political Treatise, and a Political Treatise* . New York, NY: Cosimo Classics , 2005.

Erickson, Millard J. "Biblical Inerrancy: the last twenty-five years." *Journal of the Evangelical Theological Society*, 1982: 387-394.

Erickson, Milliard J. *Christian Theology*. Grand Rapids, MI: Baker Academic, 1998.

Erickson, Richard J. *A Beginner's Guide to New Testament Exegesis*. Downers Grove: InterVarsity Press, 2005.

Esler, Philip F. *The First Christians in their Social Worlds* . New York: Taylor & Francis, 2007.

—. *The First Christians in their Social Worlds*. New York: Routledge, 1994.

Farmer, William R. *The Synoptic Problem*. Macon, Ga: Mercer University, 1976.

Farnell, F. David. "Historical Criticism vs. Grammatico-Historical Criticism?" *The Jesus Quest*, Quo Vadis Evangelicals: 503-520.

Fasold, Ralph, Jeff Connor-Linton, and ed. *An Introduction to Language and Linguistics*. Cambridge: Cambridge University Press, 2006.

Fee, Gordon D. *New Testament Exegesis: A Handbook for Studemts and Pastors*. Louisville: Westminister John Knox Press, 2002.

Ferguson, Everett. *Backgrounds of Early Christianity*. Grand Rapids, MI: Wm. B. Eerdmans, 2003.

Frame, John M. *Apologetics to the Glory of God*. Phillipsburg: P&R Publishing, 1994.

Frampton, Travis L. *Spinoza and the Rise of Historical Criticism of the Bible*. New York: T&T Clark, 2006.

Free, J. P. *Archaeology and Bible History (Revised amnd Expanded Edition)*. Grand Rapids: Zondervan, 1992.

Friedan, Betty. *The Feminist Mistique* . New York: Dell Publishing, 1963.

Friedman, Richard Elliot. *Who Wrote The Bible*. San Francisco: Harper Collins, 1997.

Friedman, Richard Elliott. *The Bible With Sources Revealed*. Northampton: Harper Collins, 2005.

Gangel, Kenneth O. *Holman New Testament Commentary: Acts*. Nashville, TN: Broadman & Holman Publishers, 1998.

Gangel, Kenneth O. *Holman New Testament Commentary, vol. 4, John* . Nashville, TN: Broadman & Holman Publishers, 2000.

—. *Holman Old Testament Commentary: Daniel*. Nashville: Broadman & Holman Publishers, 2001.

Garrett, Don. *The Cambridge companion to Spinoza*. Cambridge: Cambridge University Press, 1996.

Garrett, Duane. *Rethinking Genesis: The Sources and Authorship of the First Book of the Pentateuch* . Grand Rapids: Baker Books, 1991.

Geisler, Norman L. *Defending Inerrancy: Affirming the Accuracy of Scripture for a New Generation*. Grand Rapids, MI: Baker Books, 2012.

—. *Inerrancy*. Grand Rapids, MI: Zondervan, 1980.

Geisler, Norman L, and William E Nix. *A General Introduction to the Bible*. Chicago: Moody Press, 1996.

Geisler, Norman L. *"Inductivism, Materialism, and Rationalism: Bacon, Hobbes, and Spinoza," in The Biblical Errancy: An Analysis of Its Philosophical Roots*. Edited by Norman Geisler. Grand Rapids: Zondervan, 1981.

—. *Baker Encyclopedia of Christian Apologetics*. Grand Rapids: Baker Books, 1999.

—. *Biblical Errancy: An Analysis of Its Philosophical Roots*. Eugene, OR: Wipf and Stock Publisher, 1981.

Geisler, Norman L., and Thomas Howe. *The Big Book of Bible Difficulties*. Grand Rapids: Baker Books, 1992.

Geisler, Norman, and David Geisler. *CONVERSATION EVANGELISM: How to Listen and Speak So You Can Be Heard*. Eugene: Harvest House Publishers, 2014.

—. *CONVERSATION EVANGELISM: How to Listen and Speak So You Can Be Heard*. Eugene: Harvest House Publishers, 2009.

Geisler, Norman, and Ron Brooks. *When Skeptics Ask* . Grand Rapids, MI: Baker Books, 1996.

George, Timothy. *The New American Commentary: Galatians* . Nashville, TN: Broadman & Holman Publishers, 2001.

Gilson, Etienne, and Thomas Langan. *Modern Philosophy: Descartes to Kant*. New York: Random House, 1963.

Goodspeed, Edgar J. *Matthew, Apostle and Evangelist*. Philadelphia: John C. Winston, 1959.

Goodspeed, J. *Matthew, Apostle and Evangelist*. Philadelphia: John C. Winston, 1959.

Gorman, Michael J. *Elements of Biblical Exegesis: A Basic Guide for Students and Ministers*. Peabody: Hendrickson, 2001.

Green, Joel B, Scot McKnight, and Howard Marshall. *Dictionary of Jesus and the Gospels*. Downers Grove, IL: InterVarsity Press, 1992.

Greenlee, J Harold. *Introduction to New Testament Textual Criticism*. Peabody: Hendrickson, 1995.

Grenz, Stanley J., and Roger E Olsen. *20th Century Theology: God & the World in a Transitional Age*. Downers Gove: Intervarsity Press, 1992.

Grudem, Wayne, Leland Ryken, John C Collins, Vern S Poythress, and Bruce Winter. *Translating Truth: The Case for Essentially Literal Bible Translation*. Wheaton: Crossway Books, 2005.

Guelich, Robert A. *The Sermon on the Mount, A Foundation for Understanding*. Waco, TX: Word, 1982.

Gundry, Robert H. *The Use of the Old Testament in St. Matthew's Gospel*. Leiden: E. J. Brill, 1967.

Gundry, Robert H. "The Language Milieu of First-Century Palestine." *Journal of Biblical Literature 83*, 1964: 408.

Gunkel, Hermann (Translated by Scullion, John J. Edited by Scott, William R.). *The Stories of Genesis*. Berkeley: BIBAL, 1994.

Gunkel, Hermann. *The Stories of Genesis. Translated by John J. Scullion. Edited by William R. Scott*. Berkeley: BIBAL, 1994.

Guthrie, Donald. *Introduction to the New Testament (Revised and Expanded)*. Downers Grove, IL: InterVarsity Press, 1990.

Guthrie, George H. *The NIV Application Commentary: Hebrews*. Grand Rapids, MI: Zondervan, 1998.

Gutierrez, Gustavo. *A Theology of Liberation: History, Politics, and Salvation.* Maryknoll, NY: Orbis Books, 1988.

Habib, M. A. R. *A History of Literary Criticism and Theory from Plato to the Present.* Malden: Blackwell Publishing, 2008.

Hagner, Donald. *The New Testament, History, and the Historical Critical Method, in New Testament Criticism and Interpretation.* Grand Rapids: Baker, 2013.

Hanson, K. C., and Douglas E. Oakman. *Palestine in the time of Jesus .* Minneapolis: : Augsburg Press, 1998.

Harris, Robert Laird, Gleason Leonard Archer, and Bruce K Waltke. *Theological Wordbook of the Old Testament.* Chicago: Moody Press, 1999, c1980.

Harrison, Everett F. *Introduction to the New Testament.* Grand Rapids: Eerdmans, 1971.

Harrison, R. K. *Introduction to the Old Testament.* Massachusetts: Hendrickson, 2004.

Hasel, Gerhard F. *Understanding the Living Word of God. .* Mountain View, CA: Pacific Press, 1980.

Hayes, John H, and Carl R Holladay. *Biblical Exegesis: A Beginner's Handbook.* Lousiville, KY: Westminister John Knox Press, 2007.

Hill, Jonathan. *Zondervan Handbook to the History of Christianity.* Oxford: Lion, 2006.

Hindson, Ed, and Ergun Caner. *The Popular Encyclopedia of Apologetics: Surveying the Evidence for the Truth of Christianity.* Eugene: Harvest House, 2008.

Hoerth, Alfred. *Archaeology and the Old Testament.* Grand Rapids: Baker, 1998.

Holbert, John C, and Alyce M McKenzie. *What Not to Say: Avoiding the Common Mistakes that Can Sink Your Sermon.* Lousiville: Westminster Knox Press, 1972.

House, Paul R. *The New American Commentary: 2 Kings .* Nashville: Broadman & Holman Publishers, 2001.

—. *The New American Commentary: Vol. 8., 2 Kings.* Nashville: Broadman & Holman Publishers, 2001.

House, Paul R., and Eric Mitchell. *Old Testament Survey (2nd Edition).* Nashville, TN: B&H Publishing Group, 2007.

Howe, Thomas A. *Objectivity in Biblical Interpretation*. North Charleston: CreateSpace, 2015.

Hume, David. *An Enquiry Concerning Human Understanding (vol. 35)*. Chicago: Great Books of the Western World, 1952.

Hume, David, and Adam Smith. *An Enquiry Concerning Human Understanding: And Selections from a Treatise of Human Nature*. New York: Barnes & Noble Library of Essential Reading, 2004.

Hutchison, John C. "Darwin's Evolutionary Theory and 19th-Century Natural Theology." *Bibliotheca Sacra 152*, July-September 1995: 334.

Huxley, Thomas H. *Science and Christian Tradition*. New York: D. Appleton, 1899.

Jeremias, Joachim. *New Testament Theology*. New York: Charles Scribner's Sons, 1971.

John, Robert H. *Evangelicals at an Impasse: Biblical Authority in Practice*. Atlanta: John Knox, 1979.

Johnson, Phillip E. *Darwin on Trial. Second Edition*. Downers Grove: InterVarsity, 1993.

Johnson, S. Lewis. *The Old Testament in the New: An Argument for Biblical Inspiration Contemporary Evangelical Perspectives*. Grand Rapids: Zondervan, 1980.

Kaiser Jr., Walter C. *The Old Testament Documents: Are They Reliable & Relevant?* Downer Groves: InterVarsity Press, 2001.

Kaiser, Christopher B. *Creational Theology and the History of Physical Science: The Creationist Tradition from Basil to Bohr*. Leiden: Brill, 1997.

Kaiser, Walter C, and Moises Silva. *Introduction to Biblical Hermeneutics: The Search for Meaning*. Grand Rapids: Zondervan, 1994, 2007.

Käsemann, Ernst. "The Problem of the Historical Jesus," in *Essays on New Testament Themes*. Translated by W. J. Montague. Philadelphia: Fortress Press, 1982.

Kass, Leon R. *The Beginning of Wisdom: Reading Genesis*. New York: Free Press, 2003.

Kassian, Mary A. *The Feminist Mistake*. Wheaton, IL: Crossway Books, 2005.

Keener, Craig S. *The IVP Bible Background Commentary: New Testament.* Downer Groves, IL: InterVarsity Press, 1993.

Keil, Carl Friedrich, and Franz Delitzsch. *Commentary on the Old Testament.* Peabody, MA: Hendrickson, 1996.

—. *Commentary on the Old Testament.* Peabody, MA: Hendrickson, 2002.

Kelber, Wegner H. *The Oral and the Written Gospel.* Philadelphia: Fortress, 1983.

Keller, Werner. *Archaeology & Science Delve 4,000 Years into the Past to Document THE BIBLE AS HISTORY (2nd Revised ed.).* New York: Hodder and Stoughton, 1980.

Kennedy, D. James. *Evangelism Explosion.* Wheaton, IL: Tyndale House Publishers, 1977.

Kenneth, Boa., and Kruidenier. *Holman New Testament Commentary: Romans, Vol. 6.* Nashville, TN: Broadman & Holman, 2000.

Kimel Jr., Alvin F. Kimel Jr., and ed. *This Is My Name Forever: The Trinity & Gender Language for God.* Downers Grove: InterVarsity Press, 2001.

Kissling, Paul J. *The College Press NIV commentary: Genesis.* Joplin, MO: College Press Pub. Co., 2004.

Kistemaker, Simon J, and William Hendriksen. *New Testament Commentary: vol. 15, Exposition of Hebrews.* Grand Rapids: Baker Book House, 1953-2001.

Kitchen, K A. *On the Reliability of the Old Testament.* Grand Rapids: Eerdmans, 2003.

—. *The Ancient Orient and the Old Testament.* Chicago: Tyndale Press, 1966.

Kitchen, K. A. *Ancient Orient and Old Testament.* Downers Grove, IL: InterVarsity Press, 1975.

—. *The Ancient Orient and Old Testament.* Downers Grove, IL: InterVarsity Press, 1975.

Koehler, Ludwig. "Problem in the Study in the Language of the Old Testament." *Journal of Semitic Studies*, 1956: 3-24.

Koehler, Ludwig, Walter Baumgartner, M E J Richardson, and Johann Jakob Stamm. *The Hebrew and Aramaic Lexicon of the Old Testament.* Leiden; New York: E. J. Brill, 1999.

Krentz, Edgar. *The Historical-Critical Method*. Philadelphia: Fortress Press, 1975.

—. *The Historical-Critical Method*. Philadelphia: Fortress Press, 1975.

Kümmel, Werner Georg. *The New Testament: The History of the Investigation of Its Problems*, trans. S. McLean Gilmour and Howard C. Kee. Nashville: Abingdon Press, 1970.

Kugel, James L. *How to Read the Bible: A Guide to Scripture, Then and Now*. New York: Free Press, 2008.

Ladd, George Eldon. *The New Testament and Criticism*. Grand Rapids: Eerdmans, 1967.

Language, John Peter. *A Commentary on the Holy Scriptures: Genesis*. Bellingham: Logos Research Systems, 1939, 2008.

Lantz, Charles Craig. *Hermeneutics: The Art and Science of Biblical Interpretation*. Seattle, WA: Create Space, 2012.

Larsen, L. David. *The Evangelism Mandate*. Wheaton: Crossway Books, 1992.

Larson, Knute. *Holman New Testament Commentary, vol. 9, I & II Thessalonians, I & II Timothy, Titus, Philemon*. Nashville, TN: Broadman & Holman Publishers, 2000.

Lasor, William Sanford, David Allan Hubbard, and Frederic Williams Bush. *The Message, Form, and Background of the Old Testament: Old Testament Survey (2nd ed.)*. Grand Rapids: Wm. B. Eerdmans, 1996.

Lawrence, Paul, and Alan Millard. *The IVP Atlas of Bible History*. Downers Grove, IL: Intervarsity Press, 2006.

Lea, Thomas D. *Holman New Testament Commentary: Hebrews, James*. Nashville, TN: Broadman & Holman Publishers, 1999.

—. *Holman New Testament Commentary: Vol. 10, Hebrews, James*. Nashville, TN: Broadman & Holman Publishers, 1999.

Lea, Thomas D., and Hayne P. Griffin. *The New American Commentary, vol. 34, 1, 2 Timothy, Titus*. Nashville: Broadman & Holman Publishers, 1992.

Legaspi, Michael C. *The Death of Scripture and the Rise of Biblical Studies*. Oxford: Oxford University Press, 2010.

Lemche, Niels Peter. *The Old Testament Between Theology and History: A Critical Survey*. Louisville: Westminster John Knox Press, 2008.

Lenski, R. C. H. *Interpretation of the I & II Epistles of Peter the Three Epistles of John, and the Epistle of Jude.* Minneapolis: Augsburg Fortress, 1945, 2008.

—. *The Interpretation of The Acts of the Apostles.* Minneapolis, MN: Ediciones Sigueme, 1961.

Licona, Michael R. *The Resurrection of Jesus, A New Historiographical Approach.* Downers Grove: InterVarsity Press, 2010.

Lightfoot, J. B. *Essays on the Work Entitled Supernatural Religion.* London: Macmillan and Co., 1889.

Lightfoot, Neil R. *How We Got the Bible.* Grand Rapids, MI: Baker Books, 1963, 1988, 2003.

Lightfoot, Richard H. *History and Interpretation in the Gospels.* New York and London: Harper and Brothers, 1934.

Lightfoot, Robert H. *History and Interpretation of the Gospels.* (New York and London: Harper and Brothers, 1934.

Lindsell, Harold. *The Battle for the Bible.* Grand Rapids: Zondervan, 1976.

Linnemann. *Is There A Synoptic Problem? Rethinking the Literary Dependance of the First Three Gospels.* Grand Rapids, MI: Baker Book House, 1992.

Linnemann, Eta. *Biblical Criticism on Trial: How Scientific is "Scientific Theology"?* Grand Rapids: Kregel, 2001.

—. *Historical Criticism of the Bible: Methododology or Ideaology?* Grand Rapid, MI: Kregel Publications, 1990.

Longman III, Tremper. *How to Read Genesis.* Downers Groves, IL: Intervarsity Press, 2005.

Longman, III, Tremper. *Literary Approaches to Biblical Interpretation.* Grand Rapids: Zondervan Publishing House, 1987.

Longman, Tremper III. *Reading the Bible: With Heart & Mind.* Colorado Springs: NavPress, 1997.

Longman, Tremper III, and Raymond B Dillard. *An Introduction to the Old Testament.* Grand Rapids: Zondervan, 2006.

MacArthur, John. *The MacArthur Bible Commentary.* Nashville: Thomas Nelson, 2005.

Machen, J. Gresham. "Christianity and Culture." *Princeton Theological Review,* 1913: 7.

—. *The Christian Faith in the Modern World.* Grand Rapids: Eerdmans, 1965 [1936].

Maier, Gerhard. *The End of the Historical-Critical Method. Translated by Edwin W. Leverenz and Rudolf F. Norden.* St. Louis: Concordia, 1977.

Maier, Herhard. *The End of the Historical-Critical Method.* St. Loius, MO: Concordia Publishing House, 1974.

Malina, Bruce.J. *The Social Gospel of Jesus: The Kingdom of God in Mediterranean Perspective.* Minneapolis: Fortress Press, 2001.

Marshall, I. Howard. *A Critical and Exegetical Commentary on the Pastoral Epistles.* New York, London: T&T Clark LTD, 2004.

—. *Historical Criticism, Iin New Testament Interpretation.* Grand Rapids: Eerdmans, 1977.

Martin, D Michael. *The New American Commentary 33 1, 2 Thessalonians .* Nashville, TN: Broadman & Holman, 2001, c1995 .

Mathews, K. A. *The New American Commentary vol. 1A, Genesis 1-11:26 .* Nashville: Broadman & Holman Publishers, 2001.

Matthews, K. A. *The New American Commentary Vol. 1B, Genesis 11:27-50:26.* Nashville: Broadman and Holman Publishers, 2001.

Mayers, Mark K. *Christianity Confronts Culture: A Strategy for Crosscultural Evangelism.* Grand Rapids : Zondervan, 1987.

McCue, Rolland. *Promises Unfulfilled: The Failed Strategy of Modern Evangelism.* Greenville, SC: Ambassador Group, 2004.

McGrath, Alister. "Why Evangelicalism is the Future of Protestantism." *Christianity Today,* June 19, 1995: 18-23.

McKay, K. L. *A New Syntax of the Verb in New Testament Greek.* New York: Peter Lang, 1994.

McKenzie, Stephen L, and Stephen R Hayes. *An Introduction to Biblical Criticism and Their Application: To Each its Own Meaning.* Louisville: John Knox Press, 1999.

McKnight, Edgar V. *Postmodern Use of the Bible: The Emergence of Reader-Oriented Criticism.* Nashville: Abingdon Press, 1988.

—. *What is Form Criticism?* Philadelphia: Fortress, 1969.

McKnight, Edgar V. *"Form and Redaction Criticism."* The New Testament and Its Modern Interpreters. Philadelphia: Fortress Press, 1989.

McRaney, William. *The Art of Personal Evangelism.* Nashville: Broadman & Holman, 2003.

McRay, John. *Archaeology and the New Testament.* Grand Rapids: Baker House Books, 1991.

Melick, Richard R. *The New American Commentary: vol. 32, Philippians, Colissians, Philemon.* Nashville, TN : Broadman & Holman Publishers, 2001.

Metzger, Bruce M. *The Text of the New Testament: Its Transmission, Corruption, and Transmission.* New York: Oxford University Press, 1964, 1968, 1992.

Metzger, Bruce M. *A Textual Commentary on the Greek New Testament.* New York: United Bible Society, 1994.

Mirriam-Webster, Inc. *Mirriam-Webster's Collegiate Dictionary. Eleventh Edition.* Springfield: Mirriam-Webster, Inc., 2003.

Morgan, Robert. *"Rudolf Bultmann," in The Modern Theologians, vol. 1 in An Introduction to Christian Theology in the Twentieth Century. Edited by David F. Ford.* New York: Basil Blackwell, 1989.

Morgenthaler, Sally. *Worship Evangelism.* Grand Rapids: Zondervan Publishing House, 1995.

Morris, Henry M. *The Genesis Record: A Scientific and Devotional Commentary on the Book of the Beginnings.* Grand Rapids: Baker Books, 2007, 1976.

Morris, Leon. *The Gospel According to Matthew.* Grand Rapids, MI: Inter-Varsity Press, 1992.

Mounce, Robert H. *Matthew, vol. 1 in the New International Biblical Commentary. Edited by W. Ward Gasque.* Peabody, MA: Hendrickson, 1991.

Mounce, William D. *Mounce's Complete Expository Dictionary of Old & New Testament Words.* Grand Rapids, MI: Zondervan, 2006.

Mounce, William D. *Basics of Biblical Greek Grammar.* Grand Rapids: Zonervan, 2009.

Myers, Allen C. *The Eerdmans Bible Dictionary .* Grand Rapids, Mich: Eerdmans, 1987.

Nagel, Thomas. *The View from Nowhere.* New York: Oxford University Press, 1986.

Neil, Stephen, and Tom Wright. *The Interpretation of the New Testament, 1861-1986. Second Edition.* Oxford: Oxford University, 1988.

Nicholson, Ernest. *The Pentateuch in the Twentieth Century: The Legacy of Julius Wellhausen.* New York: Oxford University Press, 1998.

Niessen, Richard. "The virginity of the `almah in Isaiah 7:14." *Bibliotheca Sacra 137* , 1980: 133-50.

Nineham, D. E. "Eyewitness Testimony and the Gospel Tradition—I." *Journal of Theological Studies 9* , April 1958: 13.

Oden, Thomas C. *Ministry Through Word and Sacrament, Classic Pastoral Care.* New York: Crossroad, 1989.

Orchard, Bernard. *J. J. Griesbach: Synoptic and Text - Critical Studies .* Cambridge: Cambridge University Press, 1776-1976, 2005.

Orchard, Bernard, and Thomas R. W. Longstaff. *J. J. Griesbach: Synoptic and text-critical studies 1776-1976.* Cambridge: Cambridge University, 1978.

Osborne, Grant R. *THE HERMENEUTICAL SPIRAL A Comprehensive Introduction to Biblical Interpretation (2nd Edition).* Downers Grove, IL: InterVarsity Press, 2006.

Oswalt, John N. *The NIV Application Commentary: Isaiah.* Grand Rapids, MI: Zondervan, 2003.

Outlaw, W. Stanley. *The Book of Hebrews .* Nashville, TN: Randall House, 2005.

Packer, J. I. *Evangelism and Sovereignty of God.* Downers Grove, II: InterVarsity Press, 1961.

Packer, J. I. *Evangelism and the Sovereignty of God.* Downers Grove, IL: InterVarsity Press, 1979.

Perrin, Norman. *Rediscovering the Teaching of Jesus.* New York: Harper and Row, 1976.

—. *What is Redaction Criticism?* Philadelphia: Fortress, 1969.

Pink, Arthur Walkington. *An Exposition of Hebrews.* Swengel, PA: Bible Truth Depot, 1954.

—. *Objections to God's Sovereignty Answered.* Bellingham: Logos Bible Software, 2005.

Polhill, John B. *The New American Commentary 26: Acts.* Nashville: Broadman & Holman Publishers, 2001.

Porter, Stanley E. *Handbook to Exegesis of the New Testament.* Leiden, NY: Koninklijke, 1997.

Posterski, C. Donald. *Reinventing Evangelism.* Downers Grove, IL: InterVarsity Press, 1989.

Powell, Doug. *Holman QuickSource Guide to Christian Apologetics.* Nashville, TN: Holman Reference, 2006.

Pratt Jr, Richard L. *Holman New Testament Commentary: I & II Corinthians, vol. 7.* Nashville: Broadman & Holman Publishers, 2000.

Pratt Jr, Richard L. *I & II Corinthians, vol. 7, Holman New Testament Commentary .* Nashville, TN: , 2000: Broadman & Holman Publishers, 2000.

Rainer, S. Thomas. *Evangelism in the Twenty-First Century.* Wheaton, IL: Harold Shaw Publishers, 1989.

Rainer, Thom S. *Surprising Insights From the Unchurched and Proven Ways to Reach Them.* Grand Rapids, MI: Zondervan, 2001.

Ramm, Bernard. *Protestant Biblical Interpretation: A Textbook of Hermeneutics, 3rd rev. ed.* Grand Rapids, MI: Baker, 1999.

Rast, Walter E. *Tradition History and the Old Testament.* Philadelphia: Fortress Press, 1972.

Reginald H. Fuller, The New Testament in Current Study. New York: Charles Scribner's Sons, 1962.

Reid, Alvin. *Introduction to Evangelism.* Nashville: Boardman & Holmes , 1998.

Reid, Alvin L. *Radically Unchurched: Who They are and How to Reach Them.* Grand Rapids: Kregel, 2002.

Rendtorff, R. "The Problem of the Process of Transmission in the Pentateuch." *JSOT,* 1990: 101.

Reyburn, William David, and Euan Mc G. Fry. *A Handbook on Genesis (UBS Handbook Series).* New York: United Bible Societies, 1997.

Richards, E. Randolph. *Paul And First-Century Letter Writing: Secretaries, Composition and Collection.* Downers Grove: InterVarsity Press, 2004.

Richardson, A, W Schweitzer, and ed. *Biblical Authority for Today.* Philadelphia: Westminster Press, 1951.

Roberts, Alexander, James Donaldson, and Cleveland Coxe. *The Ante-Nicene Fathers Vol.I: Translations of the Writings of the Fathers Down to A.D. 325* . Oak Harbor: Logos , 1997.

Robertson, A. T. *An Introduction to the Textual Criticism of the New Testament.* London: Hodder & Stoughton, 1925.

Robertson, A.T. *Word Pictures in the New Testament.* Oak Harbor, MI: Logos Research Systems, 1933, 1997.

Robinson, G. L., and R. K. Harrison. *The International Standard Bible Encyclopedia, vol. 2.* Grand Rapids: Eerdmans, 1982.

Robinson, John A. T. *Can We Trust the New Testament? "The New Testament Dating Game," Time.* Grand Rapids: Eerdmans, 1977.

—. *Redating the New Testament.* Philadelphia: Fortress, 1976.

Rogers, Jack B, and Donald K. McKim. *The Authority and Interpretation of the Bible, An Historical Approach.* New York: Harper & Row, 1979.

Rooker, Mark F. *The New American Commentary, vol. 3A, Leviticus.* Nashville: Broadman & Holman Publishers, 2000.

Ropes, J. H. *The Synoptic Gospels, 2nd Impression with New Preface.* Cambridge: Harvard University, 1960.

Ruether, Rosemary Radford. *Women-Church: Theology and Practice of Feminist Liturgical Communities.* San Francisco: Harper and Row, 1986.

Russell, Letty M, and ed. *Feminist Interpretation of the Bible.* Philadelphia: Westminster Press, 1985.

Ryken, Leland. *Choosing a Bible: Understanding Bible Translation Differences.* Wheaton: Crossway Books, 2005.

—. *The Word of God in English.* Wheaton: Crossway Books, 2002.

—. *Understanding English Bible Translation: The Case for an Essentially Literal Approach.* Wheaton, IL: Crossway Books, 2009.

Sayce, A. H. *The Early History of the Hebrews.* London: Rivingtons, 1897.

Schaeffer, Francis A. *Genesis in Space and Time: The Flow of Biblical History.* Downers Groves: Intervarsity Press, 1972.

Schreiner, Thomas R. *The New American Commentary: 1, 2 Peter, Jude.* Nashville: Broadman & Holman, 2003.

Schweitzer, Albert. *The Quest of the Historical Jesus. Introduction by James M. Robinson. Trans. By W. Montgomery from the first German Edition.* New York: Macmillan, 1906, 1968.

Sisson, Dick. *Evangelism Encounter.* Chicago, IL: Victor Books, 1988.

Smith, Gary. *The New American Commentary: Isaiah 1-39, Vol. 15a.* Nashville, TN: B & H Publishing Group, 2007.

—. *The New American Commentary: Isaiah 40-66, Vol. 15b.* Nashville, TN: B&H Publishing, 2009.

Soulen, Richard N, and R. Kendall Soulen. *Handbook of Biblical Criticism. Edited by Richard N. Soulen.* Atlanta: John Knox, 1981.

Souter, Alexander. *The Text and Canon of the New Testament.* New York: Charles Scribner's Sons, 1913.

Speiser, E. A. *Genesis Anchor Bible 1.* Garden City: Doubleday, 1964.

Spinoza, Baruch. *Theological-Political Treatise, in Complete Works, trans. Samuel Shirley, ed. Michael L. Morgan.* Indianapolis: Hackett Publishing Company, 2002.

Spong, John Shelby. *Living in Sin: A Bishop Rethinks Human Sexuality. .* New York, NY: HaperCollins Publishers, 1990.

Sproul, R.C. *Knowing Scripture. .* Downers Grove, IL: Intervarsity Press, 1978.

Stanton, Elizabeth Cady. *The Woman's Bible .* Seattle, WA: Kindle Edition 2012, 1895.

—. *The Women's Bible.* Boston: Northeastern University Press, 1993.

Stein, Robert H. *A Basic Guide to Interpreting the Bible: Playing by the Rules.* Grand Rapids: Baker Books, 1994.

—. *The New American Commentary: Luke.* Nashville, TN: Broadman & Holman , 2001, c1992.

Stonehouse, , Ned B. *The Origins of the Synoptic Gospels.* Grand Rapids: Eerdmans, 1963.

Strauss, David Friedrich. *A New Life of Jesus. Authorized Translation. Second Edition.* Williams and Norgate: Covent Garden, 1879.

—. *The Life of Jesus Critically Examined. Edited by Peter C. Hodgson. Translated by George Eliot.* Philadelphia: Fortress, 1972.

Streeter, Burnett H. *The Four Gospels, A Study of Origins.* London: Macmillan, 1953.

Streeter, Burnett Hillman. *The Four Gospels, A Study of Origins*. London: Macmillan and Co., 1924.

Stuart, Douglas. *Old Testament Exegesis: A Handbook for Students and Pastors (Fourth Edition)*. Louisville: Westminister John Knox Press, 2009.

Tacitus. *The Histories, Books IV-V, Annals Books I-III (Loeb Classical Library No. 249)*. Cambridge, MA: Harvard University Press, 1931.

Taylor, Vincent. *The Formation of the Gospel Tradition*. London: Macmillan, 1953.

Tenney, Merrill C. et. al. *Zondervan Pictorial Encyclopedia of the Bible*. Grand Rapids: Zondervan, 1975.

Terry, Milton S. *Biblical Hermeneutics: A Treatise on the Interpretation of the Old and New Testaments*. Grand Rapids: Zondervan, 1883.

Theissen, Gerd. *Psychological aspects of Pauline Theology*. Philadelphia, PA: Fortress Press, 1987.

—. *Sociology of Early Palestinian Christianity.* . Philadelphia, PA : Fortress Press, 1977.

—. *The Social Setting of Pauline Christianity.* . Philadelphia, PA : Fortress Press, 1982.

Theissen, Gerd, and Annette Mertz. *The Historical Jesus: A comprehensive Guide*. Minneapolis, MN: Augsburg Fortress, 1998.

Thiselton, Anthony C. *The Two Horizons: New Testament Hermeneutics and Philosophical Description* . Grand Rapids: Eerdmans, 1980.

Thomas, Robert L. "Current Hermeneutical Trends: Toward Explanation or Obfuscation?" *JETS* , 1996: 241-256.

—. *Evangelical Hermeneutics*. Grand Rapids: Kregel Publications, 2002.

—. *Three Views of the Origins of the Synoptic Gospels*. Grand Rapids, MI: Kregel, 2002.

Thomas, Robert L. ""Current Hermeneutical Trends: Toward Explanation or Obfuscation?" *JETS 39*, June 1996: 241-256.

Thomas, Robert L. "Current Hermeneutical Trends: Toward Explanation or Obfuscation?" *JETS 39* , June 1996: 241-256.

—. *Revelation 1-7: An Exegetical Commentary* . Chicago, IL: Moody Publishers, 1992.

Thomas, Robert L., and F. David Farnell. *THE JESUS CRISIS: The Inroads of Historical Criticism in Evagelical Scholarship*. Grand Rapids, MI: Kregel Publications, 1998.

Torrey, Reuben A., and Edward D. Andrews. *DIFFICULTIES IN THE BIBLE Alleged Errors and Contradictions: Updated and Expanded Edition*. Cambridge: Christian Publishing House, 2012.

Turner, Henry E. W. *Historicity and the Gospel*. London: A. R. Mowbray, 1963.

Vine, W E. *Vine's Expository Dictionary of Old and New Testament Words*. Nashville: Thomas Nelson, 1996.

Virkler, Henry A, and Karelynne Gerber Ayayo. *Hermeneutics: Principles and Processes of Biblical Interpretation*. Grand Rapids, MI: Baker Academic, 1981, 2007.

Wainwright, William J, and ed. *The Oxford Handbook of Philosophy of Religion*. New York: Oxford University, 2005.

Walker, Williston, Richard A Norris, David W Lotz, and Robert T. Handy. *A History of the Christian Church, 4th ed.* New York: Charles Scribner's Sons, 1985.

Wallace, Daniel. *Greek Grammar Beyond the Basics*. Grad Rapids: Zondervan, 1996.

Walls, David, and Max Anders. *Holman New Testament Commentary: I & II Peter, I, II & III John, Jude.* Nashville: Broadman & Holman Publishers, 1996.

Walsh, Jerome T. *Old Testament Narrative: A Guide to Interpretation.* Louisville: Westminster John Knox Press, 2009.

Walton, John H. *Zondervan Illustrated Bible Backgrounds Commentary (Old Testament) Volume 1: Genesis, Exodus, Leviticus, Numbers, Deuteronomy*. Grand Rapids, MI: Zondervan, 2009.

—. *Ancient Near Eastern Thought and the Old Testament*. Grand Rapids: Baker Academic, 2006.

Walton, John H. "Isaiah 7:14: what's in a name?" *Journal of the Evangelical Theological Society 30*, 1987: 289-306.

—. *Zondervan Illustrated Bible Backgrounds Commentary (Old Testament) Volume 5: The Minor Prophets, Job, Psalms, Proverbs, Ecclesiastes, Song of Songs*. Grand Rapids, M: Zondervan, 2009.

Walton, John H. *THE NIV APPLICATION COMMENTARY Genesis*. Grand Rapids: Zondervan, 2001.

Walton, John H., and Sandy. D. Brent. *The Lost World of Scripture, Ancient Literary Culture and Biblical Authority.* Downers Grove: InterVarsity Press, 2013.

Walton, John H., Victor H. Matthews, and Mark W Chavalas. *The IVP Bible Background Commentary: Old Testament.* Downers Grove: IVP Academic, 2000.

Weber, Stuart K. *Holman New Testament Commentary, vol. 1, Matthew.* Nashville, TN: Broadman & Holman Publishers, 2000.

Wegner, Paul D. *A Student's Guide to Textual Criticism of the Bible: Its History Methods & Results.* Downers Grove: InterVarsity Press, 2006.

Wellhausen, Julius. *Prolegomena to the History of Israel .* New York: BiblioBazzar, 1878, 2009.

Westcott, B. F., and Hort F. J. A. *The New Testament in the Original Greek, Vol. 2: Introduction, Appendix.* London: Macmillan and Co., 1882.

Wheelock, Frederic M, and Richard A Lafleur. *Wheelock's Latin, 7th ed.* New York: Harper Collins, 2011.

Whiston, William. *The Works of Josephus.* Peabody, MA: Hendrickson, 1987.

Whitney, Donald S. *Spiritual Disciplines for the Christian Life with Bonus Content (Pilgrimage Growth Guide).* Colorado Springs, CO: Navpress, 1991.

Wolf, Herbert M. "Solution to the Immanuel Prophecy in Isaiah 7:14-8:22." *Journal of Biblical Literature 91 ,* 1972: 449-56.

Wood, D R W. *New Bible Dictionary (Third Edition).* Downers Grove: InterVarsity Press, 1996.

Woodhead, Linda. "Spiritualising the Sacred: A Critique of Feminist Theology." *Modern Theology,* 1997: 197.

Wright, N. T. *Hebrews for Everyone.* London: Westminster John Knox Press, 2003.

Yarbrough, Robert W. "Evangelical Theology in Germany." *Evangelical Quarterly LXV ,* October 1993: 329, 353.

Young, Pamela Dickey. *Feminist Theology/Christian Theology: In Search of Method.* Eugene: Wipf and Stock, 1990.

Zodhiates, Spiros. *The Complete Word Study Dictionary: New Testament.* Chattanooga: AMG Publishers, 2000, c1992, c1993.

Zuck, Roy B. *Basic Bible Interpretation: A Prafctical Guide to Discovering Biblical Truth.* Colorado Springs: David C. Cook, 1991.

www.ingramcontent.com/pod-product-compliance
Lightning Source LLC
Chambersburg PA
CBHW022003090426
42741CB00007B/877